JN074722

EAST ASIAN STRATEGIC REVIEW 2022

The National Institute for Defense Studies, Japan

Edited by:
The National Institute for Defense Studies
5-1 Ichigaya Honmura-cho, Shinjuku-ku, Tokyo 162-8808, Japan
URL: www.nids.mod.go.jp

Published by:
Interbooks Co., Ltd.
Kudan-Crest Bldg 6F, 5-10 Kudan-Kita 1-chome,
Chiyoda-ku, Tokyo 102-0073, Japan

Phone: +81-3-5212-4652
URL: https://www.interbooks.co.jp
books@interbooks.co.jp

ISBN 978-4-924914-78-0

The National Institute for Defense Studies
East Asian Strategic Review 2022

Printed in Japan

Preface

The National Institute for Defense Studies (NIDS) celebrates its 70th anniversary this year. Our predecessor National Safety College was founded in 1952. The *East Asian Strategic Review (EASR)* commenced publication in 1996 as part of an effort to foster mutual understanding and build trust with neighbors and regional countries in the post-Cold War era, and this edition marks the 26th year of publication. Over these years, the strategic geography of "East Asia" has expanded, and Japan's security challenges have become increasingly complex and diverse.

The world after the novel coronavirus disease (COVID-19) will be defined by an era of "great power competition." Great power competition refers to a geo-strategic contest for influence among the great powers. At the same time, it is a contest between democratic values, such as freedom of expression and open economy and society, and authoritarian values, like state-led economic growth and public order. Unlike the Cold War period, however, we live in a globalized world where trade, investment, and private-sector production networks have made states interdependent. Today, if some states were to attempt to manipulate this economic interdependence to gain technological superiority and convert it into military superiority, it might be of great concern. Such an attempt would constitute a major challenge to the "free and open system" that has sustained our prosperity.

EASR analyzes aspects of the great power competition from the perspective of its actors—the United States, China, and Russia—and how countries in the region are caught in this competition. The first two chapters address the changes taking place in the era of great power competition in the Greater Middle East, where U.S. engagement has grown since 2001. Chapter 1, which focuses on Afghanistan, examines the intentions of stakeholders—the United States, China, Russia, Iran, Pakistan, and India. It sheds light on the negative aspects of great power politics that impede cooperation even against a shared terrorist threat. Chapter 2 regarding the Middle East analyzes the 2020 normalization of relations between four Arab states and Israel through U.S. President Donald Trump's mediation. It explains that Arab diplomacy was conducted without any linkage to progress in Israeli-Palestinian peace negotiations and marks a shift in conventional diplomacy.

Chapter 3 onwards analyzes key events in 2021 by country or region. Chapter 3 discusses how China, mindful of the competition with the United States, urges independent development of science and technology and is strengthening its strategic partnership with Russia. Chapter 4 compares North Korea, which continues to develop missiles by exploiting the cracks of the great power competition, and South Korea, which maintains a conciliatory policy toward North Korea detached from the great power competition. Chapter 5 looks at the situation in Myanmar and the South China Sea issue. It postulates that, despite the existence of the ASEAN regional framework, China's deep involvement makes it difficult to exert diplomatic pressure on the Armed Forces of Myanmar. Chapter 6 assesses Russia's perception of the international order as revealed by its new National Security Strategy. The issue of Ukraine forms the core of Russia's perceptions of traditional geo-strategic competition with the West. Chapter 7 analyzes strategic competition with China from the U.S. perspective and describes efforts to strengthen security cooperation for maintaining the international order. Chapter 8 presents Japan's options in the era of great power competition.

The scholarly analyses presented in *EASR* are solely those of individual researchers, and the views expressed do not necessarily represent the official position of the Government of Japan or the Ministry of Defense. *EASR*'s standing as an academic work is further made explicit by specifying the contributors and their responsible parts as well as providing citations at the end of each chapter.

This edition was authored by: Kurita Masahiro (Chapter 1); Nishino Masami (Chapter 2); Iida Masafumi and Iwamoto Hiroshi (Chapter 3); Akutsu Hiroyasu and Murooka Tetsuo (Chapter 4); Matsuura Yoshihide and Tomikawa Hideo (Chapter 5); Hasegawa Takeyuki and Sakaguchi Yoshiaki (Chapter 6); Kikuchi

Shigeo (Chapter 7); and Takahashi Sugio (Chapter 8). It was edited by Masuda Masayuki, Arakaki Hiromu, Satake Tomohiko, Tanaka Ryosuke, Asami Asaki, Aizawa Riho, Oguma Shinya, and Yoshida Tomoaki.

In the era of great power competition, it is our hope that *EASR* will cultivate awareness of the East Asian strategic environment and promote an intellectual discourse for further improving the security policy of Japan.

Izuyama Marie
Editor-in-chief
Director, Security Studies Department
March 2022

Contents

Chapter 1

Great Power Politics over Afghanistan after the U.S. Withdrawal

KURITA Masahiro

Summary

As U.S. forces were withdrawing from Afghanistan, the Taliban, an insurgent group in the country, took over its capital Kabul on August 15, 2021, leading to the collapse of the internationally backed democratic government of the country. With its forces withdrawn, the United States is pursuing measures for containing terror threats originating from Afghanistan through an "over-the-horizon" approach. The key stakeholders in the region favoring engagement with the Taliban are Pakistan, which has maintained close ties with the Taliban; China, which fears the spillover of terrorism and extremism to the neighboring Xinjiang Uyghur Autonomous Region; Russia, which worries about destabilization of its Central Asian allies; and Iran, which is concerned about the safety of Shia Muslims in Afghanistan. Meanwhile, India, which strenuously supported the former democratic regime, watches the Taliban takeover with wariness.

What these six countries call on the Taliban to do are not so far apart from each other: containing the threat of terrorism originating from Afghanistan, establishing an ethnically inclusive political structure, and respecting the rights of minorities and women—albeit with differences in order of priority and degree. Nevertheless, the six countries are not aligned in how to deal with the Taliban in practice. China, Russia, and Iran, the countries willing to embrace the Islamist group, have touted the rapid collapse of the western-backed democratic regime in Kabul and the Taliban's return to power as a failure of the United States and criticize Washington's reluctance to engage with the Taliban. However, at least to the point of writing, even the countries favoring engagement have not been able to secure what they demanded from the Taliban. The latitude for the Taliban to meet the demands of the key stakeholders is constrained in part by the growing presence of the Islamic State Khorasan Province (ISKP), an Islamist movement that challenges the Taliban.

There are some efforts to align the respective approaches toward the Taliban among the key stakeholders, including hosting multilateral meetings that transcend their differences in stance, which raises the hope for the emergence of cooperation involving all of the key stakeholders. In reality, however, the issue of how to deal with Afghanistan under the Taliban is more likely to become an additional source of conflict among the regional countries and between the United States and China and Russia, which are already in a strategic competition.

First press conference by the Taliban after the takeover of Kabul, August 17, 2021 (Kyodo)

Keywords

Afghanistan Taliban Islamic State Khorasan Province United States
Pakistan China Russia Iran India

1. The Taliban's Takeover of Kabul

On August 15, 2021, the Taliban, an Afghan insurgent group ousted from power in 2001, seized control of the capital, Kabul, and President Ashraf Ghani fled the country, resulting in the unexpectedly rapid collapse of its internationally backed democratic regime. This happened as the Joseph Biden administration, having inherited the 2020 U.S.-Taliban peace agreement, was withdrawing the U.S. forces from Afghanistan by the deadline of August 31, 2021.

Since the takeover of Kabul, the Taliban have sought to set themselves apart from their previous reign from 1996 to 2001. The group announced respect for women's rights and amnesty for Afghans who had cooperated with the previous government, pledged to not allow anyone to use the Afghan soil for activities against other countries, and expressed its intention to form an inclusive government that would not be dominated by the Taliban and ethnic Pashtuns, from which most of the members of the group hail. Nevertheless, the interim government that has since been announced by the Taliban is far from inclusive, and the future of the Afghan state is becoming increasingly uncertain.

Meanwhile, the rapidly evolving situation brings attention to the moves of not only the United States but also the key stakeholders around Afghanistan. The actors that have a role in the Afghanistan issue are wide-ranging, with even small, geographically distant countries such as Qatar playing an important part. That said, the key stakeholders that can influence the course of the Afghan state are the five countries that U.S.

U.S. Marine Corps deployed to the airport in Kabul (Balkis Press/ABACA/Kyodo News Images)

Secretary of State Antony Blinken mentioned when proposing a conference hosted by the United Nations (UN) on peace in Afghanistan. These countries are: Pakistan, China, and Iran, which share a border with Afghanistan; Russia, which backs the Central Asian Republics on Afghanistan's northern border; and India, which has historically had close ties with Afghanistan.

The questions here are as follows. How do the United States and these five countries view the Taliban-controlled Afghanistan? What interests do they have, and how are they responding to the developments in the country? Furthermore, what are the implications of the relationships and interactions among the key stakeholders for the future trajectory of the Afghan state and, conversely, what will be the impacts of the developments in Afghanistan on their relationships? This chapter addresses these questions.

2. U.S. Policy toward Afghanistan

(1) The Two Decades of War on Terror in Afghanistan

The history of U.S. engagement with Afghanistan traces back to the 1980s. In response to the Soviet military intervention in Afghanistan to support its communist government in late 1979, the United States launched a proxy war against the Soviet forces in the country, backing Islamic militants in cooperation with its ally Pakistan. After the Soviet withdrawal, however, Washington lost interest in Afghanistan, which would be mired in civil war in the first half of the 1990s. In this process, the Taliban rose to power and declared establishment of the Islamic Emirate of Afghanistan in 1996. The Islamist group ruled the country with their radical interpretation of Islamic law, including suppression of human rights, and sheltered Osama bin Laden, the leader of the international terrorist outfit al Qaeda, which fueled concern in the United States.[1]

Against this backdrop, the September 11 terrorist attacks on the United States occurred in 2001. Washington demanded that the Taliban hand over bin Laden who masterminded the attacks, along with other members of the al Qaeda leadership, but the Taliban refused. Consequently, the George W. Bush administration declared a "Global War on Terror" and launched military operations in Afghanistan in October. The United States and its allies of the North Atlantic Treaty Organization (NATO), in collaboration with the Northern Alliance that had been resisting the Taliban rule in Afghanistan, quickly overthrew the Taliban government. In December 2001, an interim government was formed based on an agreement among the major factions in the country, excluding the Taliban. By 2004, progress was made in establishing a democratic regime, including adoption of a new constitution and the election of Hamid Karzai in the first presidential election.

The Taliban, however, did not simply disappear. Their leadership and fighters fled across the border into western Pakistan. They resurrected their organization under the protection and support of Pakistan's Inter-services Intelligence (ISI) and gradually expanded their influence from southern Afghanistan through cross-border attacks. By 2006, the deterioration of security conditions in Afghanistan was evident.[2]

In an effort to push back the Taliban's growing influence, the United States and NATO allies stepped up counterinsurgency operations and increased their troop strength. The most dramatic move was the 30,000-strong surge announced by the Barack Obama administration at the end of 2009. At this time, it was unveiled that the transfer of security authority to the Afghan government and the gradual drawdown of U.S. forces would begin in July 2011. In May 2014, it was announced that the U.S. and NATO combat operations in Afghanistan would be completed in the end of the year. It was also announced that less than 10,000 troops would remain to train the Afghanistan National Defense and Security Forces (ANDSF) and engage in counterterrorism operations against al Qaeda and allied groups. Most of these troops were to withdraw by the end of 2016. In line with this plan, the combat operations of NATO forces, including U.S. forces, ceased by the end of 2014. In the meantime, the United States killed al Qaeda leader bin Laden in Pakistan in May 2011.

Since 2015, however, the Taliban gained further momentum, and the Islamic State Khorasan Province (ISKP), a branch of the self-styled Islamic State (IS), entered Afghanistan, negating the plan to withdraw U.S. forces by the end of 2016. Although U.S. President Donald Trump had championed during his electoral campaign to end the war in Afghanistan, he ordered a U.S. troop surge soon after taking office and stepped up military operations not only against al Qaeda and its affiliates and ISKP, but also against the Taliban.[3]

As it appeared that stabilization of Afghanistan was difficult, the United States began pursuing direct peace talks with the Taliban in 2018 brokered by Pakistan, a country with influence over the Islamist group. The talks culminated in the February 2020 U.S.-Taliban peace agreement signed in Doha, Qatar. The agreement stipulated that the United States and its allies and partners withdraw their forces from Afghanistan within 14 months. Meanwhile, the Taliban promised to take steps to prevent any of its members as well as any group or individual, including al Qaeda, from using the soil of Afghanistan to threaten the security of the United States and its allies, and to start intra-Afghan negotiations with the government in Kabul on March 10. There were also classified annexes that included a commitment by the Taliban to refrain from attacking foreign military forces.[4]

However, a peace process based on this agreement was fraught with uncertainties from the beginning. The intra-Afghan talks between the Taliban and the government faced challenges even in their commencement. The Taliban did not slow their offensive against the ANDSF and were constantly reported as maintaining ties with al Qaeda. It was later suggested the agreement created a perception of abandonment among the Afghan government and the ANDSF, which in turn hastened their collapse.[5]

Nonetheless, the Biden administration, inaugurated in January 2021, continued the drawdown of U.S. forces, albeit with an extended deadline. Its position was clear: the goals that the United States had envisioned at the beginning of this war in 2001—bringing the perpetrators of the 9/11 attacks to justice and reducing the threat of terrorism originating from Afghanistan—were already achieved, and it was the right and the responsibility of the Afghan people to choose how the Afghan state should be run, with all the necessary tools which had already been provided by the international community.[6] Though U.S. forces continued to attack the Taliban

Figure 1.1. Number of troops and casualties of U.S. forces in Afghanistan

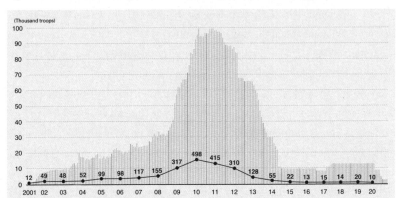

Note: The bar graph shows the number of troops (left axis), and the line graph shows the number of casualties.

Source: Compiled by the author based on Twitter, @AFP, July 6, 2021.

fighters to support the Afghan government during the withdrawal process,[7] they did not militarily stop the Taliban from taking control of Kabul. Amidst the chaos that followed the fall of the capital, the withdrawal of U.S. forces was completed on August 30.

(2) U.S. Policy toward Afghanistan after the Taliban Takeover

President Biden explained that the U.S. military withdrawal was necessary because, while the threat of terrorism has spread across the world over the past two decades and can no longer be contained effectively through large-scale troop deployments in Afghanistan, other strategic challenges have emerged, such as the intensifying competition with China and Russia and the threat of cyberattacks and nuclear proliferation. Biden categorically stated that the sole vital interest the United States has in Afghanistan is to prevent the country from becoming a hotbed of terrorism again and serving as a launchpad for terrorist attacks on the United States and friendly countries.[8]

The shift in focus from the two-decade war on terror in the Greater Middle

East, including Afghanistan, to the great power competition with China and Russia is part of the long-term trend in U.S. security policy articulated in the 2017 National Security Strategy under the previous administration. Notwithstanding the mixed views on how the withdrawal process was handled, few Americans advocate for continuing to put significant energy and security resources into Afghanistan. Washington calls on the Taliban to not shelter terrorist organizations, respect human rights, especially women's and minorities' rights, and establish an inclusive government. It maintains, however, that they should be pursued "through diplomacy, economic tools, and rallying the rest of the world for support."[9]

The al Qaeda core has not abandoned its stronghold in Afghanistan despite U.S. military pressure. This is also why they have been contained by U.S. counterterrorism operations in Afghanistan.[10] In one to two years' time, however, al Qaeda is expected to resurrect itself up to the level of being able to attack the U.S. mainland.[11] Furthermore, ISKP, hostile toward the United States like al Qaeda, has resurged since 2020, albeit weakening from 2016 to 2020 under attacks by U.S. forces, ANDSF, and the Taliban. ISKP carried out a suicide bombing near Kabul airport in August 2021. There are indications that it has planned terrorist attacks in countries beyond Afghanistan for the past several years.[12] In congressional testimony in October 2021, a senior official of the U.S. Department of Defense said ISKP could acquire the capability to attack the U.S. mainland in around six months.[13]

The U.S. government attests that these threats can be dealt with through an "over the horizon" approach, without a military presence in Afghanistan. Many have, however, pointed out the difficulties involved.[14] While counterterrorism operations using either drones or carrier-based aircraft in the Indian Ocean are not impossible, the deployment of aircraft carriers could hinder carrier operations in the Pacific. And while drone operations are seemingly promising, the United States does not have bases in neighboring countries to operate them. The option of borrowing bases in Central Asian countries, used in the early stages of the war on terror, has been met with strong opposition from Russia, which exerts influence on these countries. Although drones can be operated from U.S. bases in the Gulf states, they are geographically distant and doing so would be operationally inefficient. Above all, the United States critically lacks the intelligence-gathering capabilities needed to carry out an attack, having neither a base in Afghanistan for U.S. intelligence operations, nor local partners, such as the Afghan government and military, intelligence agencies, and Afghan collaborators. Senior U.S. military officials and others acknowledge that the over-the-horizon approach will not be easy to accomplish at this time.[15]

A key question, then, is to what extent the Taliban are willing and able to fulfill their commitment to prevent international terrorist attacks originating from Afghanistan, as was included in the peace agreement with the United States. To examine this question, the responses to al Qaeda and ISKP need to be considered separately. The Taliban and ISKP are enemies and have engaged in fierce fighting with each other, which raises the expectation that the Taliban have willingness to dislodge ISKP.[16]

Even so, it is questionable what the Taliban can do alone against ISKP, which has been contained in part by the counterterrorism operations of the U.S. forces and ANDSF.[17] Following the suicide bombing in late August 2021, ISKP has continued to wage attacks in Afghanistan targeting the Taliban and minorities, including bombings of Shia mosques in Kunduz and Kandahar and an assault on a military hospital in Kabul. In November, the UN special representative for Afghanistan expressed the view that the Taliban have been unable to contain ISKP, which has expanded its presence to nearly every province in Afghanistan and whose number of terrorist attacks in 2021 reached 334, more than five times the number in 2020.[18] Although the Taliban conduct mop-up operations against ISKP and play up their achievements, the operations are said to be so crude that they may inversely help ISKP's recruitment.[19] Furthermore, members of the military and intelligence agencies of the former government are reportedly joining ISKP fearing the Taliban's retribution.[20]

Perhaps in light of the Taliban's shortcomings, Mark Milley, chairman of the U.S. Joint Chiefs of Staff, mentioned shortly after the withdrawal that U.S. forces may coordinate with the Taliban on campaigns against ISKP.[21] U.S. forces and the Taliban have a record of effectively fighting together against ISKP.[22] The hurdles to U.S.-Taliban cooperation nevertheless remain high, considering the stated aim of the Taliban insurgency—driving out foreign troops from Afghanistan—and the propaganda war waged by ISKP, claiming the Taliban are a U.S. ally and not a true jihadist organization.[23] The Taliban, for their part, have refused to cooperate with

Foreign Minister Qureshi of Pakistan visiting Kabul, October 2021 (Xinhua/Kyodo News Images)

the United States, insisting they can deal with ISKP on their own. The commander of the U.S. Special Operations Command has said as well that the Taliban are not a partner in counterterrorism.[24]

Meanwhile, the Taliban have maintained cooperative ties with al Qaeda, despite their commitments under the U.S.-Taliban peace agreement.[25] Underlying this are the Taliban's receipt of diverse support from al Qaeda and their view that cooperating with the group is essential for surviving the competition with ISKP and other potential adversaries.[26] A senior Taliban official has asserted that the agreement with the United States does not include an obligation to sever ties with third parties, and the Taliban have reportedly sent a notice to foreign militant groups, including al Qaeda, to register. In view of such information, the best that can be hoped for under the peace agreement is limited to the Taliban monitoring the activities of the groups while tolerating their presence in Afghan territory, and preventing international terrorist attacks.[27]

It is unknown at this time whether such measures will be sufficient to address the threat of international terrorism by al Qaeda and its affiliates. Indeed, the Taliban do not share al Qaeda's goal of global jihad and, insofar as they seek international recognition of the Taliban-led government, there is some rationale for believing they have a motive to prevent the use of Afghan soil for terrorist attacks on other countries.[28] Even then, it is doubtful that the Taliban, an insurgent group for the past two decades, can act as a governing entity and sufficiently curb international terrorism of not only al Qaeda but also other terrorist organizations in the territory. Moreover, al Qaeda's polarized chain of command is believed to make it difficult for the Taliban to monitor and control its activities.[29] Exercising excessive control may propel al Qaeda and its affiliates to turn against the Taliban and become a threat to the group.[30]

Nevertheless, as long as difficulties are entailed in conducting an effective counterterrorism operation "over the horizon," the United States does not have the option of totally ceasing to motivate the Taliban to honor their pledge of preventing terrorism. The United States can use both stick and carrot to accomplish this, including recognizing the Taliban government, unfreezing the Afghan central bank's assets in the United States, imposing additional unilateral or multilateral sanctions or lifting them, and providing humanitarian assistance and economic aid.

These are, however, not necessarily easy tools to utilize. Many of them are subject to certain constraints given the increasingly serious and deteriorating humanitarian and economic situation in Afghanistan due to the collapse of the government. Since the tools are also used to encourage the Taliban to form an inclusive government and respect human rights, the necessary coordination among the different goals will be challenging. Above all, the effectiveness of these tools in motivating the Taliban to curb terrorism and, furthermore, form an inclusive government and respect human rights will largely depend on the approach taken by other key stakeholders, the majority of which are conspicuously positive about engaging with the Taliban compared to Washington.

3. Key Stakeholders' Policy toward Afghanistan

(1) Pakistan

Pakistan is arguably one of the countries with the greatest influence over Afghanistan under the Taliban, owing to the covert support it has provided to the group, despite its official denial. In the West's proxy war against the Soviet Union in the 1980s, Pakistan directly provided support to Islamist militants in Afghanistan, including those who later formed the core of the Taliban and al Qaeda.[31] During the subsequent Afghan civil war in the 1990s, Pakistan helped the Taliban seize power. After the 9/11 attacks in 2001, Islamabad outwardly cooperated with the U.S. war on terror and severed ties with the Taliban, but clandestinely sheltered fleeing Taliban leadership and fighters and provided sanctuary along the border, training, financing support, and advice.[32] This double-dealing led to the deterioration of its relations with Kabul and Washington; however, since 2018, Pakistan has leveraged its influence to help realize the U.S.-Taliban peace talks, at the request of the Trump administration.

Behind Pakistan's backing of the Taliban is the concept of "strategic depth" widely espoused in the country. While Pakistan has a longstanding and serious territorial dispute with India over the sovereignty of Kashmir, it has also faced border challenges from Afghanistan. This has raised concerns in Pakistan that its interests would be violated via Afghanistan if India and Afghanistan were to collude. In particular, Islamabad has fears about interference in the Pashtun and Baloch separatist movements in the western area bordering Afghanistan. To prevent this, Pakistan—especially its Army—has felt it necessary to intervene in Afghanistan to establish a pro-Pakistan regime and exclude India's influence from the country.[33]

This foundation, coupled with the close ties developed with India by the Afghan democratic government under both Karzai and Ghani, led some Pakistanis to welcome its collapse.[34] After the Taliban takeover of Kabul, the Pakistani government said it would not rush to recognize the Taliban regime, but it has also urged the international community to "give Taliban a chance."[35]

This longstanding close relationship with the Taliban is unique to Pakistan and may give the country an advantage over other key stakeholders in shaping the future of Afghanistan. Additionally, members of the Haqqani Network, who are particularly close to the Pakistani security establishment within the Taliban, hold key posts in the interim government announced in September 2021.

That said, Pakistan's influence over the Taliban is not so absolute as to steer it freely. The previous Taliban government refused to recognize Pakistan's border claims, as did successive Afghan governments. Nor did the Taliban agree to extradite bin Laden immediately after the 9/11 attacks, despite Pakistan's persuasion. Above all, as discussed below, the Taliban to this day have maintained ties with the Tehrik-i-Taliban Pakistan (TTP), a notorious militant group which has targeted the Pakistani government and military.

Pakistani influence over the Taliban, by no means absolute, is expected to decline further with the group's takeover of Afghanistan and the withdrawal of U.S. forces. During its insurgency, the Taliban were significantly dependent on Pakistan's support, especially its provision of a sanctuary across the border, which could be leveraged by Pakistan to influence the Taliban.[36] Besides, the Taliban leadership and their families were sheltered in Quetta in southwest Pakistan, enabling the country to put pressure on the Taliban.[37] Now that the group controls most of Afghanistan and has become its governing entity, however, Pakistan's backing will become less valuable to the Taliban. While they will continue to fight ISKP, the Taliban have little necessity for a sanctuary on the Pakistani side of the border if there is hardly any need to fear airstrikes by ANDSF and the U.S. forces. Once Afghanistan stabilizes under Taliban rule, the leadership will likely repatriate their families to the country. Furthermore, other countries have begun to provide some support to the Taliban that seized power.[38] The Taliban, for their part, do not wish to depend on Pakistan and have sought to diversify their international patronage.[39] If this is realized, Pakistan, which has hardly any comparative advantage in the field of statebuilding, will not be indispensable for the Taliban.

As its influence diminishes, Pakistan will be pressed to address two issues in its relations with Afghanistan under the Taliban. The first is the threat of terrorism emanating from Afghanistan. Threat here refers to that posed by TTP and the Balochistan Liberation Army (BLA). TTP, a terrorist outfit that campaigns for Islamic rule in Pakistan and has deep ties with al Qaeda, caused a havoc by conducting numerous deadly attacks in Pakistan from 2007 to 2014. Then it sustained great losses due to the counterterrorism operations by the Pakistani military and U.S. forces and fled to Afghanistan; however, TTP resurrected itself there and has intensified cross-border attacks from Afghanistan to Pakistan since around 2019.[40] Notwithstanding the extensive support they have received from Pakistan, the Taliban have maintained a close relationship with TTP, to which the Pakistani government and military are implacably hostile.[41] Seeking to emulate the Taliban's "success," TTP has further stepped up its offensive in 2021.[42] On the other hand, BLA advocates for the secession and independence of Balochistan province in southwestern Pakistan, and in recent years, has been known for conducting attacks on Chinese interests in the country. BLA has also carried out cross-border attacks from Afghanistan into Pakistani territory.

Since BLA seemingly does not have close ties to the Taliban, the Taliban are reportedly enhancing their crackdown on BLA in response to Pakistan's request.[43] However, it will not be easy to elicit an effective response to TTP from the Taliban, considering Pakistan's failure to force the Taliban to sever ties with TTP or adequately contain it even when the Taliban were more dependent on Pakistan's support to sustain their insurgency. After placing Kabul under their control, the Taliban stated that "The issue of the TTP is one that Pakistan will have to deal with" and opted for brokering peace talks between the Pakistani government and TTP rather than cracking down on or expelling the latter.[44] This effort resulted in the announcement on November 8 by the Pakistani government that a one-month ceasefire would take effect with TTP and that it was pursuing dialogue with the group, but the dialogue went nowhere and TTP announced the resumption of attacks on December 9, condemning the government for violating the terms of the dialogue.[45]

The Pakistani government has reached a peace agreement nine times in the past with anti-state Islamist militant groups including TTP, none of which have lasted. Even if a new peace deal with TTP is materialized, some of its subgroups dissatisfied with the peace process are likely to break away and continue their attacks or join ISKP, given the highly decentralized nature of TTP.[46] Many TTP defectors have already joined ISKP, which conducts terrorist attacks also in Pakistan.[47] Given the loss of the U.S. military's counterterrorism operations that had traditionally dealt significant blows to TTP and other terrorist outfits, Pakistan will face an increased threat of terrorism.

The second issue is refugees from Afghanistan. After the Taliban's takeover of Afghanistan, Pakistan has urged the international community for measures to prevent a humanitarian crisis. While Islamabad's desire may be to prevent the collapse of Pakistan-backed Taliban rule, it appears there is also an intention to avoid a large influx of refugees due to a worsening humanitarian situation. The number of refugees to Afghanistan's neighboring countries did not surge immediately after the fall of Kabul.[48] Nevertheless, the number of refugees is expected to increase as the humanitarian situation in Afghanistan deteriorates.

Pakistan is already home to 1.4 million Afghan refugees and does not intend to host new refugees without the capacity to absorb more.[49] That said, if the situation devolved into a refugee crisis, the resulting chaos in the border region would force the Pakistani government to deploy significant military forces there to ensure stability. Such measures along the border between northwestern Pakistan and Afghanistan could, however, provoke a backlash from local Pashtuns, who have strong antipathy toward the federal government of Pakistan. This could increase support for the Pashtun Tahafuz Movement (PTM), which the Pakistani government has been trying to suppress in recent years.[50]

Concerns over the refugee issue are thought to be one of the reasons why Pakistan, like the international community, is calling on the Taliban to establish an inclusive political structure. Despite its close ties with the Taliban, Pakistan has repeatedly called for the establishment of an inclusive government, stirring resentment among the Taliban.[51] An Afghan government that is at least to some extent ethnically inclusive would be desirable for Pakistan, as it could bring stability to the country and prevent another civil war, thereby allowing Islamabad to avoid a refugee crisis.[52]

Given these issues and the recognition of the limits of its influence, Pakistan has refrained from unilaterally recognizing the Taliban government and has urged the international community to continue engagement with the Islamist group. Moreover, Pakistan is working in tandem with countries that, though harboring some concerns over the Taliban's Afghanistan with respect to counterterrorism and inclusive political structure, are more forward-leaning about engaging with the Taliban compared to the West. These countries are China, Russia, and Iran.

(2) China

Beijing's policy on Afghanistan has been strongly defined by its concerns on stability in the Xinjiang Uyghur Autonomous Region adjacent to Afghanistan, not to say China has no economic interests in the country.[53] Chinese authorities have forcefully suppressed the smoldering separatist movement in Xinjiang where Muslims are the majority, which led to an Afghan policy prioritizing the insulation of Xinjiang against instability originating from neighboring Afghanistan—in particular, the prevention of Afghanistan's transformation into a base for Uyghur dissidents.

As part of this policy, China began to develop relations with the Taliban. During the Soviet intervention in Afghanistan in the 1980s, Uyghur militants joined the anti-Soviet jihad and established ties with other Islamic militant groups that later became active in Central and South Asia, including Afghanistan.[54] Knowing this connection, China reached out to those militant groups in the 1990s, through the intermediary of Pakistan's ISI, to prevent them from turning hostile toward China and to isolate Uyghur outfits from the network of Islamist militant groups. Among such groups are al Qaeda and the Taliban, the latter of which were sheltering the Uyghur separatist militant group, the Eastern Turkistan Islamic Movement (ETIM).[55] This effort resulted in the Taliban assuring the Chinese that they would not allow anyone to use the Afghan soil in a way that infringed on Chinese interests.[56]

After the Taliban regime was overthrown in 2001, China was cooperative toward the U.S.-led nation-building in Afghanistan. It quickly recognized the transitional government and, though refusing to join the International Security Assistance Force (ISAF), offered aid and investment to the country.[57] Meanwhile, Beijing continued to harbor ambivalence toward the U.S. military presence in Afghanistan. While China feared that a hasty withdrawal of the U.S. forces would destabilize the western neighbor, it also considered that the U.S. presence itself was a destabilizing factor that distorts Afghan politics and that the purpose of the United States stationing troops there was to control China's backyard.[58] In the 2010s, China started to strengthen relations with the Taliban, perceiving that much of Afghanistan would inevitably come under Taliban control and that cooperation between Afghan militant groups and Uyghurs must be thwarted. Eventually, China also began to use its relationship with the Taliban as leverage to facilitate peace talks between the Islamist group and the Afghan government.[59] In this process, Taliban officials started to visit China, and in late July 2021, Wang Yi, state councilor and minister of foreign affairs, met with the visiting Taliban delegation.

Due to this background, immediately after the fall of Kabul, the reaction from the Chinese Foreign Ministry was largely positive. It expressed hopes for continuing the development of cooperative relations with Afghanistan and an intention to play a role in the country's reconstruction, noting the Taliban said they hope to grow friendly relations with China.[60] Meanwhile, Beijing condemned the U.S. intervention in Afghanistan, saying it had only left the country in chaos.[61]

That said, setting rhetoric aside, the terror threat from Afghanistan after the U.S. withdrawal is a great concern for China. ETIM, which China views with most hostility, was sometimes targeted by U.S. counterterrorism operations in Afghanistan because the group had worked with the Taliban and its affiliates.[62] Going forward, however, there will no longer be such operations.

China, wary of the spillover of instability from the post-U.S. Afghanistan, has been preparing for dealing with the increased terror threat from before. In addition to strengthening surveillance of the Sino-Afghan border to prevent militant groups from crossing the border, Beijing has taken measures to protect against penetration via Tajikistan, with which it shares a far longer border than with Afghanistan. China installed a monitoring outpost in the border area in Tajikistan, conducted counterterrorism exercises with the country, and in 2016, launched a quadrilateral counterterrorism framework comprised of China, Tajikistan, Afghanistan, and Pakistan. In October 2021, a senior official from the Tajik Internal Affairs Ministry said China is expected to build an outpost for the Tajik special forces unit near

Tajikistan's border with Afghanistan.[63] Joint counterterrorism measures have also been espoused with Russia and enshrined in the framework of the Shanghai Cooperation Organization (SCO), which includes both China and Russia. More recently, China and Russia jointly conducted an exercise based on scenarios related to terrorism in northwest China in August and the eight SCO member states staged a counterterrorism exercise in southwest Russia in September 2021.

In parallel with these measures, it is also essential for China to prevent Afghanistan from becoming a base for anti-Chinese terror groups. The Taliban reassured during their delegation's visit to China in July 2021 that they would not allow anyone to use the Afghan soil for activities against China.[64] Moreover, after the takeover of Kabul, a Taliban spokesperson told the Chinese newspaper *Global Times* that many ETIM members had already left Afghanistan.[65] He declined to say, however, whether the Taliban would hand over ETIM members if China were to request it in the future.

Regarding ETIM, a May 2021 report submitted to the UN Security Council states that the group has several hundred members in Badakhshan and other provinces and has ties to groups such as al Qaeda and ISKP.[66] There are also reports that ETIM had joined the Taliban's fight against ANDSF.[67] The authenticity of the Taliban's claim about ETIM leaving Afghanistan cannot be verified, and the Taliban spokesperson did not give the exact number of ETIM members who are believed to have left Afghanistan.[68] Furthermore, another news report suggests that the Taliban government did not expel Uyghur militants but merely relocated them from Badakhshan province neighboring China to different areas in Afghanistan.[69] In the late 1990s, the previous Taliban government, at the request of China, urged ETIM to cease its anti-China activities. This resulted only in ETIM members being subsumed into the Islamic Movement of Uzbekistan (IMU), which was also active in Afghanistan.[70]

For China, the terror threat originating from Afghanistan is not limited to ETIM. Since the late 2000s, China has become unable to deflect the hostility of Islamist militant groups, even with Pakistan's mediation.[71] Al Qaeda has often expressed solidarity with anti-China jihad and Uyghur militants following the 2009 Urumqi riots.[72] The self-styled Islamic State has also viewed China as an enemy alongside the United States, India, and Israel, and in 2017, issued a message threatening retaliation for China's repression of Uyghurs.[73] In addition, unless Islamabad succeeds in containing the threats of TTP, it is highly likely that China-related targets in Pakistan will be attacked by the group. This has been the case in the past. In 2012, TTP killed a Chinese tourist, claiming it was a retribution for the killing of Uyghurs in Xinjiang. In April 2021, TTP bombed a hotel in Quetta where the Chinese ambassador to Pakistan was staying. The recent growing attention on Chinese human rights abuses in the Xinjiang Uyghur Autonomous Region is likely to aggravate the hostility toward China from jihadist groups.

China is determined not to follow the footsteps of the United States and the Soviet Union, which became bogged down to a protracted, unwinnable war through direct military intervention in Afghanistan.[74] Neither do the Taliban plan to cooperate with other countries in counterterrorism and intelligence.[75] Thus, Beijing faces the question of how to get the Taliban to seriously address the anti-China terror threat.

One of the tools likely to be used as leverage is the provision of the economic benefits, in which China has comparative advantage, along with the well-established channels that Pakistan, China's foremost ally, maintains with the Taliban. China indeed announced $31 million in humanitarian assistance right after the Taliban takeover, which was followed by the China-Taliban agreement in October 2021 to establish a working level mechanism to strengthen dialogue. A Chinese state-run newspaper reported that Chinese businesses are exploring investment opportunities in Afghanistan under Taliban rule.[76] The Taliban, for their part, have pinned high hopes on China in this respect.

However, the effectiveness of such an approach is debatable. As in the case of the United States, even if the Taliban wish to curb terrorist attacks from Afghanistan against China, it is doubtful that the Taliban have the capacity to accomplish this, including constraining the activities of its adversary, ISKP. The group has attempted to capitalize on the Taliban's cooperative stance with China. In its statement of responsibility for the October 2021 mosque bombing in Kunduz, northern Afghanistan, ISKP stated that the perpetrator was a Uyghur and described the attack as a retribution against the Shia Muslims and the Taliban, alleging that they are expelling Uyghurs in response to demands from China. It is pointed out that ISKP is trying to position itself as a protector of Uyghurs and seek to attract Uyghur militants.[77]

Meanwhile, the limits of Taliban's ability to contain the threat of anti-China terrorism raise another challenge for Beijing: the security of Chinese interests in Afghanistan. Unless their security is ensured, it is natural for China to be cautious about making actual investments. However, the conundrum here is that, in that case, China will not be able to use economic incentives as leverage to stir the Taliban.

The extent to which China is interested in Afghanistan's economic potential itself remains questionable. Due to security and corruption issues in Afghanistan, Chinese investment in the country has been exceedingly limited vis-à-vis its potential. The Belt and Road Initiative (BRI) memorandum signed in 2016 has not led to any concrete projects, and the copper mining and oil field drilling projects for which Chinese companies were awarded contracts around 2010 have made little progress.[78] This was when the Taliban had assured the security of the copper mining project.[79] The scarcity of China's contribution to Afghanistan's economic reconstruction has even attracted criticisms from the United States.[80]

As investment projects under BRI in neighboring Pakistan typify, despite its willingness to launch eye-catching economic initiatives in an unstable environment, China is noticeably cautious about the actual implementation of investment projects under such circumstances. For the foreseeable future, a variety of investment proposals is likely to be put forward by China and used as tools for Beijing to court the Taliban. However, whether the proposals will actually proceed to implementation is another matter.

Meanwhile, China is pursuing cooperation and coordination on this issue with Pakistan, Russia, and Iran, countries which share the basic tenets of the policies toward the Taliban—urging the Islamist group to curb terrorism and establish an inclusive regime, while criticizing the United States and its allies for their reluctance to engage with the Taliban.[81] This approach can be construed as China's attempt at gaining more effective collective leverage against the Taliban.

(3) Russia

Relations between the Taliban and Russia were formerly hostile. The failure of the Soviet intervention left Moscow with an aversion to any involvement in Afghanistan. The late 1990s, however, saw the rise of the Taliban which had links to international Islamic militant groups and Chechen dissidents, prompting Russia to back the anti-Taliban Northern Alliance, together with Iran, India, and Central Asian countries.[82] At the time, Afghanistan was turning into a base for militant groups that sought to destabilize Central Asian Republics, which Russia considers as under its sphere of influence, and Russia itself, such as IMU whose targets were Tajikistan, Uzbekistan, and Kyrgyzstan. For this reason, Russia welcomed the toppling of the Taliban regime by the United States and NATO after the 9/11 attacks.[83]

But, not long thereafter, Russia developed mixed feelings about the U.S. presence in Afghanistan. It recognized that the U.S. military presence kept the Afghan state from collapsing and prevented instability from spilling over into neighboring Central Asian countries and beyond into Russian borders. Like China, however, Russia became wary of the U.S. presence, viewing it as an attempt to secure American influence in central Eurasia.[84] This concern, coupled with the pessimistic view over the sustainability of the democratic regime in Kabul and emergence of ISKP as a common threat to the Taliban and Russia, drove the latter to build relations with the Taliban. Russia opened back channels with the Islamist group in 2015 and began to host dialogues between the Taliban and Afghan government officials in 2018.[85] At the same time, Russia explored solutions to the Afghan issue under multilateral initiatives, such as regional frameworks with the participation of China, India, Pakistan, Iran, and Central Asian countries, as well as the Troika of U.S.-China-Russia.

Because of this backdrop, Moscow largely welcomed the Taliban's takeover of Kabul.[86] Russia has aligned its approach toward the Taliban with countries like

China and Pakistan, favoring engagement with the group. Moscow provided humanitarian assistance to Afghanistan in November 2021. The Taliban, for their part, have emphasized their good relations with Russia and assured that they would not allow anyone to use the Afghan soil for attacks against Russia and its neighbors.[87]

At the same time, however, Russia's moves reveal wariness toward Taliban-ruled Afghanistan. Russia has long developed cooperation with individual Central Asian Republics, as well as within the framework of the Collective Security Treaty Organization (CSTO), on responses to contingencies and terrorist attacks on the border between Afghanistan and Central Asia.[88] The measures Moscow has taken since August 2021 include exercises with Tajikistan and Uzbekistan, respectively, and the intensification CSTO exercises for responding to the terror threat spilling over from Afghanistan.[89] After the fall of Kabul, Russia reached an agreement with India, a country also wary of the Taliban, to strengthen intelligence cooperation on Afghanistan and terrorism, and confirmed with China on strengthening responses to terrorism and narcotics originating in Afghanistan.[90]

What Russia worries is that terrorism and extremism will spread to Central Asian countries adjacent to Afghanistan and to Russia itself.[91] Its concern is reportedly centered not on the Taliban exporting terrorism but on Afghanistan becoming a breeding ground for terrorism due to the Taliban's limited governing capacity.[92] Moreover, among the Central Asian countries, Tajikistan in particular has accepted some Afghan refugees since the Taliban's takeover of Kabul, raising concern of the infiltration of terrorists disguising themselves as refugees.[93]

Afghanistan is home to various militant groups that target Central Asian countries and Russia, including ISKP and IMU, the latter of which has several hundred members.[94] Russia has partnered with the Taliban in dealing with ISKP and thus has shown confidence in the Taliban's sincerity to contain the rival jihadist group.[95] As already noted, however, the Taliban's ability as a governing entity to deal with ISKP is unknown.

Meanwhile, Russia faces the challenge of getting the Taliban to form an ethnically inclusive government. Russia is working in tandem with countries like China, Pakistan, and Iran in this respect, but Moscow has been especially vocal about the importance of this issue.[96] Underlying this are considerations for Tajikistan and Uzbekistan, which have a strong interest in ensuring that ethnic Tajiks and Uzbeks are not persecuted in Afghanistan, as well as concerns that a political setup that is not representative of Afghanistan's ethnic diversity would be unsustainable and could lead to a civil war.[97] In this regard, Tajikistan in particular adopts a hard-line stance against the Taliban. When the Taliban announced the interim government in September 2021, Russia refused to call it an inclusive setup, adding that it will continue to call on the Taliban to establish a government that represents all ethnic groups.[98]

The experience in the Soviet era has kept Russia wary of direct involvement in Afghanistan,[99] and the influence Russia alone could have on the Taliban is less than Pakistan and China's. That said, Russia has a prominent presence in multilateral diplomacy on Afghanistan. In October 2021, Russia held a meeting of an extended Troika of U.S.-China-Russia-Pakistan (the United States was absent) as well as a Moscow Format meeting participated by China, India, Pakistan, Iran, five Central Asian countries, and the Taliban. The joint statement of the latter calls on the Taliban to form an inclusive government and urges the international community to provide humanitarian assistance to Afghanistan.[100] Russia has participated in almost all of the high-level meetings on Afghanistan that have been held by the key stakeholders since the Taliban's takeover of Kabul.

(4) Iran

Iran, bordering western Afghanistan, has considerable political clout in the country through religious and cultural bonds with the Hazara and other Shia Muslims, who make up nearly 20% of Afghanistan's population, and with the Tajiks in the country who speak the Persian language of Dari.[101] Relations between Iran and the Taliban have transformed dramatically over the past two decades. In the 1990s, the relationship was hostile. Iran provided substantial support to Burhanuddin Rabbani's government and subsequently the Northern Alliance, formed in northern Afghanistan by the factions that had constituted the Rabbani government after it was ousted from Kabul. Some say such Iran's support far exceeded what Pakistan provided for the Taliban.[102] Meanwhile, the Taliban, a Sunni Islamist movement, was hostile to Shia-dominated Iran and persecuted the Shia Hazara minority in Afghanistan. In 1998, Iran threatened a war against the Taliban with the mobilization of its military in response to the killing of Iranian diplomats and a journalist in northern Afghanistan.

Against this backdrop, Iran cooperated with the U.S. overthrow of Taliban rule and the establishment of a new regime in Afghanistan in 2001. However, as relations with the United States deteriorated over nuclear and other issues, Iran subsequently began to view U.S. forces in Afghanistan as a threat and shifted to building relations with the Taliban through dialogue and limited military assistance, while maintaining relations with the government of Kabul.[103] From the mid-2010s, Iran and the Taliban started cooperating to eliminate ISKP, a group that harbors far stronger hostility toward Shia-dominated Iran than the Taliban does, in the Iran-Afghanistan border areas controlled by the Taliban.[104]

For this reason, the Iranian reaction to the Taliban's seizure of power was generally favorable. President Ebrahim Raisi hailed the U.S. failure as an opportunity to forge a lasting peace in Afghanistan.[105]

Now that U.S. forces have withdrawn, Iran's concern is with preventing the Taliban and other Sunni Islamist organizations, such as ISKP, from persecuting Afghan Shia Muslims and conducting terrorist attacks against Iran from Afghanistan.[106] So far, the Taliban have taken some measures to reassure Tehran, such as appointing a Hazara as governor and allowing Shia religious events. The Taliban seem to try not to unnecessarily antagonize Tehran, given its record of supporting the anti-Taliban Northern Alliance and the importance of economic relations with Iran, especially trade.[107] It is doubtful, however, that such rational calculations are shared down to the lowest levels of the group, with reports that Taliban members have been killing Hazara people since August 15.[108]

Even more unclear is the suppression of other Sunni Islamist organizations. Iran has developed some kind of relationship with al Qaeda, albeit that does not mean the latter is simply a proxy for Tehran,[109] which keeps the risk of al Qaeda infringing on Iranian interests low. ISKP is a real threat, however. The jihadist group has repeatedly targeted Hazara people in Afghanistan, including the May 2021 terrorist attack on a school and the October suicide bombing in Kunduz. It is an irony that Tehran, which used to hope for the U.S. withdrawal, has to face an increased threat of terrorism now—it was the U.S. counterterrorism operations that had kept ISKP at bay in Afghanistan.

Iran, like Pakistan, also has concerns over the influx of refugees from Afghanistan. To date, Iran has accepted the second largest number of Afghan refugees after Pakistan. Many Afghan refugees have sought refuge in Iran because of the relative ease of crossing the border. The Iranian government fears, however, that ISKP might infiltrate among the refugees.[110] Although Iran has closed its borders as the Taliban advanced toward Kabul in August 2021, claiming it cannot accept any more refugees, more are expected to arrive in Iran if the humanitarian situation in Afghanistan continues to deteriorate.[111] In November 2021, it was estimated that 4,000 to 5,000 Afghan refugees were crossing the border into Iran every day.[112]

The establishment of an inclusive Afghan government is also a key concern for Iran, which has links to the Hazaras and Tajiks, and Tehran has been urging the Taliban for its realization. Following the announcement of the interim government in September 2021, Iran openly criticized its composition as not inclusive, calling on the Taliban once again to form a government that has representation from all political and ethnic groups in Afghanistan.[113] Earlier, Iran condemned in strong terms the Taliban's use of force to suppress the National Resistance Front comprised mainly of Tajiks, which attempted to resist the Taliban until the end in Afghanistan's Panjshir Province.[114]

So far, Iran has remained steadfast in addressing these challenges through engagement with the Taliban rather than confrontation. In addition to providing humanitarian assistance, the October 2021 talks between the Iranian mission and the Taliban resulted in several agreements on economic relations, including facilitation of border trade.[115] In November, an agreement was reached to supply 100 megawatts of electricity to the national electric power company of Afghanistan, which has had difficulty paying for imported electricity since the Taliban takeover.[116] Furthermore, Iran has tried to coordinate its Afghan policy with other stakeholders, hosting a foreign ministers' meeting of Afghanistan's neighbors at the end of October participated by China, Russia, Pakistan, Tajikistan, Uzbekistan, and Turkmenistan.

As regards its potential, Tehran has many levers it can use to put pressure on the Taliban. Iran's network in Afghanistan consists mainly of the Hazara and Tajik minorities but also extends to the dominant Pashtuns.[117] Economically, Iran is Afghanistan's key trading partner, and it is virtually impossible to reach the sea from Afghanistan without transiting Iran or Pakistan, making Iran critically important for any other external powers to implement connectivity projects involving Afghanistan.

In addition, Iran maintains a hard-power instrument that could be utilized inside Afghanistan. The Iranian Revolutionary Guard Corps (IRGC) has deployed the Fatemiyoun Brigade, a militia made up of Afghan Hazara immigrants and refugees to Iran, to support the Assad regime in the Syrian civil war since 2013, reportedly sending a total of 50,000 fighters. The fighters have been being pulled back, however, as the Syrian civil war loses momentum, and observers have suggested they may be used in Afghanistan instead.[118] The foreign minister of Iran once suggested that the Afghan democratic government use the Fatemiyoun Brigade to deal with ISKP.[119] If Iran's interests were to be seriously harmed in and by Afghanistan under Taliban rule, it is conceivable that Iran could resort to pressure tactics using these levers.

(5) India

India was among the countries that supported the anti-Taliban Northern Alliance in the 1990s. Although Pakistan's intervention in Afghanistan, including support for the Taliban, has been driven by the perceived "Indian threat," Delhi, which had developed close relations with successive Afghan governments before the Taliban took power in 1996, had historically been not so enthusiastic about leveraging its ties with Kabul against Islamabad.[120]

But, in the late 1980s and onwards, India realized how detrimental an Afghanistan with Pakistan's significant influence could be—not only for Delhi's clout in the country, but also for India's own security. Completing the anti-Soviet proxy war in Afghanistan, Pakistan diverted the assets it had developed for supporting jihad from the country to Kashmir. The Pakistan Army and ISI trained fighters in Taliban-ruled Afghanistan to send to support the massive insurgency that was raging in Indian-administered Kashmir and also deployed Islamic militants who had previously fought Soviet forces to Kashmir.[121] Although the Taliban themselves were not systematically involved in the Kashmir insurgency, India, which heightened concerns on this development and viewed the Taliban as a puppet of Pakistan, supported the Northern Alliance in an effort to contain the Islamist group.[122]

Therefore, after the 9/11 attacks, India looked favorably upon the democratic regime in Afghanistan that was established with the backing of the international community. India provided $3 billion in economic cooperation, as well as training for administrative officials and security forces.[123] Even after the Taliban resurged and Washington began to explore a peace deal with the group, Delhi did not hide its concerns over the negative impact of the U.S. withdrawal and consistently supported the Ghani administration, while refraining from building an overt relationship with the Taliban.[124] Not until June 2021 were there reports about India's moves to build relations with the group. After Kabul fell, India immediately withdrew its embassy and had no official contact with the Taliban delegation in Qatar until late August.

After retaking Kabul, the Taliban said they attached importance to their relations with India.[125] Although the group is perceived as hostile to India, in fact the Taliban have appealed to Delhi since the 1990s, hoping to reduce their dependence on Pakistan. Meanwhile, in the Indian government, there had been a growing tendency since the mid-2000s to view the Taliban as a reasonable party that can be talked with, and some behind-the-scenes contacts were reportedly made through intelligence agencies.[126] Still, there is persistent concern that a Taliban-dominated Afghanistan poses an increasing terror threat to India.

That said, it is not likely that India's worst fears will materialize—a return to the 1990s situation when Afghanistan became a hotbed of terrorism, which in turn spiraled the violence in Indian Kashmir out of control. As noted above, such developments at the time were largely spearheaded by Pakistan, which is no longer able to do the same despite maintaining relations with anti-India militant groups. The international community evidently keeps a closer eye on state sponsorship of terrorism in the wake of the 9/11 attacks. In this regard, since it was placed on the gray list of the Financial Action Task Force (FATF) in 2018, the fear of being blacklisted by the Task Force, which could result in economic suffocation, has discouraged Pakistan from making any conspicuous moves in support of terrorism.[127] Additionally, there are now powerful anti-Pakistan Islamist organizations such as TTP that did not exist in the past. They have ties to anti-India militant outfits, which are still supported by the Pakistani military and ISI, and thus bolstering support for the latter will unintentionally energize the former, leading to an escalation of terrorist attacks against Pakistan itself.[128]

Still, even if Pakistan does not substantially bolster support for anti-India militancy and the situation in Indian Kashmir does not deteriorate as it did in the 1990s, terrorist attacks in Kashmir and mainland India could still very well increase. Pakistan-based militant outfits, such as Lashkar-e-Taiba (LeT) and Jaish-e-Mohammed (JeM), which are primarily focused on attacks in mainland India and Indian Kashmir but also have a base in Afghanistan and ties to the Taliban, have gained momentum from the Taliban's success.[129] The JeM chief met with the Taliban leadership after the fall of Kabul and asked for support for the anti-India jihad in Kashmir.[130] The Taliban's wavering position on Indian rule in Kashmir, which such outfits view as oppressive to Muslims,[131] leaves open the possibility for the Taliban to step in. There also is the threat of al Qaeda and ISKP that have been freed from U.S. counterterrorism pressure.

Moreover, India is likely to have difficulties in sustaining its position as Afghanistan's main development partner, a role it has fulfilled for the past two decades. Notwithstanding the Taliban's expectations and wishes for India's continued involvement in Afghanistan's economic development,[132] it can be thwarted easily by Pakistan, which loathes India's expanding influence in Afghanistan. Even in the past two decades, all forms of Indian presence in Afghanistan have been subject to terrorist attacks by the hard-line Haqqani Network within the Taliban and Pakistan-based groups like LeT and JeM. These organizations are believed to have close ties to the Pakistani military and ISI.[133] The risk of staying in the post-U.S. Afghanistan is too great for Delhi if there is neither a pro-India government in Kabul nor U.S. forces that support it.

Meanwhile, at this time, India neither has the option to interfere in Afghanistan by supporting anti-Taliban groups. There is no powerful resistance group, and above all, even if one were to emerge, India is unable to act on its own. Its support of the Northern Alliance in the 1990s was possible precisely because of collaboration with Iran, which borders Afghanistan and has a network in the country, and with Russia, which is the backer of Central Asian Republics that lie to the north of Afghanistan.[134] Both Iran and Russia have so far chosen to engage with the Taliban.

Against this backdrop, after the Taliban's seizure of power, Indian External Affairs Minister Subrahmanyam Jaishankar made clear that India was adopting a "wait-and-watch" approach to developments in Afghanistan.[135] This may be indicative of the little room left for Delhi to act proactively; if so, however, there is also little need for India to rush into any action. Unless the situation in Kashmir in the 1990s repeats itself, the growing terror threat can still be addressed effectively with defensive measures. The fact that China and Pakistan are strengthening their engagement with the Taliban and expanding their influence in Afghanistan is a cause for concern to Delhi, but, at present, India has no means to stop this. Furthermore, while India's current approach to the Taliban differs from Russia and Iran's, Delhi still coordinates with the two on Afghanistan.[136] That both countries are working in tandem with China and Pakistan is, paradoxically, a source of reassurance for India; its partnership with Russia and Iran would enable India to grasp the situation in Afghanistan and, if the needs arise, to join the engagement camp later.

At the same time, India has gradually moved to maintain its position as a key stakeholder in Afghanistan. In early November 2021, it hosted the Regional

Security Dialogue on Afghanistan, which Iran has held twice in the past, with the attendance of national security advisors from Russia, Iran, and five Central Asian Republics. The Taliban expressed a favorable opinion of the meeting, notwithstanding that it was not invited.[137] During the Moscow Format meeting held beforehand in October, the Indian delegation held talks with the Taliban and reportedly offered humanitarian assistance, which was formally announced in November.[138] It appears that, for the foreseeable future, India's policy toward Taliban-ruled Afghanistan will be two tracks: dealing with the potential growth of the threat of terrorism resulting from the developments in Afghanistan and, simultaneously, closely following the moves of the Taliban and key stakeholders through its partnership with Russia and Iran and regional diplomacy.

4. International Politics over the Post-U.S. Afghanistan

(1) Latitude for Cooperation among the Key Stakeholders

If one takes an objective look at what the six key stakeholders for the post-U.S. Afghanistan, including the United States, demand of the Taliban following their takeover of the country, noticeable similarities can be observed. While there are differences in the order of priority, details, and degree, the six countries generally make the same three demands: containment of terrorism emanating from Afghanistan against other countries; establishment of an inclusive political structure; and respect for the rights of women and minorities. In addition, while the countries used to have varying views on the U.S. military presence in Afghanistan, they have all benefited from its existence, which helped to impede destabilization of the Afghan state and curb the threat of wide-ranging terrorism from the country.

Additionally, aside from Pakistan and Iran, which have significant influence in Afghanistan, the four remaining countries have no strong intention to deeply engage in the country and pursue anything beyond preventing or managing consequences that are detrimental to their political and security interests. There are no longer any vital U.S. national interests to be pursued in Afghanistan, other than deterring terrorist attacks from the country, as President Biden has categorically stated, and the United States has little intention of putting significant energy into Afghanistan. China may possibly be interested in Afghanistan's economic potential; however, the record of its economic activities in the country over the past two decades suggests Beijing is not strongly attracted to developing Afghanistan's economic interests per se, apart from its utility as a tool to maneuver the Taliban. As for Russia, given its experience of the failed intervention in the Soviet era, Moscow remains wary of getting involved in Afghanistan too deeply. India, which was loyal to the former democratic government until the last minute, has lost both influence in Afghanistan and the partners to maintain that influence following the Taliban's seizure of power. As such, there is no compelling reason for Delhi to become deeply involved in today's Afghanistan beyond preventing terrorism. In short, intense competition over the influence in Afghanistan among the key stakeholders—reminiscent of the 19th century "Great Game" between the British and Russian empires, which was ominously predicted to occur after the U.S. withdrawal—has so far been a far-off prospect.

Assuming the commonalities in what they demand to the Taliban, as well as the absence of the new "Great Game," it seems not inconceivable that some sort of collaboration emerges among the key stakeholders. However, the reality is that the six countries have not been able to form a common approach to deal with Afghanistan under the Taliban. The United States adopts the position that it will neither recognize the Taliban government nor provide aid that directly funds the group unless the Taliban fulfill their commitment to address the threat of terrorism, establish an inclusive government, and respect human rights.[139] China, Russia, Pakistan, and Iran similarly do not recognize the Taliban government and generally make the same demands but give priority to engaging with the Taliban. Moreover, the four countries also criticize the pressure tactics of the West, essentially backing the Taliban's demands, and call for the lifting of sanctions and the freeze on assets of the Afghan central bank.[140] The joint statement of the Moscow Format meeting hosted by Russia contains the wording, "take into account the new reality, that is the Taliban coming to power in the country."[141] At the UN Human Rights Council in October 2021, China, Russia, and Pakistan voted against the appointment of a special rapporteur on the situation of human rights in Afghanistan.

Among the factors preventing the key stakeholders from aligning their approach is their disagreement on the degree, details, and order of priority of containing terrorism, establishing an inclusive government, and respecting human rights— even though the overall directions of what each country demands from the Taliban are not so far apart from one another. In particular, clear differences exist in the weight each stakeholder attaches to the rights of women and minorities.

That being the case, what should not be overlooked here is that the issue of how to deal with Afghanistan after the Taliban takeover is now being subsumed into the competition between the United States, on the one hand, and China, Russia, and Iran—countries that have already been embroiled in a broader rivalry with Washington—on the other hand. Putting Islamabad aside (which is still an American ally), the proactive attitude of Beijing, Moscow, and Tehran on engaging with the Taliban is an extension of the relationships they built with the group while it was an anti-U.S. insurgency movement. The three capitals made rapprochement with the Taliban amid respective security concerns over the U.S. military presence in Afghanistan, albeit it might not be the sole reason. Hence, all three countries are now trying to make contrast between their willingness to embrace the new ruler in Afghanistan and reluctance of the United States and its allies, intending to exploit the collapse of the western-backed Afghan democratic regime and the Taliban's return to power as an opportunity to propagandize the failure of the United States.[142]

That said, it is another matter whether China, Russia, Pakistan, and Iran can secure what they demand from Taliban-ruled Afghanistan through actively engaging with the Taliban. Pakistan, for its part, has been unable to extract the Taliban's sincere crackdown against TTP, and it is uncertain how the Taliban will deal with ETIM as sought by China. Furthermore, the Taliban have asserted that the interim government that they announced in September 2021, which Russia and Iran criticized as not representing all political and ethnic groups in Afghanistan, is sufficiently inclusive.[143]

(2) The Taliban and the Shadow of ISKP

It is unclear to what extent the Taliban are willing to meet the demands of the key stakeholders, such as containing terrorist attacks from Afghanistan, forming an inclusive government, and respecting the rights of women and minorities. That said, even if the Taliban are willing to meet the demands, the presence of ISKP, another Islamist movement, will make it difficult.

In general, as competition between terrorist organizations intensifies, individual terrorist groups tend to escalate violence as a show of presence.[144] Although the Taliban are not oriented toward international terrorism, the presence of IS creates incentives for al Qaeda and other competing international jihadist groups to ramp up their attacks.[145]

Furthermore, ISKP has sought to attract Taliban and al Qaeda supporters by claiming that it is the true jihadist group, not the Taliban.[146] Hence, it is conceivable that, even if the Taliban were to try to constrain external terrorism by foreign militant groups in Afghan territory, dissatisfied groups and individual members will simply join ISKP. Defectors from TTP, Taliban, al Qaeda, and LeT have indeed joined ISKP.[147] While IMU has vacillated between the Taliban and ISKP, ETIM is noted to have a relationship with not only al Qaeda but also ISKP.[148]

Similar issues could arise within the ranks of Taliban as well. Cracking down on such allied militant groups or easing the harsh Taliban-style rule, including suppression of women's rights, at the request of foreign governments could create divisions within the Taliban and threaten the unity of the organization.[149] Besides, ISKP is reaching out to younger Taliban members who are ideologically more radical and are dissatisfied with their leadership's reluctance to restrict women's rights or willingness to cooperate with the United States and China. This, coupled with the high compensation ISKP is offering, has led to a large number of them joining ISKP.[150] Thus, it is becoming all the more difficult for the Taliban leadership, which values organizational unity,[151] to respond to the demands of the international community.

(3) Spillover Effects on International Relations

Given that there is little prospect of the Taliban meeting the demands of the key stakeholders, it would be ideal for the six countries to align their approaches and use pressure and engagement in a coordinated manner. Since September 2021, several multilateral meetings on Afghanistan were held in succession, including the Troika Plus meeting in November attended by the special representatives of the United States, which is wary of engagement with the Taliban, and China, Russia, and Pakistan, which are positive about engagement. It would be preferable that these developments lead to the convergence of the approach among the six.

However, their attitude hitherto suggests otherwise. Namely, the key stakeholders' demands of the Taliban—especially the one of counterterrorism, which has direct ramifications for their own security—will continue to be unmet, which in turn further complicates relations among them.

At the regional level, this could be observed in India-Pakistan and Pakistan-Iran relations. In the case of the former, if LeT or JeM, after seeing the success of the Taliban, intensifies its attacks against India, Delhi will construe that Islamabad is escalating its proxy war. Meanwhile, Pakistan, which firmly believes (albeit objectively dubious) that India is supporting TTP and ISKP, will perceive that India is stepping up the offensive if TTP attacks were to intensify. These developments will increase tension between India and Pakistan. In addition, if Iran aggressively exercises its influence or resorts to direct intervention using militias to protect the Shia minorities in Afghanistan or to eliminate the ISKP threat, this will alarm Pakistan and complicate relations between the two countries. While Iran-Pakistan relations are not necessarily adversarial, the two countries are linked to different factions in Afghanistan and within the Taliban and thus compete with each other for influence.[152]

At the global level, one can expect spillover effects on U.S.-China/Russia relations and U.S.-Iran relations. Given their efforts to contrast their willingness to embrace the Taliban with the pressure tactics of the West, Beijing, Moscow, and Tehran are likely to, at least publicly, condemn the United States and its allies for preventing the Taliban from establishing effective governance, rather than criticizing the Taliban, if the threat of terrorism from Afghanistan were to extend to the three. At the same time, China and Russia may justify their own domestic, oppressive counterterrorism policies as a response to the growing threat from Afghanistan. Yet, that logic is unacceptable to the West, which views their authoritarian way of governance as problematic. As a result, the Afghanistan issue could add another source of conflict to the already intensifying strategic competition between the United States and China/Russia/Iran.

As mentioned above, it would be an exaggeration to describe the ongoing interaction of key stakeholders over Afghanistan, especially international politics among the United States, China, and Russia, as a "Great Game." Nevertheless, coordination or cooperation among all of the key stakeholders remains difficult— more or less affected by their broader rivalry beyond the Afghan issue—and will be the same henceforth. Against this backdrop, the future of the Afghan state after the withdrawal of U.S. forces is becoming even more uncertain.

NOTES

1) Clayton Thomas et al., "U.S. Military Withdrawal and Taliban Takeover in Afghanistan: Frequently Asked Questions," Congressional Research Service (September 17, 2021), 1-2.

2) Andrew Small, *The China-Pakistan Axis: Asia's New Geopolitics* [paperback edition] (London: C. Hurst & Co. Ltd, 2020), 133.

3) Borhan Osman, "The Cost of Escalating Violence in Afghanistan," International Crisis Group (February 7, 2018).

4) Agreement for Bringing Peace to Afghanistan between the Islamic Emirate of Afghanistan Which Is Not Recognized by the United States as a State and Is Known as the Taliban and the United States of America, February 29, 2020; Clayton Thomas, "Afghanistan: Background and U.S. Policy: In Brief," Congressional Research Service (March 25, 2021), 5-6.

5) Lisa Curtis, "How America Should Deal with the Taliban," *Foreign Affairs*, September 20, 2021.

6) The White House, "Remarks by President Biden on the Drawdown of U.S. Forces in Afghanistan" (July 8, 2021).

7) CNBC, July 27, 2021.

8) The White House, "Remarks by President Biden on the End of the War in Afghanistan"

(August 31, 2021).

9)   Ibid.

10)   Afghanistan Study Group, "Afghanistan Study Group Final Report," United States Institute of Peace (USIP) (February 2021), 22-23.

11)   *New York Times*, September 15, 2021.

12)   Asfandyar Mir, "Twenty Years after 9/11: The Terror Threat from Afghanistan Post the Taliban Takeover," *CTC Sentinel* 14, no. 7 (September 2021): 37-38.

13)   Reuters, October 27, 2021.

14)   *Wall Street Journal*, August 31, 2021; *Politico*, September 3, 2021.

15)   Michael Hirsh, "U.S. Military Concedes It's Unready to Fight Terrorism from 'Over the Horizon'," *Foreign Policy*, September 30, 2021.

16)   Saurav Sarkar, "ISKP and Afghanistan's Future Security," Stimson Center (August 6, 2021).

17)   Afghanistan Study Group, "Afghanistan Study Group Final Report," 15.

18)   Reuters, November 17, 2021.

19)   Voice of America, November 10, 2021; Abdul Sayed, "The Taliban's Persistent War on Salafists in Afghanistan," *Terrorism Monitor* 19, issue 18 (September 24, 2021): 10; Oved Lobel, "The Taliban Are Losing the Fight against Islamic State," *Strategist*, December 6, 2021.

20)   *Wall Street Journal*, October 31, 2021.

21)   AP News, September 2, 2021.

22)   Michael Hirsh, "Is Islamic Terrorism Coming to the U.S. Again?," *Foreign Policy*, August 26, 2021.

23)   BBC Monitoring South Asia, September 4, 2021.

24)   National Public Radio, October 10, 2021; *Defense One*, November 20, 2021.

25)   [U.S.] Department of Defense (DOD), *Operation Freedom's Sentinel: Lead Inspector General Report to the United States Congress* (August 2021), 18-19.

26)   Barbara Elias, "Why the Taliban Won't Quit al Qaeda," *Foreign Policy*, September 21, 2021.

27)   Mir, "Twenty Years after 9/11," 31-32, 38.

28)   Afghanistan Study Group, "Afghanistan Study Group Final Report," 38; Caitlin O'Hara and Colin P. Clarke, "Thinking Long Term about the Future of Afghanistan," *Lawfare*, September 19, 2021.

29)   [U.S.] DOD, *Operation Freedom's Sentinel*, 18.

30)   Elias, "Why the Taliban Won't Quit al Qaeda."

31)   Shuja Nawaz, *Crossed Swords: Pakistan, Its Army, and the Wars Within* (Karachi: Oxford University Press, 2008), 371-375; T.V. Paul, *The Warrior State: Pakistan in the Contemporary World* (New York: Oxford University Press, 2014), 57.

32)   Afghanistan Study Group, "Afghanistan Study Group Final Report," 40-41; Bruce Riedel,

"Pakistan, Taliban and the Afghan Quagmire," Brookings Institution (August 24, 2013).

33) Zachary Constantino, "The India-Pakistan Rivalry in Afghanistan," USIP (January 2020), 9; C. Christine Fair, *Fighting to the End: The Pakistan Army's Way of War* (New York: Oxford University Press, 2014), 26, 103-104.

34) Geo News, August 16, 2021.

35) *Express Tribune*, August 29, 2021.

36) Afghanistan Study Group, "Afghanistan Study Group Final Report," 38.

37) *Dawn*, March 2, 2016.

38) Elizabeth Threlkeld and Grace Easterly, "Afghanistan-Pakistan Ties and Future Stability in Afghanistan," USIP (August 2021), 20.

39) Afghanistan Study Group, "Afghanistan Study Group Final Report," 39.

40) Amira Jadoon, "The Evolution and Potential Resurgence of the Tehrik-i-Taliban Pakistan," USIP (May 2021), 3-15.

41) United Nations Security Council (UNSC), Letter dated 20 May 2021 from the Chair of the Security Council Committee established pursuant to resolution 1988 (2011) addressed to the President of the Security Council, S/2021/486 (June 1, 2021), 19.

42) BBC, October 13, 2021.

43) *Nikkei Asia*, October 15, 2021.

44) *News*, August 29, 2021; *Dawn*, November 14, 2021.

45) Voice of America, December 9, 2021.

46) Antonio Giustozzi, "The Resurgence of the Tehrik-i-Taliban Pakistan," Royal United Services Institute (RUSI) (August 12, 2021).

47) Catrina Doxsee, Jared Thompson, and Grace Hwang, "Examining Extremism: Islamic State Khorasan Province," Center for Strategic and International Studies (CSIS) (September 8, 2021).

48) Reuters, September 10, 2021.

49) Aljazeera, September 20, 2021.

50) Threlkeld and Easterly, "Afghanistan-Pakistan Ties," 19.

51) *Daily Times*, September 20, 2021.

52) Umair Jamal, "Iran and Pakistan: Bilateral Bonding over the Taliban," *Diplomat*, September 28, 2021.

53) Zhao Huasheng and Andrew C. Kuchins, "China and Afghanistan: China's Interests, Stances, and Perspectives," CSIS (March 2012), 3.

54) Small, *The China-Pakistan Axis*, 74-75.

55) Ibid., 80-82.

56) Abdul Salam Zaeef, *My Life with the Taliban* (London: C. Hurst and Co. Ltd., 2010), 135.

57) Tiffany P. Ng, "China's Role in Shaping the Future of Afghanistan," Carnegie Endowment for International Peace (September 1, 2010), 3-4.

58) Yun Sun, "How China Views the U.S. Withdrawal from Afghanistan," *War on the Rocks*, May 13, 2021.

59) Vanda Felbab-Brown, "A BRI(dge) too Far: The Unfulfilled Promise and Limitations of China's Involvement in Afghanistan," Brookings Institution (June 2020), 2-5.

60) [China] Ministry of Foreign Affairs (MFA), "Foreign Ministry Spokesperson Hua Chunying's Regular Press Conference on August 16, 2021" (August 16, 2021).

61) [China] MFA, "Foreign Ministry Spokesperson Hua Chunying's Regular Press Conference on August 17, 2021" (August 17, 2021).

62) *Washington Post*, February 10, 2018; *Dawn*, August 24, 2012.

63) *Tajikistan Newsline*, October 29, 2021.

64) *Dawn*, July 28, 2021.

65) *Global Times*, September 9, 2021.

66) S/2021/486, 19-20.

67) *Nikkei Asia*, August 11, 2021.

68) *Global Times*, September 17, 2021.

69) Radio Free Europe/Radio Liberty, October 5, 2021.

70) Small, *The China-Pakistan Axis*, 76, 129-130.

71) Ibid., 87-88.

72) Reuters, October 7, 2009; Animesh Roul, "Al-Qaeda and Islamic State Reinvigorating East Turkistan Jihad," *Terrorism Monitor* 17, issue 10 (May 17, 2019): 8.

73) Tushar Ranjan Mohanty, "Balochistan: The Chinese Chequered," *South Asia Intelligence Review* 15, no. 51 (June 19, 2017).

74) Kevin Schwartz, "China's Evolving Security Presence in Afghanistan and Central Asia," *China Brief* 21, issue 2 (February 4, 2021): 34.

75) *Global Times*, September 9, 2021.

76) *Global Times*, August 24, 2021.

77) Aljazeera, October 8, 2021.

78) Felbab-Brown, "A BRI(dge) too Far," 8-9.

79) CNBC, December 16, 2016.

80) [U.S.] Department of State, "A Conversation with Ambassador Alice Wells on the China-Pakistan Economic Corridor" (November 21, 2019).

81) *SCMP*, September 17, 2021; *Financial Times*, September 23, 2021.

82) David G. Lewis, "Return to Kabul? Russian Policy in Afghanistan," *Security Insights*, George C. Marshall European Center for Security Studies (June 2020), 1-3.

83) Small, *The China-Pakistan Axis*, 76; "Adapting to a New Reality in Afghanistan," International Institute for Strategic Studies (August 20, 2021).

84) Alexey Kupriyanov and Alexey Davydov, "A Russian View," in *2021: Afghanistan's Year of Reckoning*, eds. Rakesh Sood et al., Observer Research Foundation (April 2021), 16-17.

85) Michael Kofman, Aaron Stein, and Yun Sun, "After Withdrawal: How China, Turkey, and Russia Will Respond to the Taliban," *War on the Rocks*, August 31, 2021.

86) Tass, August 16, 2021.

87) AP News, July 9, 2021.

88) Umida Hashimova, "Russia, Central Asian States Worry about Instability in Afghanistan," *Diplomat*, May 3, 2021.

89) Radio Free Europe/Radio Liberty, August 30, 2021; Radio Free Europe/Radio Liberty, September 7, 2021.

90) *Economic Times*, September 10, 2021; *Moscow Times*, August 25, 2021.

91) Kofman, Stein, and Sun, "After Withdrawal."

92) Dara Massicot, "Can a Pragmatic Relationship with the Taliban Help Russia Counter Terrorism?," *National Interest*, September 3, 2021.

93) United Nations High Commissioner for Refugees, "Afghanistan Situation External Update: 1 October 2021" (October 1, 2021), 3; Ibid.

94) Mir, "Twenty Years after 9/11," 36-37.

95) Tass, August 16, 2021.

96) Aljazeera, September 26, 2021.

97) Samuel Ramani, "Russia and the Taliban: Prospective Partners?," RUSI (September 14, 2021); Kupriyanov and Davydov, "A Russian View," 17.

98) Tass, September 17, 2021.

99) Afghanistan Study Group, "Afghanistan Study Group Final Report," 42.

100) Anadolu Agency, October 19, 2021; [Russia] Ministry of Foreign Affairs (MFA), "Joint Statement of the Participants in the Moscow Format Consultations on Afghanistan, Moscow, 20 October 2021" (October 20, 2021).

101) Alireza Nader et al., *Iran's Influence in Afghanistan: Implications for the U.S. Drawdown* (Santa Monica: RAND Corporation, 2014), 5-7.

102) Avinash Paliwal, *My Enemy's Enemy: India in Afghanistan from the Soviet Invasion to the US Withdrawal* (London: Hurst & Company, 2017), 117.

103) Nader et al., *Iran's Influence in Afghanistan*, 5-16.

104) Yochi Dreazen, "Exclusive: Iran Teams with Taliban to Fight Islamic State in Afghanistan," *Foreign Policy*, May 26, 2016.

105) Reuters, August 16, 2021.

106) Radio Free Europe/Radio Liberty, August 18, 2021.

107) Borzou Daragahi, "Iran Spent Years Preparing for a Taliban Victory. It May Still Get Stung.," Atlantic Council (August 20, 2021).

108) Amnesty International, "Afghanistan: 13 Hazara Killed by Taliban Fighters in Daykundi Province – New Investigation" (October 5, 2021); Amnesty International, "Afghanistan: Taliban Responsible for Brutal Massacre of Hazara Men – New Investigation" (August 19, 2021).

109) Bryce Loidolt, "Al-Qaeda's Iran Dilemma: Evidence from the Abbottabad Records," *Studies in Conflict & Terrorism* (2020): 1-28; Asfandyar Mir and Colin P. Clarke, "Making Sense of Iran and al-Qaeda's Relationship," *Lawfare*, March 21, 2021.

110) Fatemeh Aman, "The Afghan Refugee Crisis: What Does It Mean for Iran?," Middle East Institute (September 20, 2021).

111) *Nikkei Asia*, September 7, 2021.

112) Reuters, November 10, 2021.

113) Aljazeera, September 9, 2021.

114) *News*, September 7, 2021.

115) *Nation*, November 22, 2021; ABC News, October 6, 2021.

116) Tolo News, November 11, 2021.

117) Nader et al., *Iran's Influence in Afghanistan*, 5-7.

118) Sudha Ramachandran, "The Shia Fatemiyoun Brigade: Iran's Prospective Proxy Militia in Afghanistan," *Terrorism Monitor* 19, no. 6 (March 26, 2021): 3-5.

119) Tolo News, December 21, 2020.

120) Paliwal, *My Enemy's Enemy*, 38-41, 47-55.

121) V.K. Sood and Pravin Sawhney, *Operation Parakram: The War Unfinished* (New Delhi: Sage Publications, 2003), 34.

122) Paliwal, *My Enemy's Enemy*, 99, 112-113.

123) Constantino, "The India-Pakistan Rivalry in Afghanistan," 4, 17.

124) Ibid., 7; Afghanistan Study Group, "Afghanistan Study Group Final Report," 42.

125) *Indian Express*, August 30, 2021.

126) Paliwal, *My Enemy's Enemy*, 213-236.

127) *Indian Express*, July 20, 2019.

128) C. Christine Fair, "Explaining Support for Sectarian Terrorism in Pakistan: Piety, Maslak and Sharia," *Religions* 6, no. 4 (December 2015): 1139.

129) Mir, "Twenty Years after 9/11," 37; Jared Schwartz and Yelena Biberman, "A Divided Taliban Could Unleash a New Proxy War in Afghanistan," Atlantic Council (June 29, 2020); Sushant Singh, "Afghanistan Shows the Limits of India's Power," *Foreign Policy*,

April 22, 2021.

130) *India Today*, August 27, 2021.

131) *India Today*, September 3, 2021.

132) *Indian Express*, August 30, 2021.

133) *Dawn*, September 22, 2011; *Fair, Fighting to the End*, 251-252.

134) Paliwal, *My Enemy's Enemy*, 132.

135) *New Indian Express*, August 27, 2021.

136) *Economic Times*, September 23, 2021; *Hindu*, December 7, 2021.

137) NDTV, November 12, 2021.

138) *Business Standard*, October 21, 2021; *Deccan Herald*, November 18, 2021.

139) P. Michael McKinley, "Afghanistan's Looming Catastrophe," *Foreign Affairs*, December 3, 2021.

140) *Financial Times*, September 23, 2021; *Moscow Times*, October 25, 2021; *Dawn*, September 16, 2021.

141) [Russia] MFA, "Joint Statement of the Participants in the Moscow Format Consultations on Afghanistan, Moscow, 20 October 2021" (October 20, 2021).

142) NBC News, September 9, 2021.

143) Anadolu Agency, November 12, 2021.

144) Justin Conrad and Kevin Greene, "Competition, Differentiation, and the Severity of Terrorists Attacks," *Journal of Politics* 77, no. 2 (2015): 546-561.

145) Mir, "Twenty Years after 9/11," 39-40.

146) Amira Jadoon and Andrew Mines, "The Taliban Can't Take on the Islamic State Alone," *War on the Rocks*, October 14, 2021.

147) Doxsee, Thompson, and Hwang, "Examining Extremism."

148) UNSC, Letter dated 15 July 2021 from the Chair of the Security Council Committee pursuant to resolutions 1267 (1999), 1989 (2011) and 2253 (2015) concerning Islamic State in Iraq and the Levant (Da'esh), Al-Qaida and associated individuals, groups, undertakings and entities addressed to the President of the Security Council, S/2021/655 (July 21, 2021), 15; S/2021/486, 20.

149) "Terrorism Monitor Interview with Dr. Antonio Giustozzi," *Terrorism Monitor* 19, issue 17 (September 7, 2021): 7; Andrew Watkins, "An Assessment of Taliban Rule at Three Months," *CTC Sentinel* 14, no. 9 (November 2021): 12.

150) *Nikkei Asia*, November 19, 2021.

151) Watkins, "An Assessment of Taliban Rule at Three Months," 3.

152) Ali Fatollah-Nejad and Hamidreza Azizi, "Iran and the Taliban after the US Fiasco in Afghanistan," Middle East Institute (September 22, 2021); Antonio Giustozzi, "Russia

and Iran: Disappointed Friends of the Taliban?," RUSI (September 30, 2021).

Chapter 2

Progress in the Normalization of Relations between the Arab Countries and Israel

The 2020 Abraham Accords and
Subsequent Developments

NISHINO Masami

The Abraham Accords signing ceremony at the White House, September 15, 2020 (CNP/DPA/Kyodo News Images)

Summary

In 2020, relations between the Arab countries and Israel underwent changes with mediation by the U.S. Trump administration. Starting in August, four Arab countries—the United Arab Emirates (UAE), Bahrain, Sudan, and Morocco—decided to normalize relations with Israel in succession. Ever since Israel was founded in 1948, the Arab countries and Israel have fought a number of Arab-Israeli wars, and until 2020, Egypt and Jordan were the only two Arab countries that had normalized relations with Israel.

Traditionally, most Arab countries took the position that establishment of diplomatic relations with Israel would be conditioned on progress in Israeli-Palestinian negotiations and the creation of a Palestinian state. The recent normalization of relations, however, had nothing to do with the progress of the negotiations, signifying the Arab countries have departed from the traditional position.

The Arab countries that normalized relations with Israel had something to gain from the United States. Other Arab countries did not condemn the normalization of relations and may themselves decide to normalize ties with Israel. Hamas in the Gaza Strip exchanged fire with Israel in May 2021. Nevertheless, this engagement did not stem the trend of improving relations between the Arab countries and Israel.

From 2000 to 2001, Israel and Palestine held negotiations on the creation of a Palestinian state with the mediation of the U.S. Clinton administration but were unable to reach an agreement. Furthermore, in 2007, the Palestinian territories were divided into the West Bank, self-governed by the Fatah-led Palestinian National Authority, and the Gaza Strip, under the effective control of Hamas. Since then, talks between Palestine and Israel have stagnated further. Meanwhile, some Arab countries and Israel improved their relations behind the scenes in the 2010s. The lack of prospect for progress in Israeli-Palestinian negotiations on the creation of a Palestinian state, combined with some Arab countries' wish to improve relations with Israel, were behind the recent wave of normalization agreements.

Keywords

Israel | Arab | Palestine | Middle East | Abraham Accords

1. From the Founding of Israel to the Oslo Accords

The successive persecution of Jews in Europe and Russia in the latter part of the 19th century triggered Zionism, a Jewish nationalist movement to create a Jewish State. They chose to establish the new state in Palestine, where a Jewish kingdom existed in ancient times, and began immigrating there in 1882.

Palestine was placed under the British mandate after World War I. As Jewish immigration continued, clashes grew between the Jews and the original Arab inhabitants in Palestine (Palestinians). In the 1930s, Britain restricted Jewish immigration. During World War II, large numbers of Jews enlisted and fought in the British Armed Forces in order to gain military experience. Yet, even after the war, Britain continued to impose the immigration restrictions, inciting the Jews in Palestine to launch an armed struggle against the British mandatory authorities in October 1945. No longer able to contain the situation, Britain referred the matter of the future of Palestine to the United Nations (UN) in February 1947. In November, the UN adopted a resolution partitioning Palestine into two states, the Jewish State and the Arab State, with the Jerusalem area under international trusteeship.[1] The Jews accepted the resolution, but the Arabs rejected it.[2]

In May 1948, the British mandate ended, and the Jews declared independence of the new state of Israel. Not recognizing Israel, Egypt and other Arab states mounted a military attack on the country, triggering the First Arab-Israeli War. Conversely, the United States and the Soviet Union quickly recognized the state. Israel gradually gained the upper hand in the war after purchasing weapons from Czechoslovakia, and the war de facto ended in January 1949. Within Palestine, the Arab country of Egypt occupied the Gaza Strip, while Transjordan occupied the West Bank, including East Jerusalem. Israel acquired the rest of the land, including West Jerusalem.[3] In short, Israel gained a larger area of Palestine than that allocated in the UN Partition Plan for Palestine. Many Arabs (Palestinians) fled Israel and entered the West Bank, Gaza Strip, and neighboring Arab countries as refugees.[4] Thus originated the Palestinian refugee issue that continues to this day.

Following the subsequent Suez Crisis of 1956, or the Second Arab-Israeli War, Israel launched a preemptive attack on Egypt, Jordan, Syria, and other Arab countries in 1967 in response to Egyptian military threats, triggering the Third Arab-Israeli War. By this time, the Arab countries were supported by the East (Soviet Union) and Israel was supported by the West (United States and Europe). The Third Arab-Israeli War is also called the Six-Day War because Israel won the war in six days. In this war, Israeli forces occupied the West Bank, including East Jerusalem, the Gaza Strip, the Golan Heights in Syria, and the Sinai Peninsula in Egypt.[5] In other words, Israel took control of the entire Palestine as well as the surrounding areas.

Until the Third Arab-Israeli War, the Arab countries appear to have aimed for the overthrow of Israel. That is to say, the survival of Israel was considered the point of contention until then. With Israel's astounding victory in the Third Arab-Israeli War, however, Israel's survival was no longer a point of contention. From then on, the true point of contention shifted to the extent of Israel's territory, i.e., where the borders should be drawn. After the war, in November 1967, UN Security Council Resolution 242 was adopted, calling for Israeli forces to withdraw from territories occupied in the war. The resolution can be construed as requiring Israel to withdraw from the West Bank and Gaza Strip in Palestine. This led to the later two-state concept of establishing a Palestinian state in the West Bank and Gaza Strip. In 1969, the United States became almost the sole arms supplier to Israel, and U.S.-Israeli relations have since grown even closer.

Then, in 1973, Egypt and Syria mounted a surprise attack on Israel from the north and south, causing the sudden outbreak of the Fourth Arab-Israeli War. In this war, the Arab countries were able to demonstrate their military capabilities for the first time. Egypt was thus able to claim victory in the war, and afterwards, used this as leverage to embark on peace negotiations with Israel. In 1978, Egyptian President Anwar Sadat and Israeli Prime Minister Menachem Begin, through the mediation of U.S. President Jimmy Carter, held negotiations at Camp David in the United States and reached an agreement. Based on this agreement, the Treaty of Peace between the Arab Republic of Egypt and the State of Israel was signed at the White House in 1979.[6] In this way, the United States has played a mediating role in the Middle East peace process since the 1970s.

Accordingly, Egypt became the first Arab country to normalize relations with Israel, and Israel returned the Sinai Peninsula to Egypt. With Egypt's departure from the Arab coalition, the rest of the Arab countries no longer had a chance to win against Israel. For this reason, in the wake of the Fourth Arab-Israeli War, no war has broken out involving full exchange of fire between the regular military forces of the Arab countries and Israeli forces. In protest over Egypt's unilateral signing of the peace treaty, the other Arab countries suspended Egypt's membership in the Arab League from 1979 to 1989. The peace treaty was met with opposition within Egypt as well, and President Sadat was assassinated in 1981.

In 1982, Israeli forces advanced into Lebanon with the aim of expelling the Palestine Liberation Organization (PLO). The PLO was a Palestinian political organization that was based in Lebanon at the time. As a result, the PLO leadership was forced out of Lebanon and relocated to Tunisia, losing geographical contact with Palestine. Subsequently, in 1987, the Palestinian resistance movement against Israel, the intifada, was launched in the Israeli-occupied West Bank and Gaza Strip, heightening international sympathy for the Palestinians. Although the West Bank was annexed by Jordan in 1950 after the First Arab-Israeli War, Jordan relinquished sovereignty over the West Bank in 1988.

Later, in 1990, when Iraq occupied Kuwait and the Gulf Crisis broke out, Iraq advocated a linkage theory linking Israel's withdrawal from territories occupied after the 1967 Third Arab-Israeli War and Iraq's withdrawal from Kuwait. In turn, the PLO supported Iraq. In the ensuing 1991 Gulf War, U.S. and other multinational forces liberated Kuwait, and Iraq was defeated. The PLO fell short of its intention to use Iraq as leverage to defuse the situation. Meanwhile, the victorious United States stepped up diplomatic activities, creating a negotiating environment between Israel and the Palestinians.

In January 1993, Israel and the PLO began secret negotiations in Oslo through Norwegian mediation. The talks were successful. In September, Israel and the PLO mutually recognized each other and signed the Declaration of Principles on Interim Self-Government Arrangements (Oslo Accord) at the White House. Under this agreement, it was decided that the Palestinians would govern themselves in the West Bank and Gaza Strip, that interim self-government would begin in Jericho in the West Bank and in the Gaza Strip, and that the interim period would be five years, during which the Israelis and the Palestinians would negotiate the permanent status. The matters of Jerusalem, Palestinian refugees' right to return, settlements in the West Bank and Gaza Strip, and the borders were to be discussed in the negotiations on the permanent status. The Oslo Accord thus established the policy of the two-state solution, whereby Israel would coexist with the Palestinian state, consisting of the West Bank and Gaza Strip.

Following progress in Israeli-Palestinian reconciliation, Jordan and Israel signed a peace treaty in 1994, making Jordan the second Arab country to normalize relations with Israel.

2. Stagnation of the Peace Process

Ever since these developments, however, negotiations between the Palestinians and Israelis did not make steady progress, nor did the normalization of relations between the Arab countries and Israel.

On May 4, 1994, Israel and the PLO signed an agreement in Cairo. This date marked the beginning of the five-year interim period stipulated in the Oslo Accord.[7] In the same month, self-government began in the Gaza Strip and Jericho.

In September 1995, Israel and the PLO signed the Israeli-Palestinian Interim Agreement on the West Bank and the Gaza Strip (Oslo II).[8] Under the agreement, the West Bank was divided into three areas: Area A, where the Palestinian National Authority has administrative and police authority; Area B, where the Palestinian National Authority has administrative authority and both Israel and the Palestinian National Authority have police authority; and Area C, where Israel has administrative and police authority. Areas A and B have a total area equivalent to around 30% of the entire West Bank. Furthermore, the agreement stipulated the withdrawal of Israeli forces from the six cities of Jenin, Tulkarm, Nablus, Qalqilya, Ramallah, and

Figure 2.1. Israel and Palestinian
territories

Bethlehem in Area A and from 450 towns and villages in Area B, as well as the holding of elections after the withdrawal.

Then, in November, an advocate of the peace process, Israeli Prime Minister Yitzhak Rabin of the Labor Party, was assassinated. Israeli Foreign Minister Shimon Peres of the Labor Party succeeded as prime minister and maintained the peace process. In January 1996, elections for the president of the Palestinian National Authority and elections for the Palestinian Legislative Council (the equivalent of parliament) were held in the West Bank and Gaza Strip. PLO Chairman Yasser Arafat was elected in the former, and Fatah, led by PLO Chairman Arafat, won a majority of seats in the latter.

From February to March 1996, the Palestinian Islamist organization Hamas carried out suicide terrorist attacks targeting Israelis. Under its principles, Hamas does not recognize Israel's existence and rejects a peace process that is based on the Oslo Accords.

Under these circumstances, in the Israeli prime ministerial election in May 1996, incumbent Prime Minister Peres was defeated, and Benjamin Netanyahu, leader of the Likud Party against the Oslo Accords, was elected. Yet, the peace process was maintained due to the United States' exercise of influence on Israel.

Nevertheless, on May 4, 1999, the five-year interim period stipulated in the Oslo Accord elapsed without any progress in the negotiations. In the Israeli prime ministerial election on May 17, incumbent Prime Minister Netanyahu was defeated, and Ehud Barak, leader of the Labor Party, was elected.

Israel and the PLO continued negotiations mediated by the United States. It is thought that, at the time, the Bill Clinton administration aspired to resolve the Palestinian matter as part of its legacy. In May 2000, Israel submitted a map showing its vision of the final territory and borders of Israel and the Palestinian state. According to this map, Israel would annex the entire West Bank area bordering Jordan, and the West Bank in the Palestinian state would be divided into four non-adjacent areas that would not border Jordan and would be completely encircled by Israel. The map was far from what the Palestinians sought, and they rejected it.

Later, at the urging of the United States, Israel made a drastic concession, agreeing to make all of the Gaza Strip and around 90% of the West Bank the territory of the Palestinian state. Additionally, Israel agreed to grant symbolic rights in East Jerusalem to the Palestinian state, out of consideration for the Palestinian claim that East Jerusalem is the capital of the future state. In July 2000, a trilateral summit was held at Camp David between U.S. President Clinton, Israeli Prime Minister Barak, and PLO Chairman Arafat. The meeting ended in failure, however, with Israel and the PLO unable to reach an agreement. Although the true reason has not been disclosed, the general understanding is that negotiations broke down due to the PLO's refusal to accept the compromise proposal presented by Israel and the United States.

Negotiations continued thereafter. But, in September 2000, when Ariel Sharon, leader of the Likud Party and opponent of peace deals, visited an area in Jerusalem considered a Muslim holy site, protests were sparked by Palestinians angered by the provocation. This is known as the second intifada. A series of Palestinian-Israeli clashes caused casualties and injuries, and public opinion once again became increasingly skeptical of the peace process.

In late January 2001, Israelis and the Palestinians held negotiations in Taba, Egypt. Israel reportedly made further concessions, proposing to make approximately 95% of the West Bank the territory of the Palestinian state, as well as to cede a portion of Israeli territory to the Palestinian state as an alternative to the approximately 5% that Israel would annex. Nonetheless, the two sides were unable to reach an agreement. The peace process lost momentum with the Clinton administration's term of office expiring in late January in the United States, while in Israel in the February prime ministerial election, Prime Minister Barak was defeated and party leader Sharon was elected. Negotiations for a final peace based on the Oslo Accords de facto ended in failure.

Subsequently, Palestinians waged a series of suicide terrorist attacks, and the Palestinian National Authority police were unable to stop them. Thus, in December 2001, Israel declared that the "Palestinian Authority is an entity that supports terrorism." It was evident Israel and the Palestinian National Authority were in a hostile relationship.

On the one hand, the Arab countries indicated they would normalize relations with Israel, in exchange for the establishment of a Palestinian state in accordance with the wishes of the Palestinians. At the Arab League summit held in Beirut in 2002, the Arab Peace Initiative was adopted. It set forth that, if Israel withdraws from occupied territories in the West Bank and Gaza Strip and establish a Palestinian state in the territories, all Arab countries would establish normal relations with Israel in return.[9] This could have incentivized Israel, given that the security environment would improve if relations were normalized with all Arab countries which comprise the majority of Middle Eastern countries.

On the other hand, it appears Israel perceived that the breakdown in negotiations was due to the Palestinians' refusal to accept the Israeli concession, despite making the maximum concession in 2000–2001. On this basis, Israel determined that peace with Palestine would not be realized in the foreseeable future. Israel pushed for the construction of settlements and a separation wall in the West Bank, in order to establish a fait accompli so as not to be disadvantaged if a Palestinian state were established in the distant future. In 2002, Israel began construction of a separation wall in the West Bank as a security measure to protect its citizens from Palestinian terrorist attacks. Part of the wall was built, separating settlements in the West Bank from Palestinian residential areas. For this reason, it is noted that the separation wall was constructed to annex part of the West Bank into Israeli territory. In 2004, giving consideration to the Palestinians, the High Court of Israel issued a ruling ordering the government to change the route of the separation wall that was to be constructed near Jerusalem.[10]

For the Gaza Strip, Israel took a different approach than it did for the West Bank. In 2005, Israeli Prime Minister Sharon implemented a unilateral withdrawal from the Gaza Strip without an agreement with the Palestinian National Authority, i.e., he dismantled settlements in the Gaza Strip. The withdrawal is attributed to Prime Minister Sharon's judgment that the Gaza Strip was of little importance. As a result, the entire Gaza Strip came under Palestinian control.

As for the Palestinian side, President of the Palestinian National Authority (and PLO Chairman) Arafat died in 2004 and was succeeded by Mahmoud Abbas of Fatah.

Although the top leadership was replaced, people in the West Bank and Gaza Strip became increasingly dissatisfied with the Fatah-led self-government's failure to deliver concrete results and with the corrupt nature of Fatah. As a result, Hamas won a majority of seats in the January 2006 Palestinian Legislative Council elections. Hamas, however, does not recognize the existence of Israel and rejects the two-state solution. Consequently, hopes began to erode for the establishment of two states through negotiations between Israel and the Palestinian National Authority.

3. The Division of Palestine and Behind-the-Scenes Developments between the Arab Countries and Israel

The Palestinian territories that are considered to comprise the future Palestinian state are divided into the West Bank and Gaza Strip, which are not geographically adjacent to each other. After the Palestinian National Authority cabinet led by Hamas was inaugurated in March 2006, Hamas established its own security force, separate from the existing security force of the Palestinian National Authority. In the Gaza Strip, where Hamas is powerful, the Hamas security force clashed with the existing security force loyal to President of the Palestinian National Authority Abbas of Fatah. In January 2007, President Abbas declared the Hamas security force illegal, and the conflict between Fatah and Hamas intensified. In June, Hamas expelled Fatah and took effective control of the Gaza Strip. In response, President Abbas of Fatah dismissed Prime Minister Ismail Haniya of Hamas. Thereafter, the Palestinian National Authority headed by President Abbas of Fatah continued to govern the West Bank, while Hamas took effective control of the Gaza Strip, effectively splitting the Palestinian National Authority into two. Additionally, Israel tightened its blockade of the Gaza Strip.

Since 2006, when Hamas gained power in the Gaza Strip, the territory has further developed into a stronghold of Hamas and other Palestinian organizations to attack Israel. Attacks take a range of forms, including suicide terrorist attack, kidnapping of Israeli soldiers, and the firing of rockets into Israel. To deal with them, Israeli forces have conducted operations in the Gaza Strip.

For example, in June 2006, fighters from the Popular Resistance Committees, an organization formed by Fatah's opponents of the Oslo Accords, together with Hamas fighters penetrated into Israel from the southern part of the Gaza Strip via an underground tunnel, killing two Israeli soldiers and kidnapping one. Penetrating into Israel by digging an underground tunnel is a method often used by Palestinian organizations in the Gaza Strip, such as Hamas. To rescue the kidnapped soldier, Israeli forces launched Operation Summer Rains, and ground troops advanced into the Gaza Strip.[11]

In July 2006, while Israeli forces were executing the operation in the Gaza Strip in the south, Lebanese fighters from the Shiite organization Hezbollah crossed the border into northern Israel and waged an attack, killing eight Israeli soldiers and kidnapping two. In response, Israeli forces launched Operation Change of Direction, conducting air raids on Hezbollah outposts in Lebanese territory and sending ground troops into Lebanon.[12] At this time, Palestinian organizations, such as Hamas, and Hezbollah, both supported by Iran, attacked Israel from the north and south, forcing Israeli forces to deal with two enemies simultaneously. During this roughly one-month-long operation, Israeli forces struggled against Hezbollah, losing more than 100 soldiers and failing to rescue the two kidnapped soldiers. The two died. Two years later in 2008, in a prisoner exchange with Israel, Hezbollah returned the bodies of the two soldiers to the country. Israel released five Lebanese prisoners and repatriated them to Lebanon, and also returned numerous bodies to Lebanon, including the bodies of eight Hezbollah members.

In the Gaza Strip, Israeli forces carried out Operation Summer Rains for five months until November 2006 but failed to rescue the kidnapped soldier. Five years later, in 2011, the soldier was released, under an Israel-Hamas agreement that Israel would release 1,027 Palestinian prisoners in return for Hamas' release of the Israeli soldier. As these examples show, Israel's prisoner exchanges with Arabs, including Palestinians, have oftentimes resulted in the release of many Arabs in return for the release of a few Israelis.

Subsequently, Israeli forces conducted operations from December 2008 to January 2009 and again from July to August 2014, with ground troops advancing into the Gaza Strip.[13]

Israeli-Palestinian peace talks stagnated further. Meanwhile, the Arab countries witnessed generational changes with the passage of time. The former generation, which perpetually regarded Israel with hostility, gradually exited due to aging. In their place, the Arab countries saw the rise of a new generation not reluctant to improving relations with Israel. Among the Arab countries, this trend was pronounced in the Gulf Cooperation Council (GCC) countries. In the 2010s, relations were forged behind the scenes between some Arab countries and Israel. For example, it was reported from 2014 to 2015 that aircraft were secretly flying between Israel and the United Arab Emirates (UAE), and that the two countries were cooperating in the security field behind the scenes, with an Israeli-owned company responsible for protecting the critical infrastructure of Abu Dhabi. Furthermore, in 2017, an Israeli minister acknowledged behind-the-scenes contacts between Israel and Saudi Arabia.

A factor that facilitated the rapprochement between the GCC countries and Israel was the Joint Comprehensive Plan of Action, known as the Iran nuclear agreement, agreed to in 2015. The agreement, which eases the international community's sanctions against Iran in return for restrictions on Iran's uranium enrichment, was riddled with problems, including absence of restrictions on ballistic missiles that are the delivery means for nuclear weapons. Viewing Iran as a threat, GCC countries, such as Saudi Arabia, and Israel opposed the agreement. The agreement, as it turned out, helped bring together the two sides sharing a common threat perception.

On the surface, most Arab countries, including the GCC countries, did not have diplomatic relations with Israel, reflecting the traditional view that Israel is an enemy or a security threat for the Arab countries. In reality, however, the security threat to the GCC countries is the same as that to Israel, which is Iran. When the civil war in Yemen on the Arabian Peninsula got fully underway in 2015, Iranian-backed Houthis took effective control of the capital, Sanaa, and began attacking Saudi Arabia and other GCC countries with ballistic missiles believed to be made in Iran. These developments appear to have further encouraged the rapprochement between the GCC countries and Israel.

Thus, the tendency to view rapprochement with Israel as a taboo gradually faded in some Arab countries. In March 2018, Saudi Arabia allowed passenger flights between Israel and a third country to pass through Saudi Arabian airspace for the first time. In October 2018, an Israeli athlete won an international judo tournament in the UAE, and the Israeli national anthem was played at the venue. At the time, Israeli Culture and Sports Minister Miri Regev accompanied the athletes to the UAE, becoming the first Israeli minister to attend a sports event in the Gulf region. Also in October 2018, it was announced that Israeli Prime Minister Benjamin Netanyahu visited Oman and met with Sultan Qaboos bin Said of Oman. Nevertheless, relations between the Arab countries and Israel remained informal and did not lead to the establishment of formal diplomatic relations.

4. Normalization of UAE and Other Arab Countries' Relations with Israel in 2020

In 2020, a wind of change blew through with mediation by the Donald Trump administration of the United States. At the end of January at the White House, President Trump unveiled his vision for a comprehensive peace agreement between the Israelis and the Palestinians, Peace to Prosperity: A Vision to Improve the

Lives of the Palestinian and Israeli People, the so-called "deal of the century."[14] This peace plan favors Israel, as indicated by the fact that, of the two parties—Israel and the Palestinian National Authority—only Israeli Prime Minister Netanyahu was present at the announcement. According to the maps presented, the

U.S. President Donald Trump unveiling the peace plan, joined by Israeli Prime Minister Benjamin Netanyahu, at the White House on January 28, 2020 (CNP/DPA/Kyodo News Images)

Palestinian state in the West Bank would be surrounded by Israeli territory on its borders and would not border Jordan. Furthermore, the vision recognizes Israeli sovereignty over the settlements. Although the Palestinian National Authority wants East Jerusalem as the capital of the Palestinian state, all of the city of Jerusalem would be the capital of Israel under this plan. In addition, Abu Dis and other areas of the governorate of Jerusalem in the West Bank are identified as candidates for the capital of the Palestinian state. Prior to the vision's announcement, the United States recognized Jerusalem as the capital of Israel in December 2017, moved the U.S. embassy from Tel Aviv to Jerusalem in May 2018, and recognized Israeli sovereignty over the Golan Heights in March 2019. In November 2019, the United States announced it would not consider settlements in the West Bank as violation of international law, reversing its previous policy.

If one compares the map presented in the latest peace plan with the map of the Palestinian state purportedly presented by Israel at the end of the Clinton administration in 2001, the two have obvious differences, especially the decrease in the Palestinian state's territory in the West Bank. For this reason, President of the Palestinian National Authority Abbas rejected the plan. While the Arab League rejected it, three of its member states, Egypt, Saudi Arabia, and the UAE, responded positively to the peace plan. In other words, many Arab countries tolerated the vision.

Figure 2.2. The Palestinian state proposed in the Trump administration's "deal of the century"
(*Orange sections of the map)

Source: The White House, "Peace to Prosperity: A Vision to Improve the Lives of the Palestinian and Israeli People," January 2020, 46.

At this point, differences in position were becoming apparent between these Arab countries and the Palestinian National Authority.

Beginning in August 2020, four Arab countries decided to normalize relations with Israel in succession. First, on August 13, U.S. President Trump, Israeli Prime Minister Netanyahu, and Deputy Supreme Commander of the UAE Armed Forces and the Crown Prince of the Emirate of Abu Dhabi Muhammad bin Zayed issued a joint statement, the Abraham Accords, announcing that the UAE and Israel agreed to normalize relations. This was followed on September 11 by the announcement that Bahrain and Israel agreed to normalize relations through the mediation of President Trump. Then, on September 15, Israeli Prime Minister Netanyahu, UAE Minister of Foreign Affairs and International Cooperation Abdullah bin Zayed, Bahrain's Foreign Minister Abdullatif Al-Zayani, and President Trump gathered at the White House, and three agreements were signed: the Israel-UAE normalization agreement, the Abraham Accords Peace Agreement: Treaty of Peace, Diplomatic Relations and Full Normalization between the United Arab Emirates and the State of Israel; the Israel-Bahrain normalization agreement, the Abraham Accords: Declaration of Peace, Cooperation, and Constructive Diplomatic and Friendly Relations; and a joint declaration of the four countries, the Abraham Accords Declaration.[15] Arabs and Jews have long fought in the Arab-Israeli wars. Nevertheless, the agreements mention Arabs and Jews being descended from a common ancestor, Abraham.

Abraham is a common ancestor of the founders of the Judaism, Christianity, and Islam religions, and the agreements call for the coexistence of their respective followers in the Middle East.

Furthermore, on October 23, it was announced that Sudan and Israel agreed to normalize relations through the mediation of President Trump.[16] At a later date, Sudan signed the Abraham Accords Declaration.[17]

Additionally, on December 10, it was announced that Morocco and Israel agreed to normalize relations through the mediation of President Trump. On December 22, an Israeli delegation led by National Security Adviser Meir Ben-Shabbat and U.S. White House Senior Adviser Jared Kushner visited the Moroccan capital, Rabat, and held a meeting with King of Morocco Muhammad VI. The three countries signed a joint declaration regarding the normalization of Morocco-Israel relations. Among the Arab countries, Morocco is considered to have had relatively good relations with Israel. Even before the agreement to normalize relations, Morocco and Israel had established liaison offices in each other's countries from 1994 to 2000, and in 2003, Israeli Deputy Prime Minister and Foreign Minister Silvan Shalom visited Morocco. In February 2020, the Moroccan forces reportedly acquired Israeli-made reconnaissance drones via a third country.

In this way, four Arab countries agreed to normalize relations with Israel in a short period of time. This achievement is a legacy left by mediator President Trump. The Arab countries that agreed to normalization received something in return from the United States. The UAE is expected to able to purchase F-35 fighters from the United States. Israel, with F-35 fighters in its inventory, seeks to maintain military superiority in the region and was opposed to the acquisition of F-35 fighters by GCC countries with which it had no diplomatic relations, including the UAE. Yet, in October 2020, following the UAE-Israel normalization agreement, the United States and Israel agreed that the former would increase the military capabilities of Israel, which would allow it to maintain military superiority. Based on this agreement, Israel announced it would not oppose the U.S. sale of F-35 fighters to the UAE. In December 2021, however, Abu Dhabi reportedly informed the United States that it would suspend talks with the country to purchase F-35 fighters. The UAE, which

Figure 2.3. The Middle East

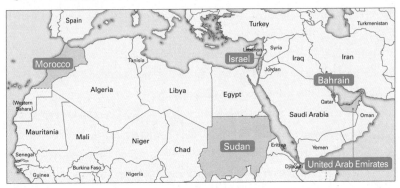

uses Chinese company Huawei's 5G communications network, was asked by the United States to take preventative measures so that F-35 fighter and other sensitive information is not leaked to China. The UAE's reluctance to comply is believed to be behind the suspension of the talks.

What Sudan received in return was its removal from the U.S. list of state sponsors of terrorism. In 1993, following a terrorist attack on the World Trade Center (later destroyed in the 9/11 attacks in 2001), the United States designated Sudan as a state sponsor of terrorism on the grounds that Sudan's Omar al-Bashir regime was harboring al Qaeda leader Osama bin Laden and others. Even after the al-Bashir regime fell in 2019, Sudan was not removed from the list of state sponsors of terrorism. But, on October 23, 2020, the date the Sudan-Israel normalization agreement was announced, President Trump signed an executive order to remove Sudan from the list, as it had completed payment of $335 million in reparations to victims of terrorist attacks, including the 1998 al Qaeda terrorist attacks on the U.S. embassies in Kenya and Tanzania, and to their families. In December 2020, the United States removed Sudan from the list of state sponsors of terrorism. Following the removal, Middle East countries on the U.S. list are Syria and Iran.[18]

Morocco received U.S. recognition of its sovereignty over the Western Sahara. When the Morocco-Israel normalization agreement was announced on December 10, 2020, President Trump announced U.S. recognition of Moroccan sovereignty over the Western Sahara, as well as an intention to open a consulate in the region.[19] The establishment of a consulate in the Western Sahara as an outpost of the U.S. Embassy in Morocco indicates the United States considers the region as Moroccan territory.

Morocco claims territorial rights over the Western Sahara, a former Spanish colony, while locally, the Polisario Front has been campaigning for its independence. The Polisario Front, which receives support from Morocco's neighbor Algeria, declared the establishment of the "Sahrawi Arab Democratic Republic" in 1976, and its government-in-exile is located in Algeria. Although the Polisario Front only controls part of the Western Sahara, the "Sahrawi Arab Democratic Republic" is recognized as a state by many African and Latin American countries and is a full member of the African Union. In addition, the UN and many Western countries adopt the position that the issues surrounding the Western Sahara should be resolved through a referendum.

In contrast, the December 22, 2020 Joint Declaration of Morocco, the United States, and Israel states, "The United States…reaffirms its support for Morocco's serious, credible, and realistic autonomy proposal as the only basis for a just and lasting solution to the dispute over the Western Sahara territory," i.e., the U.S. position that the Western Sahara matter is a matter of Moroccan domestic autonomy and not a matter of secession and independence.[20] Furthermore, the United States approved a new map that includes the Western Sahara as Moroccan territory. In such manner, Morocco gained the backing of the United States. Meanwhile, the Polisario Front and Algeria condemned the United States, and Algeria severed relations with Morocco in the following year, 2021.

A ceasefire between Morocco and the Polisario Front took effect in 1991 and lasted for 29 years until 2020. In November 2020, just before the United States recognized Moroccan sovereignty over the Western Sahara, Moroccan forces expelled Polisario Front supporters in the Western Sahara who were blocking a road leading to neighboring Mauritania. The Polisario Front then declared an end to the ceasefire. The UAE and Bahrain, which agreed to normalize relations with Israel before Morocco, subsequently opened consulates in the Western Sahara in succession. This measure was likely aimed at showing recognition of Morocco's sovereignty over the Western Sahara, and thereby, encouraging Morocco to agree to normalize relations with Israel. On November 4, 2020, the UAE opened a consulate in the Western Sahara, becoming the first Arab country to do so. In late November, it was reported that Bahrain decided to open a consulate in the Western Sahara, and the consulate was opened on December 14, following the December 10 agreement between Morocco and Israel to normalize relations.

The wave of normalization agreements in 2020 had nothing to do with the progress of the Israeli-Palestinian peace talks. This signifies that the UAE and other Arab countries have departed from their traditional position, i.e., linking progress in the Israeli-Palestinian peace talks with the normalization of relations between Israel and Arab countries. Moreover, the series of normalization of relations were essentially not condemned by other Arab countries. Rather, in September 2020, soon after the UAE-Israel normalization agreement, Saudi Arabia allowed all aircraft traveling to and from the UAE to pass through its airspace. This was, in effect, airspace clearance for aircraft flying between Israel and the UAE. In short, Saudi Arabia sought to accommodate the UAE which had normalized relations with Israel. What this implies is that Arab countries, which do not have diplomatic relations with Israel yet, perceived the following: Arab countries may normalize relations with Israel, regardless of the progress of the Israeli-Palestinian peace talks. Back when Egypt normalized relations with Israel, it was boycotted by Arab countries, and domestically, its president was assassinated. In contrast, the countries that normalized relations with Israel in 2020 have not been disadvantaged and have benefitted primarily. It is thus possible that other Arab countries may decide to normalize relations with Israel in the future. In November 2020, Israeli Prime Minister Netanyahu reportedly made a secret visit to Neom, Saudi Arabia and met with Saudi Arabia's Crown Prince Muhammad bin Salman and U.S. Secretary of State Mike Pompeo. GCC countries in particular are deepening their ties with Israel—both formal diplomatic relations and informal behind-the-scenes relations.

5. 2021 Gaza Conflict

In January 2021, President of the Palestinian National Authority Abbas announced that Palestinian Legislative Council elections would be held in May and Palestinian National Authority presidential elections at the end of July. Last held in 2005 and 2006, respectively, presidential and Legislative Council elections had not been held for many years due to the 2007 civil war. However, at the end of April 2021, President Abbas postponed both elections indefinitely. At the time, President Abbas-led Fatah was anticipated to run in the Legislative Council elections by splitting into three groups due to internal divisions. Fatah would have had a high chance of losing the elections to Hamas, and this is deemed the reason for the postponement. The postponement was therefore criticized by Hamas.

Meanwhile, from April to early May, Palestinian residents in the neighborhood of Sheikh Jarrah and Palestinians supporting them clashed with settlers and Israeli police in East Jerusalem over the Israeli authorities' eviction order against Palestinian residents. On May 7, Palestinians who had gathered for prayers at the Al-Aqsa mosque compound, considered a Muslim holy site in Jerusalem's Old City, clashed with Israeli police, and over 200 people were injured. In response to this situation, Hamas demanded that Israeli security forces withdraw from the Al-Aqsa mosque compound and the neighborhood of Sheikh Jarrah by 6 p.m. on May 10, and declared that it would wage attacks if they did not comply. On May 10, soon after the deadline unilaterally designated by Hamas expired, Hamas and the Islamist organization Palestinian Islamic Jihad (PIJ), which receives support from Iran like Hamas, fired numerous rockets from the Gaza Strip into Jerusalem and Ashkelon in southern Israel. In response, on the same day, Israeli forces launched Operation Guardian of the Walls and conducted air raids on the Gaza Strip.[21] Israeli forces intercepted many of the rockets with the Iron Dome air defense system, but some landed in Israel, partly due to Hamas' saturation attacks.

From May 11, Hamas and the Islamic Jihad expanded the scope of their attacks and fired rockets into central Israel, including Tel Aviv. On May 12, Saudi Arabia's

King Salman bin Abdulaziz expressed support for the Palestinians and condemned Israel. On May 14, ground troops of Israeli forces began shelling the Gaza Strip. In this conflict, however, the ground troops did not advance into the Gaza Strip. Advancing ground troops offers the advantage of destroying targets more reliably. Yet, it also has the disadvantage of creating more casualties and injured people among its own troops, as well as more abductees and civilian casualties. Hamas has built an extensive network of underground tunnels in the Gaza Strip, many of which have been destroyed by Israeli forces through airstrikes and artillery fire. On May 15, upon giving warning, Israeli forces launched an airstrike and destroyed a building in the Gaza Strip occupied by the Associated Press and Al Jazeera. According to Israeli forces, the building was believed to have housed a Hamas military outpost.

In this conflict, it appears that the objective of Israeli forces was to destroy the military facilities and weapons caches of Hamas, neutralize its fighters, and reduce its military capability. Hamas strengthens its military capability by stockpiling and developing weapons, such as rockets, requiring Israeli forces to destroy and weaken them every few years to decrease the threat to Israel. Meanwhile, it appears that the objective of Hamas was to bolster its presence as a challenger to Israel and to maintain effective control of the Gaza Strip. Thus, it was possible for both Israeli forces and Hamas to achieve their objectives simultaneously, leading both to later declare victory.

On May 19, U.S. President Joseph Biden held a telephone talk with Israeli Prime Minister Netanyahu and urged Israel to deescalate tensions. Israel and Hamas do not recognize each other and have no channels for direct dialogue. Therefore, Egypt, having ties to both, mediated the ceasefire. Perhaps because Israeli forces had largely achieved their operational objectives, Israel and Hamas agreed to a ceasefire, which took effect on May 21. Both Israel and Hamas declared themselves victorious. During the 11-day conflict, Hamas and the Islamic Jihad fired approximately 4,400 rockets, reportedly killing 13 people in Israel, including civilians, and more than 200 people in the Gaza Strip, including civilians. At the time of the conflict, a niece of Hamas Political Bureau Chief Haniya, the highest-ranking Hamas official, was reportedly hospitalized in an Israeli hospital. This was seemingly a humanitarian measure taken by Israel.

Although the ceasefire went into effect, there was no change in the confrontational relationship between Hamas and Israel. After the ceasefire took effect, Palestinian organizations such as Hamas launched incendiary balloons from the Gaza Strip toward Israel, causing a series of fires in southern Israel. For this reason, Israeli forces staged multiple air strikes on the Gaza Strip from mid-June.

The recent conflict in the Gaza Strip did not stem the trend of improving relations between the Arab countries and Israel. This is evidenced by their enhanced relations since then, as elaborated below. On June 29, Israeli Foreign Minister Yair Lapid became the first Israeli foreign minister to pay an official visit to the UAE and attended the opening ceremony of the Israeli embassy in Abu Dhabi. Following this, on July 14, the UAE opened an embassy in Israel in Tel Aviv. The opening ceremony was attended by Israeli President Isaac Herzog. The attendance by the president, who is the son of former Israeli President Chaim Herzog, author of *The Arab-Israeli Wars: War and Peace in the Middle East*, a fundamental book on the Arab-Israeli wars, epitomizes the improvement of relations between the Arab countries and Israel.

On July 4, a Moroccan Air Force aircraft landed at an Israeli airport, probably to participate in a multinational exercise of the Israeli Air Force. On July 25, two Israeli airlines, including EL AL, commenced direct flights between Israel and Morocco. Furthermore, in mid-August, Israeli Foreign Minister Lapid visited Rabat to meet with Moroccan Minister of Foreign Affairs and International Cooperation Nasser Bourita and attended the opening ceremony of the Israeli liaison office.

At the Tokyo Olympic Games held from July to August, Algerian and Sudanese athletes abstained from the judo event to avoid competing against Israeli athletes. While Algeria does not have diplomatic relations with Israel, Sudan agreed to normalize relations with Israel in the previous year. In Sudan, however, there is strong public opinion against normalizing relations with Israel, which is thought to have led to the abstention. On September 17, U.S. Secretary of State Antony Blinken hosted an online meeting on the first anniversary of the signing of the Abraham Accords. Israel, the UAE, Bahrain, and Morocco participated but Sudan did not.

On September 30, Israeli Foreign Minister Lapid visited Bahrain for the first time. He met with Bahrain's King Hamad bin Isa and attended the opening ceremony of the Israeli embassy. Also on September 30, Bahraini airline Gulf Air began passenger flights between Bahrain and Israel. On October 1, Expo 2020 Dubai kicked off in the UAE, and Israel participated in the Expo by opening a pavilion.

On October 3, EgyptAir began operating passenger flights between Cairo and Tel Aviv. Previously, passenger flights were formally operated by its subsidiary Air Sinai in order to keep the Egypt-Israel relationship discreet. It is believed that the operation of passenger flights switched to the parent company because relations improved between other Arab countries and Israel, making it no longer necessary to conceal the passenger flights. On December 12, Israeli Prime Minister Naftali Bennett became the first Israeli prime minister to pay an official visit to the UAE, and on the following day, December 13, met with Deputy Supreme Commander of the UAE Armed Forces and the Crown Prince of the Emirate of Abu Dhabi Muhammad bin Zayed.

In this way, the 2020 emerging trend of improved relations between the Arab countries and Israel, independent of the progress of Israeli-Palestinian peace talks, continued in 2021 despite the outbreak of the Gaza Strip conflict. This trend is expected to continue for the foreseeable future.

NOTES

1) Martin Gilbert, *The Routledge Atlas of the Arab-Israeli Conflict* (London: Routledge, 2005) 8th edition, 36.

2) Chaim Herzog, Shlomo Gazit, Michael Herzog et al., *The Arab-Israeli Wars: War and Peace in the Middle East from the 1948 War of Independence to the Present* (London: Greenhill Books, 2005), 14.

3) Gilbert, *The Routledge Atlas of the Arab-Israeli Conflict*, 46.

4) Ibid., 47.

5) Ibid., 68.

6) Treaty of Peace between the Arab Republic of Egypt and the State of Israel, March 26, 1979.

7) Agreement on the Gaza Strip and the Jericho Area, May 4, 1994.

8) Israeli-Palestinian Interim Agreement on the West Bank and the Gaza Strip, September 28, 1995.

9) "Beirut Declaration on Saudi Peace Initiative," March 28, 2002.

10) Gilbert, *The Routledge Atlas of the Arab-Israeli Conflict*, 157.

11) [Israel] Ministry of Foreign Affairs (MFA), "Kerem Shalom Attack and Kidnapping of Cpl. Gilad Shalit" (June 25, 2006); [Israel] Defense Forces Press Center, "Operation Summer Rains" (2006).

12) [Israel] MFA, "The Second Lebanon War" (July 12, 2006).

13) [Israel] Defense Forces Press Center, "Operation Cast Lead" (2009); [Israel] Defense Forces Press Center, "Operation Protective Edge" (2014).

14) The White House, "Peace to Prosperity: A Vision to Improve the Lives of the Palestinian and Israeli People" (January, 2020).

15) Abraham Accords Peace Agreement: Treaty of Peace, Diplomatic Relations and Full Normalization between the United Arab Emirates and the State of Israel, September 15, 2020; Abraham Accords: Declaration of Peace, Cooperation, and Constructive Diplomatic and Friendly Relations by the State of Israel and the Kingdom of Bahrain, September 15, 2020; The Abraham Accords Declaration, September 15, 2020.

16) The White House, "President Donald J. Trump Brokers a Historic Peace Agreement between Israel and Sudan" (October 23, 2020).

17) The Abraham Accords Declaration, January 6, 2021.

18) [U.S.] Department of State, "State Sponsors of Terrorism" (2021).

19) The White House, "President Donald J. Trump Has Brokered Peace between Israel and the Kingdom of Morocco" (December 11, 2020).

20) U.S. Embassy & Consulates in Morocco, "Joint Declaration" (December 22, 2020).

21) [Israel] Defense Forces Press Center, "Operation Guardian of the Walls" (May 2021).

Chapter 3

China

Tightening Control by the Chinese Communist Party

IIDA Masafumi (Lead author, Sections 1 and 2)
IWAMOTO Hiroshi (Section 3)

Summary

The Chinese Communist Party (CCP) celebrated its 100th anniversary in July 2021. Priding itself on turning China into a great power, the Party also tightened control and concentrated more power in the hands of General Secretary Xi Jinping. Xi aims to realize the new goal of becoming a "great modern socialist country" by 2049, the centenary of the People's Republic of China. In response to the deteriorating global landscape surrounding China's economy, Beijing unveiled a vision to make science and technology innovations that rely on state support, hoping to achieve growth led by domestic demand. In regard to Hong Kong, the CCP exerted greater control, cracking down on democratic factions and amending the electoral system, thereby shutting out democratic factions from participating in politics.

China rejects universal values, such as freedom and democracy, and continues to challenge the rules-based international order, aggravating relations with democracies including the United States. The Xi administration took a hard-line stance against the Joseph Biden administration, which is strengthening competition with China. Sanctions and retaliatory measures were also imposed against European Union members that criticized China on human rights and other issues. Meanwhile, China deepened relations with Russia and developing countries to form partnerships for countering the United States and Europe. Additionally, China intensified military pressure on Japan and Taiwan.

China is developing military legislation in the final phase of the military reforms. In doing so, the Party seeks to tighten control over the military, secure talent, and improve trainings. The People's Liberation Army (PLA) made steady progress in modernizing its equipment as well. The year 2021 saw the commissioning of a large-scale amphibious assault ship, advances in the development of drones, and numerous achievements in the space program. Furthermore, the PLA stepped up international activities. For example, through combined drills with Russia, the Shanghai Cooperation Organisation member states, and other countries, the PLA aims to enhance capabilities in counterterrorism and United Nations peacekeeping operations.

The Chinese Communist Party's centenary ceremony in Tiananmen Square (Xinhua/ Kyodo News Images)

Keywords

CCP centenary   14th Five-Year Plan   U.S.-China confrontation
Taiwan   military regulations

1. Ensuring the Party's Control

(1) The Centenary of the Chinese Communist Party

Formed in July 1921, the Chinese Communist Party (CCP) was forced to flee from the Kuomintang (KMT) forces for around two years in the mid-1930s in what became known as the "Long March." Then, with the outbreak of the Sino-Japanese War, the CCP regained its footing and won the civil war against the KMT. The People's Republic of China (PRC) was thus founded in October 1949. The CCP established the one-party system in China and maintained one-party rule even in the face of various disruptions and sacrifices, such as the Great Leap Forward, the Cultural Revolution, and the June Fourth Tiananmen Square Incident. Simultaneously, the Party realized rapid economic growth and modernized military capabilities, elevating China to the status of global power.

On July 1, 2021, the CCP held a ceremony marking its 100th anniversary in Tiananmen Square. There were some 70,000 people in attendance and commemorative flights by 71 military aircraft, including the state-of-the-art J-20 stealth fighter. At the ceremony, Xi Jinping, general secretary of the CCP and president of the PRC, delivered a speech, giving much emphasis to the Party's achievements over the past century. Xi said, when China was under foreign domination after the Opium War of 1840, the CCP brought independence to China by uniting and leading the people under the Party's "aspiration and mission," namely, to realize the "great rejuvenation of the Chinese nation." Following the era of socialist construction and the era of reform and opening up, China entered a "new era" of Xi's leadership. He declared that, in this new era, China achieved the "first centenary goal" of "building a moderately prosperous society in all respects…[and bringing] about a historic resolution to the problem of absolute poverty in China." He then indicated the Party would embark on a "new journey" to realize the "second centenary goal" of "building China into a great modern socialist country in all respects" by 2049, the 100th anniversary of the founding of the PRC.

In the same speech, General Secretary Xi most emphasized the need to uphold the strong leadership of the CCP. "Without the Communist Party of China, there would be no new China and no national rejuvenation," he noted, asserting, "The leadership of the Party is the defining feature of

General Secretary Xi delivering a speech at the CCP centenary ceremony (Xinhua/Kyodo News Images)

socialism with Chinese characteristics and constitutes the greatest strength of this system." On the "new journey," "we must uphold the Party's overall leadership and continue to enhance its leadership," urging that Xi's position be maintained as the "core" of the CCP. In short, General Secretary Xi resolved to further strengthen the system of CCP rule in China and further cement his grip on power in the Party.

In addition, General Secretary Xi revealed that he would thoroughly counter any foreign criticism of the CCP. "Any attempt to divide the Party from the Chinese people or to set the people against the Party is bound to fail," he said, stressing, "[the CCP] will not...accept sanctimonious preaching from those who feel they have the right to lecture us." "We will never allow any foreign force to bully, oppress, or subjugate us. Anyone who would attempt to do so will find themselves on a collision course with a great wall of steel forged by over 1.4 billion Chinese people." And Xi reaffirmed his determination to build a "world-class military."[1]

(2) Inward-oriented Economic Policy

Outwardly, the Xi Jinping leadership appeared firmly intent on thoroughly confronting U.S. and other foreign criticisms of the CCP rule. In response to the deteriorating global landscape surrounding China, the Xi leadership shifted economic policy to economic growth centered on domestic demand. At the Fourth Session of the 13th National People's Congress (NPC) held in March 2021, the "Outline of the 14th Five-Year Plan for national economic and social development and long-range objectives for 2035" was adopted. As a "guiding ideology," this 14th Five-Year Plan enshrines the establishment of a "new pattern of development with domestic circulation as the mainstay and domestic and international circulations reinforcing each other." In contrast, the 13th Five-Year Plan adopted in March 2016 set forth the following "guiding ideology": "we should also keep in mind the connectivity between the domestic and the world economies and…make better use of both domestic and international markets and resources." As the comparison of the two makes evident, the new policy places focus on "domestic circulation."

Regarding "domestic circulation," the 14th Five-Year Plan elaborates: "We will rely on the strong domestic market, running through all the links from production and distribution to circulation and consumption, and form a higher-level dynamic balance in which demand drives supply and supply creates demand, and promote a virtuous cycle in the national economy." Put simply, it suggests that the Party will reform the economic structure such that growth is led by domestic demand. Indeed, other economic powers, such as the United States and Japan, have domestic demand-centric growth, and it is natural that China, now the second largest economy in the world, aspires to shift to a similar economic structure. In fact, China's economic dependence on trade declined from 67% in 2006 to 32% in 2019.[2]

However, the main reason China shifted to an economic policy focused on "domestic circulation" at this time is likely to be the deteriorating global landscape surrounding the Chinese economy, including growing strategic competition with the United States, friction with democratic countries, and the global economic slowdown caused by the novel coronavirus disease (COVID-19) pandemic. In a *People's Daily* editorial on the "new pattern of development," it is noted that China faces a tough and complex situation which "requires ideological and operational preparations over a considerable length of time to cope with the changes in the external environment," and contends that the "new pattern of development" is "a major decision made to prepare for a successful endurance war."[3] Of course, for the Chinese economy it remains critical to strengthen relations with the international economy, and the Chinese government has indicated it would accelerate the opening up of its economy. Nonetheless, China is hastily shifting to a domestic demand-centric economic growth structure, anticipating that advancing economic ties with other countries will not proceed as smoothly as before.

The 14th Five-Year Plan also outlines China would enhance independent development of science and technology. The plan articulates having "science and technology self-reliance and self-improvement (科技自立自强) act as strategic support for national development." According to Zhang Tao, vice president of the Chinese Academy of Sciences (CAS), innovation in science and technology intersects with politics, economics, military, and diplomacy and has become "the main battlefield of competition and rivalry among the great powers." China, however, does not have significant capacity for innovation in key areas, is weak in basic research, and lacks human resources, according to Zhang. He notes "science and technology self-reliance and self-improvement" was proposed to overcome these weaknesses, and only by achieving this can China overcome the disadvantage of being restricted by others in key technologies, establish a science and technology innovation system befitting its status as a great power, and focus on science and technologies that are important for economic and social development as well as national security.[4]

General Secretary Xi Jinping signaled he would press forward with science and technology innovation. In a speech at a May 2021 combined meeting of the CAS, Chinese Academy of Engineering, and China Association for Science and Technology, President Xi urged Chinese scientific researchers to "strive to achieve a high level of science and technology self-reliance and self-improvement." Xi stated that in order to promote innovation in science and technology, China must bolster the "new system concentrating nationwide effort and resources" and "fully demonstrate the role of the state as the organizer of critical science and technology innovations," indicating the state would fully lead the efforts for self-reliance and self-improvement in science and technology.[5] The Xi administration may be focusing on their independent development, based on the prospect that acquiring overseas technologies would become difficult as competition increases with the United States for advanced technology. Some say "the most fundamental feature of building a new pattern of development is realizing a high level of self-reliance and self-improvement."[6] By promoting domestic economic growth through science and technology innovation, it appears China aims to bolster national strength in the face of intensifying competition with foreign countries, including the United States.

(3) Increased Clampdown on Hong Kong

The Xi Jinping administration imposed the national security law on Hong Kong in 2020. By stifling calls for democracy, the "One Country, Two Systems" arrangement that had granted Hong Kong certain political freedoms was reduced to a mere formality. In 2021, the repression of pro-democracy factions in Hong Kong increased further, and the CCP's one-party rule in Hong Kong politics was enforced.

In Hong Kong, suppression of democracy activists was stepped up. On January 6, Hong Kong authorities arrested 53 democracy activists in a single day, including former Legislative Council members, on suspicion of overthrowing the government as stipulated in the national security law. Targeted were activists who were involved in the July 2020 primary elections that were held to prevent splitting of pro-democratic votes in the Legislative Council election, which was scheduled to take place in September. On February 28, 2021, Hong Kong authorities indicted 47 of those arrested. Among the democracy activists indicted were Benny Tai, an organizer of the primary elections; Wu Chi-wai and Lam Cheuk-ting, both Legislative Council members from the Democratic Party; Au Nok-hin, a former Legislative Council member and graduate student at the University of Tokyo; and Joshua Wong, who was imprisoned after being convicted in a separate case.

In April, a Hong Kong court convicted seven people for holding unauthorized rallies, including Jimmy Lai, founder of *Apple Daily*, known for its critical stance toward China; Martin Lee, known as the "father of Hong Kong democracy"; and Lee Cheuk-yan, who had led rallies in memory of the Tiananmen Square Incident. Jimmy Lai was also convicted for holding another unauthorized rally in May. In June, Hong Kong authorities arrested five *Apple Daily* executives on charges of colluding with foreign forces in violation of the national security law. Under pressure from authorities, the *Apple Daily*, a symbol of press freedom in Hong Kong, was forced to cease publication on June 24.

The Xi administration overhauled Hong Kong's electoral system, aiming to eliminate pro-democracy factions from the political system and ensure that it is guided by the CCP. On March 30, the NPC Standing Committee decided on a new electoral system for Hong Kong. By this decision, the Election Committee, responsible for electing the chief executive, increased membership from 1,200 to 1,500, with the increased number allocated to pro-China groups. The number of Legislative Council seats rose from 70 to 90, while the number of directly elected seats decreased from 35 out of 70 to 20 out of 90. The Election Committee was newly given 40 seats. Additionally, the new Candidate Eligibility Review Committee was established to pre-screen candidates for the Election Committee and Legislative Council based on their loyalty to the Hong Kong government.[7] These changes made it difficult for pro-democracy factions critical of the CCP to run in Hong Kong elections. In the Election Committee elections held on September 19, no pro-democracy faction secured any of the 364 seats contested. The Election Committee has become dominated by pro-China factions with the exception of Tik Chi-yuen who is considered a centrist.[8] The Legislative Council election held on December 9 resulted in completely eliminating democratic factions, with voter turnout falling to a record low of 30.2%.

(4) Adoption of the Historical Resolution at the Sixth Plenary Session

The CCP held the Sixth Plenary Session of the Central Committee from November

8 to 11. The session adopted the "Resolution on the Major Achievements and Historical Experience of the Party over the Past Century" (Historical Resolution) drafted by a group headed by General Secretary Xi Jinping.[9] Only two Historical Resolutions have ever been adopted—the "Resolution on Certain Questions in the History of Our Party" adopted in 1945 under Mao Zedong and the "Resolution on Certain Questions in the History of Our Party Since the Founding of the People's Republic of China" adopted in 1981 under Deng Xiaoping, both of whom retained their position as the highest authority until their deaths. The latest Historical Resolution divided the Party's history into three periods: the period of "socialist revolution and construction" led by Mao Zedong; the period of "reform, opening up, and socialist modernization" led by Deng Xiaoping, Jiang Zemin, and Hu Jintao; and "a new era of socialism with Chinese characteristics" led by Xi Jinping. The resolution details achievements made in 13 areas in the "new era" by the CCP Central Committee, with Xi at its core. It describes that the establishment of Xi Jinping's core position on the Party Central Committee and in the Party as a whole, as well as the establishment of the guiding role of Xi Jinping Thought on Socialism with Chinese Characteristics for a New Era, are of "decisive significance" for driving forward the process of "great rejuvenation of the Chinese nation."

The adoption of the Historical Resolution further strengthened General Secretary Xi's authority within the CCP. Accordingly, he is expected to maintain his position of highest authority beyond the 20th National Party Congress to be held in 2022. The Historical Resolution sets the goal of becoming a "great modern socialist country" by around the mid-21st century while upholding the "Party's overall leadership." The Xi leadership is anticipated to continue strengthening the Party's control of politics, the economy, and society, and at the same time, keep intact its policy of taking a hard-line stance outwardly to expand China's "core interests."

2. Growing Friction with the International Community

(1) Deepening Confrontation with Democratic Countries

The relationship between the Xi Jinping administration and the former U.S. Donald Trump administration came under severe strain, with some calling it a "new Cold War." The Xi administration hoped the appointment of Joseph Biden as the new president would trigger an improvement in the bilateral relationship. Upon President Biden's inauguration, Chinese Foreign Ministry Spokesperson Hua Chunying said that the people of both China and the United States have suffered because of incitement by "a small number of anti-China politicians in the United States," and that "the Trump administration, especially Pompeo, has laid too many mines, burned too many bridges and destroyed too many roads in China-US relations, which are waiting to be cleared, rebuilt and repaired."[10] At the same time, the Chinese government announced sanctions against 28 Trump administration officials, including former Secretary of State Mike Pompeo, for violating Chinese sovereignty.[11] By placing the primary responsibility for the deterioration of China-U.S. relations on the former Trump administration, the Xi administration may have sought to find a way to improve relations with the new Biden administration. In a telephone talk with President Biden on February 11, President Xi noted "cooperation is the only right choice for both sides," and emphasized "It is crucial to show mutual respect, treat each other as equals, and properly manage and handle the differences in a constructive fashion."[12]

The Biden administration, however, shared the Trump administration's perception of China in many ways. In a foreign policy speech on February 4, President Biden referred to "the growing ambitions of China to rival the United States." "We'll also take on directly the challenges posed [to] our prosperity, security, and democratic values by our most serious competitor, China," he noted, indicating that the United States would confront these challenges.[13] In a speech on March 3, Antony Blinken, secretary of state, characterized relations with China as "the biggest geopolitical test of the 21st century." He noted "China is the only country with the economic, diplomatic, military, and technological power to seriously challenge the stable and open international system," and advocated the need to "engage China from a position of strength" by standing up for human rights abuses in the Xinjiang Uyghur Autonomous Region and for the trampling of democracy in Hong Kong, as well as by advancing cooperation with allies and partners.[14] On March 16, the United States added 24 people to the sanctions list, including Wang Chen, vice-chairman of the Standing Committee of the NPC, pursuant to the Hong Kong Autonomy Act, on the grounds that they led the enactment of the Hong Kong national security law and the repression of pro-democracy factions.[15]

The Biden administration's tough line on China led the Xi administration to take hard-line responses to the United States and not to refrain from confrontation. On March 18, a U.S.-China high-level dialogue was held in Alaska attended by Secretary of State Blinken and Jake Sullivan, national security advisor, from the United States and Yang Jiechi, director of the Central Foreign Affairs Commission General Office, and Wang Yi, state councilor and foreign minister of the PRC, from China. At the meeting, Director Yang noted that "China has Chinese-style democracy," and demanded that the United States "not complain about China's human rights and democracy." Yang further declared, "Taiwan, Hong Kong, and Xinjiang are all inalienable parts of China, and Beijing firmly opposes U.S. interference in China's internal affairs and will continue to make firm responses."[16] On July 23, as a countermeasure to the advisory document issued by the U.S. government on business risks in Hong Kong, as well as to the sanctions imposed on seven senior officials of a Chinese government liaison office, the Chinese government announced it designated seven U.S. individuals and organization on its sanctions list, including Wilbur Ross, former secretary of commerce, members of the U.S. Congress, and a human rights activist, pursuant to the Anti-Foreign Sanction Law that came into effect in June.[17]

China also stepped up its diplomatic offensive against the United States. In a July 26 meeting with Wendy Sherman, deputy secretary of state, Xie Feng, vice minister of foreign affairs, put forward two lists and demanded the United

States to take corresponding actions. The first list calls for amendments to the U.S. policy on China, including the lifting of sanctions against CCP members and senior government officials and the suspension of restrictions on Chinese companies and Chinese students. The second list is about individual matters of concern to the Chinese side, including "unfair treatment" of Chinese nationals and growing anti-Asian sentiment in the United States.[18] In addition, in a meeting with Deputy Secretary Sherman, Foreign Minister Wang Yi made three demands on the United States as bottom lines that China firmly upholds: 1) not challenge the path and system of socialism with Chinese characteristics; 2) not attempt to obstruct China's development process; and 3) not infringe upon China's state sovereignty or damage China's territorial integrity.[19]

The Xi administration appears to have set these two lists and three demands as essential conditions for advancing China-U.S. relations. In an August 29 telephone meeting with Secretary of State Blinken regarding the situation in Afghanistan, Foreign Minister Wang stated, "The Chinese side will consider how to engage with the United States based on its attitude towards China," and then requested the U.S. side to stop smearing China and "take seriously the two lists and three demands as bottom lines."[20]

On November 16, President Xi held his first virtual meeting with President Biden. During the meeting, President Xi stressed the need to build "a sound and stable China-U.S. relationship" based on the three principles of 1) respecting each other, 2) coexisting in peace, and 3) pursuing win-win cooperation. Additionally, President Xi noted that the strengthening of U.S.-Taiwan ties is "extremely dangerous," and that should Taiwan cross the red line, China "will be compelled to take resolute measures."[21] In response to President Biden's call for "common-sense guardrails" to prevent a U.S.-China conflict, President Xi noted the need to "prevent China-U.S. relations from getting out of control," but, to this end, demanded that the United States handle sensitive issues "with prudence." While the two sides agreed to continue dialogue, the meeting reaffirmed the deep-rooted confrontation between the United States and China.

China's stance to challenge universal values and the existing international order has propelled European countries to harden their policies toward China. On March 22, the Council of the European Union (EU) decided to impose sanctions on officials of the Xinjiang Uyghur Autonomous Region and the Public Security Bureau of the Xinjiang Production and Construction Corps for their involvement in human rights abuses against the Uyghurs in Xinjiang, including banning travel to and freezing assets in the EU.[22] The Chinese government responded immediately with countermeasures, announcing sanctions on ten individuals, including members of the European Parliament and the parliaments of Belgium, the Netherlands, and Lithuania, as well as on EU Council and European Parliament subcommittees and a German think tank, barring them from entering China and conducting business with Chinese companies.[23]

In retaliation, the European Parliament adopted a resolution on May 20 supporting the sanctions against China decided by the EU Council. The resolution also froze the ratification process of the EU-China Comprehensive Agreement on Investment, agreed in principle at the end of 2020, until China rescinds the sanctions against the EU.[24] As a result, it will be a long way off for the EU-China investment agreement to enter into force, which China had positioned as an important means of countering decoupling attempted by the United States.

European countries, increasingly wary of China, indicated they would strengthen coordination with the United States and other countries and increase their engagement in the Indo-Pacific region. The North Atlantic Treaty Organization (NATO) summit held on June 14 issued a joint communiqué. It characterizes China as presenting "systemic challenges to the rules-based international order," calls on China to act responsibly in the space, cyber, and maritime domains, and says NATO will deepen cooperation with Japan, Australia, and other countries to support the rules-based international order.[25] The EU-U.S. summit, held the following day, issued a joint statement expressing concerns over China's human rights abuses in Xinjiang and Tibet, pressure on democratic practices in Hong Kong, and unilateral actions that have increased tensions in the East and South China Seas. The joint statement also underscores the "importance of peace and stability across the Taiwan Strait" and states that the EU and the United States would cooperate with partner countries to realize a "free and open Indo-Pacific."[26]

On September 16, the EU released a document entitled, "Joint Communication on the EU Strategy for Cooperation in the Indo-Pacific." The EU's Indo-Pacific strategy recognizes that tensions in the East and South China Seas and the Taiwan Strait could impact the security and prosperity of the EU, and states that the EU will strengthen cooperation with its partners in the Indo-Pacific region to maintain a rules-based international order. Regarding China, it says that, while the EU will advance cooperation on common interests, it will push back in areas in which fundamental disagreements exist, such as on human rights. The strategy further notes the need to enhance naval presence as part of the EU's engagement in the Indo-Pacific region.[27] In actuality, in 2021, France dispatched the amphibious assault ship *Tonnerre* and other vessels to the Indo-Pacific region, the United Kingdom the aircraft carrier HMS *Queen Elizabeth* and other vessels, and Germany the frigate *Bayern*, all in succession. They conducted joint exercises with Southeast Asian countries, Japan, the United States, Australia, among other countries.

On September 15, the United States, the United Kingdom, and Australia announced the launch of AUKUS, a new trilateral security cooperation framework. Regarding the purpose of AUKUS, U.S. President Biden explained it was to strengthen the three countries' military capabilities and military technologies, such as cyber, artificial intelligence, quantum technologies, and undersea technologies, in order to maintain a "free and open Indo-Pacific." As the first step of this cooperation, President Biden announced the sharing of armed, nuclear-powered submarine technology with Australia.[28] A Chinese Foreign Ministry spokesperson criticized the establishment of AUKUS, asserting that the sharing of nuclear submarine-related technology with Australia would be destructive to regional peace and stability, and that the formation of an exclusive "clique" runs counters to the aspirations of the countries in the region.[29]

(2) Efforts to Gain More Partners

As rifts with democracies grow over universal values and the nature of the international order, China is focusing on gaining more partners which share a common political system and view of the international order. For China, the most important partner appears to be Russia. On March 23, Chinese Foreign Minister Wang Yi met with Russian Foreign Minister Sergey Lavrov. At the press conference following the meeting, Foreign Minister Wang underscored that strategic cooperative relations between China and Russia were strengthening and expanding. He noted that, in addition to deepening bilateral cooperation in areas such as energy, space development, and advanced technology, the two countries also share the same views on the international order, including on prioritizing non-interference in internal affairs, and that "China will work with Russia to firmly uphold the international system with the United Nations at its core, firmly uphold the international order based on international law, uphold the common values of peace, development, fairness, justice, democracy and freedom for all mankind, and join hands to build a community with a shared future for mankind."[30] The China-Russia joint statement on global governance issued after the meeting enshrines that the two countries would oppose interference in the internal affairs of sovereign nations under the pretext of "politicizing human rights issues" and "advancing democracy," and would promote the establishment of a "fair, democratic, and rational multipolar international order."[31]

In a virtual meeting held on June 28, President Xi Jinping and Russian President Vladimir Putin decided to extend the Treaty of Good-Neighborliness and Friendly Cooperation between the People's Republic of China and the Russian Federation, which had reached its 20-year expiration date. During the meeting, President Xi noted that the two countries "support each other on issues concerning each other's core interests" and safeguard the common interests of both countries. Furthermore, President Xi asserted that the two countries have "jointly safeguarded true multilateralism and international fairness and justice," and that Sino-Russian relations have set an example of a "new type of international relations." He positioned the treaty as "a vivid practice of fostering a new type of international relations and building a community with a shared future for mankind," and expressed his determination to further advance Sino-Russian relations under the treaty.[32] The bilateral cooperative relations indeed made progress in 2021. In May, a groundbreaking ceremony was held for four nuclear power reactors to be constructed in China with technical assistance from Russia.[33] The two countries are also strengthening military cooperation, as discussed later.

At the same time, China has made efforts to strengthen relations with developing countries by providing vaccines, medical supplies, and other assistance to respond to COVID-19. In his video message to the Global Health Summit on May 21, President Xi announced China would spend $3 billion over the next three years to support developing countries' COVID-19 responses and economic recovery, along with proposing to waive patents on vaccines and launch an international forum on vaccine cooperation.[34] On August 5, China held the first meeting of the International Forum on COVID-19 Vaccine Cooperation in virtual format, participated by 22 developing countries. At the forum, President Xi announced China would strive to supply two billion doses of vaccines throughout the world in the course of a year and contribute $100 million to the COVAX Facility for distributing vaccines to developing countries.[35] The participating foreign delegates "highly appreciated" China's leading role in vaccine cooperation and "thanked" China for its cooperation for developing countries, according to an article on the forum in the *People's Daily*.[36]

China's moves to gain more partners may have had some success. At June's 47th session of the UN Human Rights Council, 44 countries led by Canada issued a joint statement, criticizing human rights abuses against the Uyghurs in Xinjiang and demanding access to the Xinjiang Uyghur Autonomous Region for an assessment by the UN High Commissioner for Human Rights.[37] Meanwhile, 69 countries including China issued a joint statement, stating that the issues related to Hong Kong, Xinjiang, and Tibet are China's internal affairs and opposing interference in China's internal affairs under the pretext of human rights.[38] At the 48th session of the UN Human Rights Council held in September, Pakistan on behalf of 65 countries issued a joint statement, opposing interference in China's internal affairs related to Hong Kong, Xinjiang, and Tibet on the grounds of human rights.[39]

(3) Intimidations in China's Periphery

On the one hand, China promoted strategic cooperative relations with Russia, and through the provision of vaccines and other measures, strove to establish more partnerships with developing countries around the world. On the other hand, China continued to take hard-line and coercive actions in its periphery. Beijing unilaterally asserts sovereignty over the Senkaku Islands, an inherent part of the territory of Japan. In recent years, China has stepped up unilateral attempts to change the status quo, with government vessels and vessels belonging to the Chinese People's Armed Police Force Coast Guard Corps, also known as the China Coast Guard (CCG), entering Japan's contiguous zone and intruding into

Figure 3.1. Number of Chinese government vessels and China Coast Guard vessels that intruded into Japan's territorial sea around the Senkaku Islands

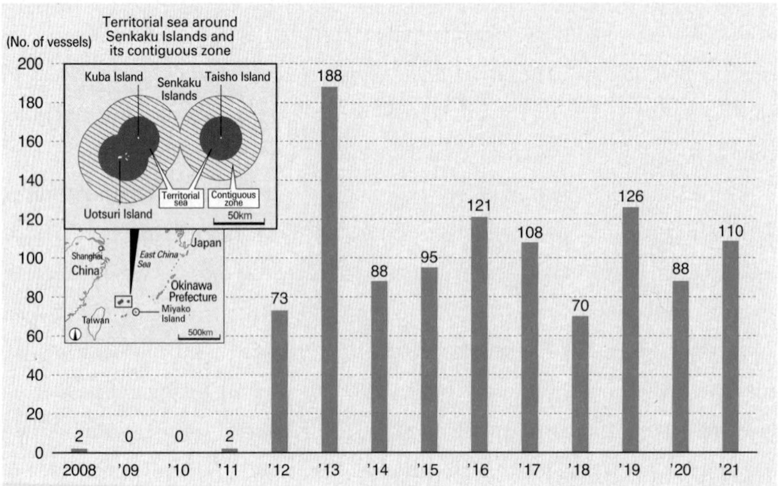

Source: Compiled by the author based on materials released by the Japan Coast Guard.

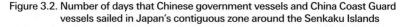

Figure 3.2. Number of days that Chinese government vessels and China Coast Guard
vessels sailed in Japan's contiguous zone around the Senkaku Islands

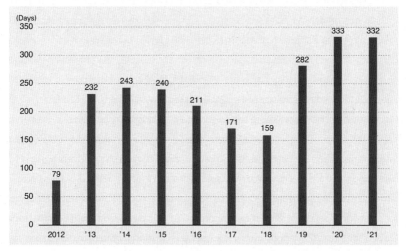

Note: The year 2012 covers the period from September 14 onwards only.
Source: Compiled by the author based on materials released by the Japan Coast Guard.

territorial waters. In 2021, CCG vessels sailed in Japan's contiguous zone on 332
days, almost the same number as in the previous year. CCG vessels persistently
navigate through Japan's contiguous zone, except when a typhoon is approaching
and so on. In 2021, the number of CCG vessels intruding into Japan's territorial
waters increased by 22 from the previous year to 110 vessels. Some CCG vessels
approached Japanese fishing vessels sailing in Japanese territorial waters. Such
actions by CCG vessels constitute a threat to Japanese sovereignty and are
drawing significant alarm. In addition, China enacted the Coast Guard Law in
February 2021. It stipulates the CCG's authority to use weapons and the duty to
remove structures set up by foreign countries. Coupled with the ambiguity of the
sea area to which the law applies, it has heightened Japan's concerns over future
CCG vessel activities in waters surrounding the Senkaku Islands.

Furthermore, the People's Liberation Army (PLA) has stepped up its activities in Japan's periphery seas and airspace. On August 24, a total of three PLA Navy (PLAN) vessels—Luyang III-class missile destroyer, Luyang II-class missile destroyer, and Jiangkai II-class frigate—sailed from the East China Sea to the Western Pacific, passing between Okinawa's main island and Miyako Island.[40] On the same day, a total of four PLAN vessels—Renhai-class missile destroyer, Luyang III-class missile destroyer, Fuchi-class replenishment ship, and Dongdiao-class intelligence collection ship—sailed from the Sea of Japan to the Western Pacific, transiting the Soya Strait.[41] On September 10, a submarine, presumed to be Chinese, sailed from the Western Pacific to the East China Sea, submerging in Japan's contiguous zone between Amami Oshima and Yokoate Island.[42] On December 16, a Chinese fleet led by the *Liaoning* aircraft carrier advanced from the East China Sea to the Western Pacific and conducted air exercises using carrier-borne fighters and carrier-based helicopters from December 19 to 20.[43] It appears these vessel activities were aimed at strengthening China's ability to deploy from coastal waters to the Western Pacific. On August 24, an unmanned aerial vehicle (UAV) believed to be China's TB-001 flew over the East China Sea.[44] On the following day, August 25, a Chinese Y-9 intelligence gathering aircraft, a Y-9 patrol aircraft, and a BZK-005 UAV flew to and back between airspace over the East China Sea and the Western Pacific, passing between Okinawa's main island and Miyako Island.[45] The following day, a

Unmanned aerial vehicle believed to be TB-001 (Joint Staff)

Chinese Y-9 intelligence gathering aircraft, a Y-9 patrol aircraft, and a Chinese UAV believed to be TB-001 made a similar flight.[46] These flights reveal the PLA's strong interest in gathering intelligence in the seas and airspace between the East China Sea and the Western Pacific, as well as expansion of the flight areas of large UAVs and improvement of their operational capabilities, such as coordination with manned aircraft.

China has intensified its military pressure on Taiwan as well. Particularly notable are the frequent flights by Chinese military aircraft in the airspace from the southwestern part of Taiwan's Air Defense Identification Zone (ADIZ), which lies between the main island of Taiwan and the Pratas Islands, to the Bashi Channel. The PLA has repeatedly conducted simultaneous flights of various military aircraft, including H-6K bomber, Y-9 patrol aircraft, Y-9 intelligence gathering aircraft, Y-8 electronic reconnaissance aircraft, KJ-500 early warning aircraft, J-10 fighter, and J-16 fighter. Thirteen and 15 PLA aircraft entered Taiwan's ADIZ on January 23 and 24, 2021, respectively.[47] On March 26, a total of 20 aircraft conducted similar flights, some of which passed through the Bashi Channel and flew to the east side of Taiwan.[48] Thereafter, PLA aircraft continued to fly in Taiwan's ADIZ: 25 aircraft in total on April 12 and 28 on June 15.[49] On October 1, Chinese National Day, a total of 38 aircraft (25 during the day and 13 at night) flew in Taiwan's ADIZ, followed by a total of 39 the next day and 56 on October 4.[50] PLAN vessels also continued to be deployed to waters surrounding Taiwan. On April 5, a fleet of six vessels led by the *Liaoning* aircraft carrier conducted exercises in the Pacific Ocean east of Taiwan.[51] On the same day, the PLA sent ten military aircraft into the southwestern airspace of Taiwan's ADIZ, applying pressure on Taiwan from the east and west. In July and August, the PLA Army's amphibious units from the Eastern Theater Command as well as Navy Marine Corps actively conducted exercises.[52]

The heightened tensions over the Taiwan Strait caused by PLA actions have aroused concerns among the international community, including Japan. The April 16 Japan-U.S. joint leaders' statement issued on the occasion of the meeting between Prime Minister Suga Yoshihide and President Biden states that the two countries "underscore the importance of peace and stability across the Taiwan Strait and encourage the peaceful resolution of cross-Strait issues."[53] The joint statement issued upon the conclusion of the May 27 summit between Japan and the EU likewise contains the wording, "underscore the importance of peace and stability across the Taiwan Strait, and encourage the peaceful resolution of cross-Strait issues."[54] Furthermore, the leaders' communiqué issued on June 13 at the Group of Seven (G7) summit in Cornwall, United Kingdom expressed a similar position.[55] Stability across the Taiwan Strait is critical not only for the security of Japan but also for the stability of the international community, and it is drawing interest and attention to the future activities of the PLA in Taiwan's periphery.

3. The People's Liberation Army's Military Capability Enhancements as the Party's Army

(1) Institutional Development to Support Military Strengthening

The Xi administration has promoted the strengthening of "law-based governance (法治)"[56] and has been developing laws related to the military. Since the end of 2015, the Xi administration has executed what has been described as the most sweeping military reforms since the founding of the PRC. So far the reforms have been carried out at the central level, known as "above the neck," including reforming the leadership and command system and reorganizing seven military area commands (MACs) into five theater commands (TCs), and at the field level, known as "below the neck," including reorganizing specific units. Institutional reforms are presently underway. The military reforms mainly cover "three campaigns," namely, 1) command structure, 2) scale and organization of the forces, and 3) institutions,[57] and have been targeted for completion by 2020. The series of reforms are currently in the final stages, with the National Defense Law amended in December 2020.

According to He Lei, vice president of the PLA's Academy of Military Science, the National Defense Law is the basic law of national defense and army building and needs to be adapted to social changes. The latest amendments fully implement the "Xi Jinping Thought on Strengthening the Military," he says, noting that the law was revised pursuant to the spirit of the CCP Central Committee and Xi Jinping.[58] The amendments wrote into the clauses Xi Jinping's name and the thoughts he advocates, and explicitly state the chairman responsibility system. While the chairman responsibility system is stipulated in the Constitution, the Central Military Commission's opinion on the system had underscored that "The army should follow Xi's command, answer to his order, and never worry him."[59] One of the objectives of revising the National Defense Law was thus to strengthen Xi Jinping's control of the military in legal terms. In addition, as interests to be safeguarded, the revised law newly added "development interests," which had been increasingly mentioned in the recent remarks and official documents of the leaders.[60] Furthermore, outer space, electromagnetic space, and cyberspace were newly listed as critical security domains alongside territorial land, territorial waters, and territorial airspace. It means the scope of national defense indicated in the 2019 defense white paper is now stipulated by law. Additionally, the amended law specifies improving the rank of military personnel and the attractiveness

Table 3.1. Major reviews and parades held on National Day and other commemorative days

	Date	Purpose and characteristic (place)
Mao Zedong	October 1, 1949 – October 1, 1959	Held every year on October 1 to celebrate the PRC's founding (Tiananmen Square)
Deng Xiaoping	October 1, 1984	35th anniversary of the PRC's founding (Tiananmen Square)
Jiang Zemin	October 1, 1999	50th anniversary of the PRC's founding (Tiananmen Square)
Hu Jintao	October 1, 2009	60th anniversary of the PRC's founding (Tiananmen Square)
	September 3, 2015	70th anniversary of Victory Day (Tiananmen Square)
	July 30, 2017	90th anniversary of the PLA's founding (Zhurihe Training Base)
	April 12, 2018	Largest-ever naval parade (South China Sea)
	April 23, 2019	70th anniversary of the PLA Navy's founding (Qingdao)
Xi Jinping	October 1, 2019	70th anniversary of the PRC's founding (Tiananmen Square)

Note: Light red cells indicate parades held under the Xi Jinping administration.

Sources: Compiled by the author based on media reports and other sources (Xinhua/Aflo, Reuters/Aflo, Universal Images Group).

of military service. Other laws with similar aims have taken effect, such as the Veterans Law since January 2021 and the Law on the Protection of the Status, Rights and Interests of Military Personnel since August. The stated purpose of these laws is to increase the personnel's sense of mission and attractiveness of the profession.[61] They are indicative of the Xi administration's commitment to securing excellent talent, which is indispensable for the country's goal of having a "world-class military."

The centenary of the CCP was China's most important event in 2021. Yet, no large-scale review or parade took place. Some believe it was to avoid the West's criticism of the one-party rule.[62] Meanwhile, some view that Xi Jinping orchestrated numerous reviews and parades in recent years in order to seize power in the military.[63] As shown in Table 3.1, large-scale reviews and parades have been held with unprecedented frequency under the Xi administration. One could deduce that a large-scale military event was not conducted for the centenary because Chairman Xi had already established an absolute position in the military and had no need to show off his leadership.

The revised National Defense Law newly stipulated loyalty to the CCP as an obligation of military personnel. In addition, China revised for the first time in ten years the Political Work Regulations of the PLA, which prescribes political work that is considered the lifeline and most distinctive characteristic of the PLA.[64] The establishment of these various military related laws has cemented Chairman Xi's position and systematically reinforced the Party's leadership over the military.

Aiming to hone the actual combat ability of the PLA, the Xi administration has also worked to improve the military training system. In February, it was reported that the Decision on Fostering a New-type Military Training System was issued upon ratification by Chairman Xi.[65] This decision stipulates that the PLA would focus on practical training, integrated training, training using science and technology, and law-based training. At the same time, institutional enhancements have been made to flexibly adapt the military to social changes. For example, the revised Law on Military Facilities Protection, which took effect on August 1, is said to reflect the growing need to adjust the arrangements for existing military facilities due to urban development and other factors.[66] The law further takes into consideration protection of the natural environment, in an attempt to balance development of military facilities with the needs of modern state building. The Military Service Law was also revised in line with the current shift in military service from a conscription system to a volunteer system.[67]

The PLA, while maintaining its nature as the Party's army with absolute obedience to the CCP, is making institutional improvements to conform to social changes. The success or failure of the military reforms is thought to depend largely on whether the Party's guidance can be strengthened while simultaneously adapting the military to a changing society.

(2) Steady Enhancements of Equipment and Other Capabilities

At the NPC in March 2021, a defense budget of approximately 1,355.3 billion

Figure 3.3. China's troop force and defense budget

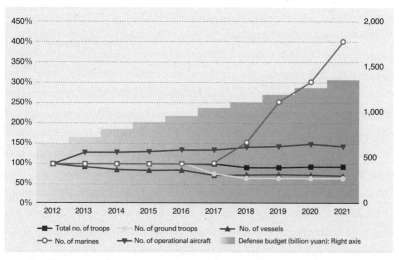

Note: The left axis shows the respective troop force (since 2012), and the right axis shows the defense budget.

Source: Compiled by the author based on each year's *Defense of Japan*.

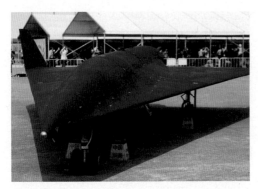

WZ-8 high-altitude and high-speed unmanned reconnaissance aircraft displayed at the China International Aviation and Aerospace Exhibition (Xinhua/Kyodo News Images)

yuan was announced for FY2021, up 6.8% from the previous year. This is higher than the economic growth target set at 6% year on year. In Figure 3.3, changes in China's troop force and disclosed defense budget are shown in a graph. While China's defense spending remains high, recent years have seen downsizing for some of the existing troop forces, alongside a marked personnel increase for the Navy Marine Corps responsible for amphibious operations. As the graph illustrates, China aims to improve its military forces in quality rather than quantity.

On April 23, the nuclear-powered submarine *Long March 18*, the amphibious assault ship *Hainan*, and the destroyer *Dalian* entered service and were delivered to the South Sea Fleet. *Hainan* is China's first large-scale amphibious assault ship, which will increase the country's amphibious operations capabilities. *Dalian* is one of PLAN's largest Renhai-class 10,000-ton destroyers, and is equipped with a 112-cell missile vertical launching system (VLS) and advanced anti-aircraft radar, among other equipment. The first Renhai-class destroyer was commissioned in January 2020 and the second in March 2021.[68] An annual report published by the U.S. Department of Defense in September 2020 notes China has the largest navy in the world.[69] With state-of-the-art vessels commissioned in succession, it can be said that PLAN is steadily upgrading in both scale and quality and significantly enhancing its overall operational capabilities.

China has also made tangible achievements in space development, which is closely linked to the military. In 2019, China became the first country in the world to successfully land a rover on the far side of the moon. In April 2021, it launched the Tianhe core module that controls the entire Tiangong space station. In June, it launched the manned spacecraft Shenzhou-12 that successfully docked with Tianhe. After about a three-month long mission, the three astronauts aboard Shenzhou-12 returned to Earth in September. In addition, on Mars, China landed Tianwen-1 in May, and the Zhurong rover conducted a topographical and geological survey. China is the third country after the former Soviet Union and the United States to land a probe on Mars and the second country after the United States to conduct an exploration mission on the planet.[70]

China's space activities have been carried out pursuant to the December 2016 white paper on space, and the space program is steadily on track. As China pushes forward to become a "space power," it may be testing technologies with direct military implications. In August 2021, China reportedly tested a hypersonic glide weapon capable of carrying a nuclear warhead, which was launched into space and landed on the ground.[71] Mark Milley, chairman of the U.S. Joint Chiefs of Staff, confirmed the test and described it as "very concerning."[72]

China's improvements in military technology were showcased at the China International Aviation and Aerospace Exhibition held in Zhuhai City, Guangdong Province in September. Several Cai Hong (Rainbow) drones were displayed. Chinese media noted on their improved range and payload, as well as their diverse missions, including high-altitude reconnaissance, anti-submarine operation, maritime patrol, and early warning.[73] J-16D, which is deemed to have been developed independently, is an electronic warfare aircraft based on the already deployed J-16 fighter. J-16D is designed to jam radars and attack the enemy's air defense system with missiles in order to secure control not only in the air and maritime but also cyber and electromagnetic domains. It is reported that J-16D may soon be deployed for operations in the periphery of Taiwan.[74] While the exhibition is considered an airshow, unmanned vessels and unmanned combat vehicles also made appearances,[75] revealing that the PLA is converting equipment into unmanned ones in a multifaceted manner.

(3) Military Activities Pursued on Hard-line and Conciliatory Fronts

As its fallout with the West deepens, China has engaged in military activities with friendly countries. In recent years, China has participated in large-scale military exercises in Russia. Since first participating in Vostok (East) 2018, China has participated in Tsentr (Center) 2019 and Kavkaz (Caucasus) 2020 and further enhanced China-Russia military cooperation.

In August 2021, the joint military exercise with Russia, Zapad/Interaction 2021, was held at the Qingtongxia training ground in China's Ningxia Hui Autonomous Region. In this exercise, a PLA maintenance squad was reportedly incorporated into a Russian armored force and acted under the command of the Russian side.[76] It is possible that field cooperation mechanisms between the two militaries have been boosted. In September, China appears to have sent observers to Zapad 2021 held in Russia and Belarus.[77] A *PLA Daily* article on Zapad/Interaction 2021 highlighted new developments in China-Russia combined exercises, namely, Russia's participation in a Chinese-led exercise held in China, as opposed to China participating in a large-scale military exercise led by Russia, as well as improvements in command and control coordination.[78] In June, the two countries issued a joint statement upon agreeing to extend the Treaty of Good-Neighborliness and Friendly Cooperation between the People's Republic of China and the Russian Federation. The statement mentions: 1) China-Russia relations have reached an unprecedented high level; 2) Russia needs a prosperous and stable China, while China needs a strong and successful Russia; and 3) the two countries will further deepen coordination and cooperation in areas such as politics, security, military, and economy and trade.[79] The strengthening of China-Russia relations, including military cooperation, is thus expected to continue.

The Ministry of National Defense cited counterterrorism as one of the objectives of Zapad/Interaction 2021, which was held in the Ningxia Hui Autonomous Region that has a large Muslim population.[80] The withdrawal of U.S. forces from Afghanistan has raised concerns that terrorist organizations may regroup.[81] By conducting the exercise, China may have sought to militarily rein in Islamic terrorist activities. Additionally, a counterterrorism exercise was conducted within the framework of the Shanghai Cooperation Organisation (SCO): the joint military exercise, Peace Mission 2021, held in Russia's Orenburg Oblast in September. Around 4,000 personnel from China, Russia, Kazakhstan, Tajikistan, Kyrgyzstan, India, Pakistan, Uzbekistan, and other countries participated (from China, 558 personnel and around 130 vehicles [equipment], mainly from the Northern Theater Command). The stated purpose of the exercise, unrelated to the regional situation, was to demonstrate the determination and actions of the SCO member states to fight terrorism.[82] The "power vacuum" created by the withdrawal of U.S. forces from Afghanistan has increased the importance of counterterrorism training for China. Hence, this type of drill may be scaled up or otherwise expanded in the future.

From September 6 to 15, Shared Destiny 2021 was held at the Queshan training ground in China's Henan Province, participated by forces from China, Mongolia, Pakistan, Thailand, and other countries. One of the stated objectives of the exercise was to increase the capabilities of peacekeeping standby forces.[83] It was the first multilateral peacekeeping field training exercise conducted in China and invited several foreign media outlets to the site.[84] Such efforts suggest the administration sought to demonstrate the PLA's elevated international standing, both domestically and globally.

China took part in the International Army Games 2021, which was held in China and other countries from August to September. The PLA sent teams to games held in Russia, Belarus, Uzbekistan, Iran, and other countries. Games held in China were participated by teams from the Russian, Belarusian, Egyptian, Iranian, Venezuelan, Vietnamese, and other forces. The Ministry of National Defense explained that China's hosting and participation in the games would promote friendly ties with foreign militaries and contribute to improving each other's capability levels.[85]

China has encouraged friendly relations with other countries in military activities while simultaneously taking a hard-line attitude. In 2020, clashes broke out at the border with India, resulting in casualties in June for the first time in 45 years. The two militaries agreed to pull out their troops in February 2021.

Chinese and Russian naval vessels sailing in formation (Joint Staff)

However, their claims conflicted at a corps commander level meeting held in October, and the two sides appear to remain in a stalemate.[86]

Meanwhile, the PLA "continued to strengthen relations" with Russian forces and conducted the bilateral naval exercise, Joint Sea 2021, in October. The purpose of the exercise was allegedly to improve the two navies' capabilities of jointly dealing with maritime security threats and preserving regional peace and stability.[87] Later, however, it was confirmed that for the first time Chinese and Russian vessels simultaneously passed through the Tsugaru Strait, sailed southward along Japan's Pacific coastline, and then navigated from the Osumi Strait to the East China Sea.[88] China called this voyage "joint maritime patrol between Chinese and Russian navies." Such large-scale and long-term activities by China and Russia in Japan's periphery are believed to be a demonstration act directed at Japan.[89]

On November 19, Chinese and Russian bombers jointly flew in the skies above the Sea of Japan and then over the East China Sea and the Pacific Ocean. China's Ministry of National Defense announced this was part of their third joint strategic air patrols.[90] The joint flight by Chinese and Russian bombers followed on from those conducted in 2019 and 2020, and it can be inferred that such flights have become routine. On November 23, Wei Fenghe, China's defense minister, and Sergei Shoigu, Russia's defense minister, held a meeting and confirmed to "continue to strengthen cooperation in strategic exercises and joint patrols."[91]

Without question, Sino-Russian cooperative relations are deepening on the military front.

NOTES

1) Xinhua Net, July 1, 2021.

2) Ren Lixuan, "Jiakuai goujian xin fazhan geju" [Accelerate the establishment of a new pattern of development], *People's Daily*, May 12, 2021.

3) Ren Ping, "Guanxi woguo fazhan quanju de zhongda zhanlüe renwu——lun jiakuai goujian xin fazhan geju" [A major strategic task related to all aspects of China's development: On accelerating the establishment of a new pattern of development], *People's Daily*, April 9, 2021.

4) Zhang Tao, "Jiakuai shixian keji zili ziqiang" [Accelerate the realization of scientific and technological self-reliance and self-improvement], *People's Daily*, May 11, 2021.

5) *People's Daily*, May 29, 2021.

6) People's Daily columnist, "Nuli shixian gao shuiping keji zili ziqiang" [Strive to achieve a high level of scientific and technological self-reliance and self-improvement], *People's Daily*, May 30, 2021.

7) *People's Daily*, March 31, 2021.

8) *South China Morning Post*, September 20, 2021; *Yomiuri Shimbun*, September 20, 2021.

9) *People's Daily*, November 17, 2021.

10) People's Daily Online, January 21, 2021.

11) *People's Daily*, January 22, 2021.

12) Xinhua Net, February 11, 2021.

13) The White House, "Remarks by President Biden on America's Place in the World" (February 4, 2021).

14) [U.S.] Department of State (DOS), "A Foreign Policy for the American People" (March 3, 2021).

15) [U.S.] DOS, "Update to Report on Identification of Foreign Persons Involved in the Erosion of the Obligations of China Under the Joint Declaration or the Basic Law" (March 16, 2021).

16) *People's Daily*, March 20, 2021.

17) *People's Daily*, July 24, 2021.

18) Xinhua Net, July 26, 2021.

19) *People's Daily*, July 27, 2021.

20) *People's Daily*, August 30, 2021.

21) *People's Daily*, November 17, 2021.

22) Council of the European Union, "EU Imposes Further Sanctions over Serious Violations of Human Rights around the World" (March 22, 2021); *Official Journal of the European Union*, Vol. 64 (March 22, 2021): 1-12.

23) [China] Ministry of Foreign Affairs, "Foreign Ministry Spokesperson Announces Sanctions on Relevant EU Entities and Personnel" (March 22, 2021).

24) European Parliament, "MEPs Refuse Any Agreement with China Whilst Sanctions are in Place" (May 20, 2021).

25) North Atlantic Treaty Organization, "Brussels Summit Communiqué" (June 14, 2021).

26) Council of the European Union, "EU-US Summit 2021 Statement: Toward a Renewed Transatlantic Partnership" (June 15, 2021).

27) European Commission, "The EU Strategy for Cooperation in the Indo-Pacific" (September 16, 2021).

28) The White House, "Remarks by President Biden, Prime Minister Morrison of Australia, and Prime Minister Johnson of the United Kingdom Announcing the Creation of AUKUS" (September 15, 2021).

29) Xinhua Net, September 16, 2021.

30) People's Daily Online, March 23, 2021.

31) *PLA Daily*, March 24, 2021.

32) *People's Daily*, June 29, 2021.

33) *People's Daily*, May 20, 2021.

34) *People's Daily*, May 22, 2021.

35) *People's Daily*, August 6, 2021.

36) *People's Daily*, August 6, 2021.

37) Government of Canada, "Joint Statement on Human Rights Situation in Xinjiang at 47th Session of UN Human Rights Council" (June 22, 2021).

38) Permanent Mission of the People's Republic of China at Geneva, "Joint Statement of 69 Countries at the Interactive Dialogue on High Commissioner's Annual Report at the 47th Session of the Human Rights Council" (June 22, 2021).

39) Permanent Mission of the People's Republic of China at Geneva, "Pakistan, on Behalf of 65 Countries, Delivered a Joint Statement against Interference in China's Internal Affairs under the Pretext of Human Rights at the Human Rights Council" (September 24, 2021).

40) Joint Staff, "Chugoku kaigun kantei no doko ni tsuite" [Movements of Chinese naval vessels] (August 25, 2021).

41) Ibid.

42) [Japan] Ministry of Defense [MOD], "Senbotsu sensuikan oyobi Chugoku kaigun kantei no doko ni tsuite" [Movements of submarine and Chinese naval vessel] (September 12, 2021).

43) Joint Staff, "Chugoku kaigun kantei no doko ni tsuite" [Movements of Chinese naval vessels] (December 17, 2021); Joint Staff, "Chugoku kaigun kantei to no doko ni tsuite" [Movements of Chinese naval vessels, aircraft, and helicopter] (December 21, 2021).

44) Joint Staff, "Suitei Chugokuki no Higashishinakai ni okeru hiko ni tsuite" [Flight by supposed Chinese aircraft over the East China Sea] (August 25, 2021).

45) Joint Staff, "Chugokuki no Higashishinakai oyobi Taiheiyo ni okeru hiko ni tsuite" [Flight by Chinese aircraft over the East China Sea and the Pacific Ocean] (August 25, 2021).

46) Joint Staff, "Chugokuki no Higashishinakai oyobi Taiheiyo ni okeru hiko ni tsuite" [Flight by Chinese aircraft over the East China Sea and the Pacific Ocean] (August 26, 2021).

47) [ROC] Ministry of National Defense (MND), "PLA aircraft entered Taiwan's southwestern ADIZ" (January 23 and 24, 2021).

48) [ROC] MND, "Air activities in the southwestern ADIZ of R.O.C." (March 26, 2021).

49) [ROC] MND, "Air activities in the southwestern ADIZ of R.O.C." (April 12 and June 15, 2021).

50) [ROC] MND, "Air activities in the southwestern ADIZ of R.O.C." (October 1, 2, and 4, 2021).

51) *Global Times* (Chinese), April 6, 2021.

52) *Global Times*, July 18, 2021.

53) [Japan] Ministry of Foreign Affairs (MOFA), "U.S.-Japan Joint Leaders' Statement" (April 16, 2021).

54) [Japan] MOFA, "The 27th Japan-EU Summit" (May 27, 2021).

55) [Japan] MOFA, "Carbis Bay G7 Summit Communiqué" (June 18, 2021).

56) Iwamoto Hiroshi, "Chugoku no kokka senryaku 'gunmin yugo' ni kansuru tenbo" [Prospects for China's "military-civil fusion" national strategy], *NIDS Commentary* (December 24, 2020).

57) China Military Online, November 15, 2018.

58) *PLA Daily*, January 13, 2021.

59) *People's Daily*, November 6, 2017.

60) Furuya Koichi, "Chugoku ga mamorou to suru 'hatten rieki' to wa nanika" [What are the "development interests" that China seeks to protect], *Toa* [East Asia] no. 643 (January 2021): 52-53.

61) *PLA Daily*, June 12, 2021.

62) *Nikkei Shimbun* (online), March 23, 2021.

63) *Sankei Shimbun* (online), September 22, 2019.

64) *PLA Daily*, February 20, 2021.

65) *PLA Daily*, February 21, 2021.

66) Government of China, "Wei guofang he jundui xiandaihua jianshe tigong jianqiang falü baozhang—youguan bumen fuzeren jiu guofang junshi lifa xiangguan wenti huida jizhe tiwen" [Providing strong legal protection for modernization of national defense and armed forces: Responsible persons from relevant departments answer reporters' questions on issues related to national defense and military legislation], Central People's Government website (July 31, 2021).

67) China News Online, August 26, 2021.

68) [Japan] MOD, *Defense of Japan 2021* (Tokyo: Ministry of Defense, 2021), 65.

69) [U.S.] Department of Defense, *Military and Security Developments Involving the People's Republic of China 2020* (September 1, 2020), ii.

70) *Mainichi Shimbun* (online), May 15, 2021.

71) *Financial Times*, October 17, 2021.

72) Bloomberg.com, October 27, 2021.

73) People's Daily Online, September 30, 2021.

74) Xinhua Net, September 27, 2021.

75) Xinhua Net, September 29, 2021.

76) *PLA Daily*, August 14, 2021.

77) Красная звезда, от 10 сентября 2021г.

78) *PLA Daily*, August 12, 2021.

79) [China] Ministry of Foreign Affairs, "Zhonghua renmin gongheguo he Eluosi lianbang guanyu 'Zhong E mulin youhao hezuo tiaoyue' qianshu 20 zhounian de lianhe shengming" [Joint statement of the People's Republic of China and the Russian Federation on the 20th anniversary of the signing of the 'Treaty of Good-Neighborliness and Friendly Cooperation between the People's Republic of China and the Russian Federation'] (June 28, 2021).

80) [China] Ministry of National Defense (MND), "Regular Press Conference of the Ministry of National Defense on July 29" (July 29, 2021).

81) NHK News, September 30, 2021.

82) *PLA Daily*, September 11 and 25, 2021.

83) *PLA Daily*, September 6, 2021.

84) Xinhua Net (Japanese), September 7, 2021; [China] MND, "Guofangbu jieshao

'gongtong mingyun-2021' guoji weihe shibing yanxi tedian" [Ministry of National Defense introduces the characteristics of 'Shared Destiny-2021' international peacekeeping exercise] (September 30, 2021).

85) [China] MND, "Regular Press Conference of the Ministry of National Defense on July 29" (July 29, 2021).

86) *Asahi Shimbun* (online), October 11, 2021.

87) *PLA Daily*, October 15, 2021.

88) Joint Staff, "Chugoku oyobi Roshia kaigun kantei no doko ni tsuite" [Movements of Chinese and Russian naval vessels] (October 18, 21, and 23, 2021).

89) [Japan] MOD, "Boei daijin kisha kaiken" [Press conference by the Minister of Defense] (October 26, 2021).

90) Xinhua Net, November 19, 2021.

91) *People's Daily*, November 24, 2021.

Chapter 4

The Korean Peninsula

Missile Diversification in North and South Korea

AKUTSU Hiroyasu (Lead author, Section 1)
MUROOKA Tetsuo (Section 2)

Summary

In 2021, which marked the tenth anniversary of President of the State Affairs Kim Jong Un's succession to power, North Korea focused on diversifying missile capabilities (including launch methods). Such efforts were in line with Kim's report made at the 8th Congress of the Workers' Party of Korea in January. The report unveiled his aims to launch new type ballistic missiles, new type long-range cruise missiles, railway-borne missiles, the Hwasong 8 hypersonic missile, and new type surface-to-air missiles. Against this backdrop, the International Atomic Energy Agency and the South Korean Armed Forces' Joint Chiefs of Staff revealed there were indications of operation of nuclear facilities in North Korea.

North Korea adopts a "dialogue and confrontation" policy with the United States while it began to show flexibility with South Korea. Pyongyang, for example, reversed its reluctance to President Moon Jae-in's proposal to declare an end to the Korean War and restored the inter-Korean lines of communication, all the while maintaining readiness to counter South Korean military threats. In addition, the North Korean and Chinese leaders reaffirmed their cooperation in July, on the 60th anniversary of the Sino-North Korean Mutual Aid and Cooperation Friendship Treaty. Due to the novel coronavirus disease (COVID-19) pandemic and other circumstances, however, it did not lead to the full resumption of bilateral trade.

In South Korea, President Moon Jae-in entered the final year of his term in 2021 retaining more power than previous presidents. The presidential election was a contest between Lee Jae-myung, the candidate of the progressive ruling party, the Democratic Party of Korea, and Yoon Suk-yeol, the candidate of the conservative opposition party, the People Power Party. If the former wins, President Moon's conciliatory North Korea policy will be upheld fundamentally, while if the latter wins, there may be a change in policy leading to stronger backlash from North Korea.

President Moon made a series of efforts to realize the "end-of-war declaration" for the Korean War. The idea was to revive the stalled inter-Korean and U.S.-North Korea relations. However, the "end-of-war declaration" was not realized in 2021 amid the halt in U.S.-North Korea dialogue. While adopting a conciliatory North Korea policy, the Moon administration sought to diversify strike capabilities, such as submarine-launched ballistic missiles (SLBM), and extend the range of missiles and increase their yield in order to deal with "threats from all directions," which include not only North Korea but also neighboring countries.

Defense Development Exhibition "Self-Defense 2021" (KCNA/Kyodo)

Keywords

missile diversification   end-of-war declaration

ROK presidential election   SLBM

1. North Korea's Missile Diversification and Hard-line and Soft-line Policies toward the United States and South Korea

(1) Accelerated Missile Development

The succession of President of the State Affairs Kim Jong Un as supreme leader marked the tenth anniversary in 2021. During this year, North Korea more actively developed missiles and missile capabilities, so as to build on the achievements and overcome the challenges laid out by Kim in his January report at the 8th Congress of the Workers' Party of Korea (WPK).[1] Table 4.1 below lists the main achievements in military technology and capabilities that were outlined in the report.

Table 4.1. Main achievements in defense technology claimed by North Korea (last five years)

Main achievements
Developed and perfected the super-large multiple launch rocket system (MLRS)
Developed and perfected the new type tactical missile and medium-range cruise missile capable of carrying conventional warheads
Completed development and research of warheads, including the guidance technology for multi-warhead missile and the supersonic gliding flight warhead for new type ballistic missiles, and started preparations for their prototype production
Set goals for the modernization of medium-sized submarine armaments
Completed design and research of the new nuclear-powered submarine and reached the final examination stage
Perfected designs of electronic weapons, unmanned striking equipment, means of reconnaissance and detection, and military reconnaissance satellite

Source: Compiled by the author based on KCNA, January 9, 2021.

The challenges are listed in Table 4.2.

As of October 2021, North Korea's missile and nuclear-related activities since March can be understood as efforts to verify the achievements and resolve the challenges detailed in the aforementioned report. Test firings were conducted that showcase the increasing variety and diversity of North Korea's missile capabilities, including launch methods, such as new type ballistic missiles, new type long-range cruise missiles, railway-borne missiles, hypersonic missiles, and new type surface-to-air missiles. Table 4.3 lists North Korea's missile launches in 2021 as of October.

Table 4.2. Main challenges facing defense technology claimed by North Korea (next five years)

Main challenges
Making nuclear weapons smaller, lighter, and tactical
Improving precision to strike and annihilate any strategic target within a 15,000-kilometer range
Developing and introducing the supersonic gliding flight warhead in a short period
Issues related to possessing nuclear-powered submarines and underwater-launch nuclear strategic weapons (significant for improving long-range nuclear striking capability)
Securing reconnaissance and information gathering ability by operating a military reconnaissance satellite in the near future
Promoting development of reconnaissance means, including reconnaissance drones capable of precision reconnaissance up to 500 kilometer depth into the front
Realizing intelligent, precise, unmanned, high-performance, and lightweight equipment as a basic task facing defense science and technology

Source: Compiled by the author based on KCNA, January 9, 2021.

On March 25, North Korea fired a total of two missiles in an eastward direction from the vicinity of Sondok on the country's east coast. The missiles were of the same type as the new type ballistic missile unveiled on January 14 during a military parade held in conjunction with the 8th Party Congress. Both missiles flew around 450 kilometers at an altitude of less than 100 kilometers, a lower trajectory than that of North Korean Scuds, and landed outside Japan's exclusive economic zone (EEZ). According to North Korea's Academy of National Defense Science (ANDS), the missiles fired were a "newly developed new-type tactical guided projectile," constituting a weapon system which improved the warhead weight to 2.5 tons, and accurately hit targets that were

Table 4.3. North Korea's major missile launches in 2021 (including those announced by North Korea)

Date	Type, altitude, flight distance
March 25	Two new type ballistic missiles, altitude below 100 kilometers, flight distance approx. 450 kilometers
September 11 and 12	Two new type long-range cruise missiles, altitude unknown, flight distance 1,500 kilometers
September 15	Two new type railway-borne ballistic missiles, maximum altitude approx. 50 kilometers, flight distance approx. 750 kilometers
September 28	One Hwasong 8 hypersonic missile, altitude unknown, flight distance unknown
September 30	One new type surface-to-air missile, altitude unknown, flight distance unknown
October 19	One new type SLBM, maximum altitude approx. 50 kilometers, flight distance approx. 600 kilometers

Sources: Compiled by the author based on KCNA and Ministry of Defense of Japan.

600 kilometers away in the Sea of Japan.[2] ANDS mentioned that the test-firing confirmed the reliability of the improved solid-fuel rocket engine through engine ground jet tests and their test-firing processes, and reconfirmed the irregular orbit features of the low-altitude gliding leap type flight mode. It assessed, "The development of this weapon system is of great significance in bolstering up the military power of the country and deterring all sorts of military threats existing on the Korean Peninsula."

On September 13, North Korea's ANDS announced the successful test-firing of newly developed new type long-range cruise missiles on September 11 and 12. The announcement reported that the launched cruise missiles flew 1,500 kilometers in 7,580 seconds along an elliptical and figure-eight trajectory and hit their targets. It further cited that long-range cruise missiles had been under development for two years as part of a core project of national defense. "The missile has strategic significance in giving us an effective means of deterrence to suppress the military activities of hostile forces and ensure our security," ANDS assessed.

North Korea has been developing anti-ship cruise missiles for coastal defense based on Russian-made models, and they are known to have been test-fired since the 1990s.[3] Under the Kim Jong Un regime, North Korea announced the launch of five new type anti-ship cruise missiles in February 2015,[4] three anti-ship cruise missiles in June 2015,[5] and several surface-to-ship cruise missiles in June 2017.[6] While North Korea had launched short-range cruise missiles, this was the first time it announced the launch of long-range cruise missiles. When North Korea announced test launches of cruise missiles, it released photos showing the missile hitting its target. For example, when a cruise missile was fired from Wonsan in eastern North Korea into the Sea of Japan in June 2017, it announced that the missile "flew in a precise circle and detected and hit the target ship floating on the east sea of Korea" and published photos of the missile in the *Rodong Sinmun*.[7] Following the test-fire on September 11, however, no such photos were published. Despite North Korea's assessment that the test-fire was a success, the launch may have failed and thus photos cannot be released. If so, North Korea will likely repeat the test-firing until it is able to release images showing it was successful. Furthermore, if North Korea recognizes that cruise missiles are not subject to the United Nations (UN) Security Council resolutions, the hurdle to repeat the launch may not be very high.

In addition, North Korea launched two more ballistic missiles on September 15. North Korea announced that the railway-borne missile regiment of the Korean People's Army used a railway-borne missile system to fire the missiles, which flew approximately 800 kilometers and hit their targets.[8] The missiles flew along an irregular trajectory and are estimated to have fallen within Japan's EEZ, about 300 kilometers north of

A railway-borne missile being launched (KCNA/Kyodo)

Hegura Island off Japan's Noto Peninsula.

Such a railway-borne system, previously developed by the former Soviet Union, is not a new idea or technology. Radio Free Asia (RFA) reported in 2016 that North Korea had begun developing railway-borne missiles.[9] This report suggests that China's refusal to export large-vehicle mobile launchers to North Korea prompted Pyongyang to begin developing a train-based mobile launcher. According to the report, one of North Korea's technological challenges at the time was figuring out how to load a 100-ton class long-range missile onto a North Korean freight car with a maximum payload of around 60 tons.

Meanwhile, on September 15, the day North Korea launched the railway-borne missiles, South Korea (also referred to as the Republic of Korea or ROK) announced the successful underwater test-fire of a submarine-launched ballistic missile (SLBM). The SLBM test-fired by South Korea "looked somewhat like a poor weapon without all its shape and far from an underwater weapon," said ANDS President Jang Chang Ha on September 20. Judging it was "clearly not SLBM" and was a tactical ballistic missile with a range "less than 500 km," he assessed "Such meaningless missile is just for 'bragging' and 'self-comforting.'"[10] It cannot "be an effective military attack means in a war," President Jang analyzed, noting, "we have meditated over its [South Korea's] purpose of giving attachment to the development of submarine-launched weapon system."

Furthermore, North Korea announced ANDS launched the newly developed Hwasong 8 hypersonic missile on September 28.[11] Kim Jong Un's January report had foreshadowed the introduction of the hypersonic missile "in a short period" (see Table 4.1). The North Korean announcement said the test-firing "ascertained the stability of the engine as well as of missile fuel ampoule that has been introduced for the first time."

Pak Jong Chon, a member of the Presidium of the Political Bureau and secretary of the WPK who observed the test-firing with leading officials of the national defense science sector, reportedly "referred to the strategic importance of developing and field deploying hypersonic missiles, as well as to the military significance of turning all missile fuel systems into ampoules."[12] North Korea's announcement, however, did not make any mention of such military significance. Simply put, fuel ampoule is a technology that keeps liquid fuel in the missile for a certain period of time, instead of having to inject liquid fuel into the missile just before the launch.[13] "Ampoulization" allows for more instantaneous missile launches. The ROK Joint Chiefs of Staff assessed, "This missile is in the early stages of development, and it will take a considerable period of time for it to be deployed in actual warfare." Nevertheless, some ROK experts fear the ampoulization technology will make it difficult to detect signs of North Korean missile launches.[14]

Shortly after the September 28 launch, Kim Song, North Korea's ambassador to the UN, delivered a speech at the UN General Assembly in New York. In the speech, he asserted North Korea's right to self-defense and weapons testing, and underscored North Korea's right to "develop, test, manufacture, and possess" weapons systems.

North Korea announced on October 1 that it launched a new type anti-aircraft missile for air defense on the previous day, September 30.[15] According to the announcement, the test launch was conducted to verify "comprehensive combat performance" and opened prospects for the missile's practical use. North Korea appears to be attempting to improve Anti-Access/Area Denial capabilities using cruise missiles for coastal defense and surface-to-air missiles for air defense.

Lastly, North Korea announced that ANDS test-fired a new type SLBM on October 19.[16] According to the Ministry of Defense of Japan, North Korea launched one SLBM eastward from the vicinity of Sinpo on the eastern side of the Korean Peninsula. The missile is estimated to have flown on an irregular trajectory for approximately 600 kilometers at an altitude of up to around 50 kilometers before falling into the Sea of Japan east of the Peninsula.[17] North Korea's announcement states the new type SLBM was launched from the "8.24 Yongung" ship from which ANDS conducted its first successful SLBM test-firing five years ago. The announcement also mentions, "Many advanced control guidance technologies have been introduced, including flank mobility and gliding skip mobility."

The UN Security Council did not issue a statement condemning neither North Korea's September 15 and 28 ballistic missile and other launches, nor its October 19 SLBM launch. This was reportedly because of China and Russia's opposition to the issuance of such statements.[18] This attitude of the two countries is, in effect, decreasing the international community's ability to restrain missile launches by North Korea.

Meanwhile, regarding nuclear development, Sweden's Stockholm International Peace Research Institute (SIPRI) reported on June 14 that North Korea's estimated nuclear weapon inventory increased from 30–40 warheads in the previous year to 40–50 warheads as of January 2021.[19] On August 27, the International Atomic Energy Agency (IAEA) released a report stating there were indications that the 5,000 kW graphite moderated reactor at North Korea's nuclear facility in Yongbyon had been restarted.[20] Additionally, on October 8, Won In-choul, chairman of the ROK Joint Chiefs of Staff, revealed that an audit of the National Defense Committee of the National Assembly found on October 6 that the nuclear facility in Pyongsan in southern North Korea was in normal operation. "It continues to produce nuclear materials, such as uranium and plutonium," and "Ore mined in Pyongsan, where a uranium refinery plant is believed to be located, is being supplied to the nuclear facility," he said. He further revealed that North-South denuclearization negotiations have been stalled for a long time.[21] In light of the Kim Jong Un regime's default course of action and his January report at the 8th Party Congress, North Korea is unlikely to agree to denuclearization in the form demanded by the United States and the ROK. This was reaffirmed by the report of the Joint Chiefs of Staff regarding the stalemate in denuclearization negotiations.

Going forward, there are several possibilities for North Korea's moves for its nuclear and missile programs. Assuming North Korea makes good on the January report at the 8th Party Congress, it could remain consistent with its established policy of increasing the variety and diversity of nuclear weapons and missiles. For example, it may launch SLBMs or ballistic missiles it calls "satellites" and conduct test flights of reconnaissance drones. In other words, North Korea may conduct cruise missile test flights and test-firings of ballistic missiles along irregular trajectories, aiming to further improve the capabilities that were considered as achievements. Of course, in the absence of a summit meeting or an official high-level dialogue with the Joseph Biden administration, the North's firing of an intercontinental ballistic missile (ICBM) in anticipation of a strong reaction from the United States cannot be ruled out. In any event, North Korea is anticipated to continue with efforts to improve its military technology.

New types of North Korean weapons were unveiled at the Defense Development Exhibition "Self-Defense 2021" on October 11 (the exhibition ran until October 22). While North Korea did not hold a military parade on October 10, which marked the 76th anniversary of the WPK's founding, these weapons were ultimately showcased at the exhibition to domestic and international audiences. North Korea's ambitions to improve military technology to strengthen military capabilities against the United States and South Korea were underscored once again in President Kim's speech at the exhibition. Alongside stressing the need to deter war on the Korean Peninsula, President Kim justified that the North's defense capabilities must continue to be strengthened, on the grounds that the ROK is aspiring to improve combat capabilities by introducing stealth fighters, high-altitude reconnaissance drones, and a large number of high-tech weapons under strong U.S. patronage.[22] "The United States has frequently sent signals that it is not hostile to our state, but its behaviours provide us with no reason why we should believe in them," he said, reiterating his distrust of the United States. In addition to ICBMs believed to be the Hwasong 17 and Hwasong 15 types, several strategic and tactical weapons were shown in the "Self-Defense 2021" video, including what seems to be the Hwasong 8 hypersonic missile launched in September.[23] Missile launches were concentrated in September and continued until October 19 while the exhibition was ongoing. North Korea is thought to have showed off the missiles at the exhibition in order to impart a stronger impression of its defense technological achievements to domestic and international audiences.

(2) Hard-line and Soft-line Policies toward the United States and South Korea
On the one hand, North Korea ignored the Biden administration's informal attempts to make contact with Pyongyang before it officially took office, and continued to repeatedly criticize the United States' North Korea policy. On the other hand, the supreme leader, President Kim Jong Un, indicated in June 2021 that he would prepare for both dialogue and confrontation with the new U.S. administration. As this illustrates, North Korea appears to be taking both hard-line and soft-line approaches with the United States as of date.

President Moon Jae-in proposed to declare the termination of the Korean War in his speech at the 76th Session of the UN General Assembly in New York on September 21. On September 23, North Korea's vice minister of foreign affairs issued a statement that called the proposal "premature."[24] However, on the same day, Kim Yo Jong, vice department director of the WPK Central Committee, released a statement suggesting a flexible stance, noting North Korea was "ready to discuss" the issue on the condition that the South scraps its "double standards" and hostile policy toward North Korea.[25] Furthermore, on September 29, President Kim Jong Un delivered a policy speech on the second day of the 5th Session of the 14th Supreme People's Assembly of the DPRK, in which he stated that the communication lines that have been suspended over the U.S.-South Korea combined exercises would be reactivated in early October.[26] With regard to the "independent reunification of the country," President Kim stated in his report in January, "Whether the north-south relations can be restored and invigorated or not entirely depends on the attitude of the south Korean authorities." Without a resumption of dialogue with the United States, North Korea may be beginning to show a flexible attitude toward South Korea in order to achieve some results in the tenth year of President Kim Jong Un's reign as supreme leader. As indicated by President Kim's remarks at "Self-Defense 2021," however, North Korea appears to be increasingly wary of

South Korea's increased combat capability.

As regards North Korea-China relations, President Kim Jong Un sent a congratulatory telegram to Chinese President Xi Jinping on the 60th anniversary of the Sino-DPRK Mutual Aid and Cooperation Friendship Treaty on July 11. In the telegram, he recognized that "the hostile forces become more desperate in their challenge and obstructive moves" and said he intends to continue to develop the bilateral relationship.[27] Likewise, in his congratulatory telegram to President Kim, President Xi expressed hope for advancement of the bilateral relationship.[28] Prior to the first U.S.-North Korea summit in June 2018, President Kim visited China in May, following on from his visit in March, during which he and Xi held a meeting and agreed to coordinate closely. Nevertheless, amid the COVID-19 pandemic and other disruptions, trade between China and North Korea did not fully resume by the end of 2021.[29]

2. The Moon Jae-in Administration's Appeasement Policy toward North Korea and Defense Capability Enhancement

(1) President Moon Jae-in's Retention of Political Power and the Presidential Election Outlook

In South Korea, the Moon Jae-in administration entered its de facto final year in 2021, and fierce competition for the next presidential seat unfolded between the candidates of the ruling progressive party, the Democratic Party of Korea (DPK), and the largest conservative opposition party, the People Power Party (PPP). Whether or not the new government that takes office in May 2022 will remain progressive or shift to conservative will probably make a difference in inter-Korean relations, the U.S.-ROK alliance, and South Korea's defense capability enhancement, and by extension, affect the security environment in Northeast Asia.

The ROK Constitution limits the presidential term to one five-year term. Partly for this reason, successive presidents have become "lame ducks" at the end of their terms, unable to fully implement their policies amid faltering approval ratings. President Moon Jae-in had a formidable approval rating of over 80% when he took office in May 2017, but it began to decline in 2018. While his approval rating temporarily surged during the second quarter of 2020, boosted by the COVID-19 control measures of his administration, disapproval began to exceed approval from December 2020. The primary reason for disapproval was the administration's failure to curb real estate prices, which surged beyond the reach of the middle class.[30] Furthermore, the public became disheartened by the revelations of scandals among administration and ruling party officials, despite President Moon's commitment to equality and fairness.

That said, in the second quarter of his fifth year in office, President Moon's approval rating was 39% (53% disapproved; Gallup Korea poll). This compares favorably with the ratings of Presidents Roh Moo-hyun (24% approved, 66% disapproved) and Lee Myung-bak (25%, 58%) during a similar period and for Park Geun-hye (12%, 80%) before her impeachment (December 2016).[31] The DPK, which backs the Moon administration, still maintained a single-party majority in the National Assembly, although it was defeated by the PPP in the April 2021 mayoral elections in the two largest cities, Seoul and Busan.[32] In addition, in the presidential election campaign, as shown below, the DPK candidate was in a close race with the PPP candidate. With these conditions in place, President Moon retained political power to a degree rarely seen in a South Korean president near the end of his term. As a result, he was able to maintain a conciliatory North Korea policy, as discussed in the next section.

DPK candidate Lee Jae-myung and PPP candidate Yoon Suk-yeol shaking hands on November 24, 2021, Seoul (Yonhap News Agency/Kyodo News Images)

In the second half of 2021, both parties

held preliminary elections to choose their candidate for the next presidential election. As their respective candidates, the DPK chose then Governor of Gyeonggi Province Lee Jae-myung on October 10, and the PPP chose former Prosecutor General Yoon Suk-yeol on November 5. Lee trailed Yoon in approval ratings, despite polls showing a strong desire for change from a progressive to a conservative government.[33] Both candidates were beset by allegations against themselves and their families. Additionally, Yoon repeatedly made gaffes, resulting in intensified internal strife within the party and a drop in approval rating. In January 2022, the approval rating for Ahn Cheol-soo, leader of the centrist People Party, rose sharply, making the outcome still unpredictable.[34]

Lee and Yoon's campaign pledges diverge considerably on the foreign and security policies of South Korea. Depending on who is elected president, the policies on North Korea, the United States, China, and Japan could differ significantly. The North Korea policy of Lee Jae-myung encourages its denuclearization through the easing of economic sanctions and provision of assistance to North Korea, with the condition (snapback) that sanctions will be immediately reimposed if North Korea violates its commitments. Lee is attempting to do what the Moon Jae-in administration could not realize due to failure to obtain U.S. support. As such, it is expected that South Korea will experience challenges in coordinating with the United States and other countries that do not support North Korea's nuclear armament. Lee intends to meet in person with the U.S. president and President Kim Jong Un to make progress on denuclearization.[35]

Meanwhile, Yoon Suk-yeol proposes to disable North Korea's nuclear weapons and missiles by expanding Korean Air and Missile Defense (KAMD) and "ROK-U.S. extended deterrence," as well as provide economic assistance commensurate with progress in North Korea's denuclearization.[36] When such an initiative was tried in the past by the Lee Myung-bak administration, it was met with opposition from North Korea, and inter-Korean relations fell into a stalemate. The same situation could well repeat itself. Furthermore, Yoon pledges to establish a permanent three-way dialogue channel between North and South Korea and the United States in Panmunjom.

Regarding policies toward the United States and China, Lee's policy is that, while the United States is the only ally, the ROK has a strategic partnership with China and does not have to choose one country or the other.[37] Additionally, he has pledged to realize the early transition of wartime operational control (OPCON).[38] Meanwhile, Yoon gives top priority to the alliance with the United States, including strengthening "ROK-U.S. extended deterrence" and considering the ROK's participation in the Japan-Australia-India-U.S. cooperation framework (the Quad). He advocates that the ROK-China relationship should be one of "mutual respect," based on his assessment that the ROK's position was downplayed during the Moon Jae-in administration. Furthermore, he indicated he would not be bound by the "Three Nos," announced by the Moon administration in October 2017 with China in mind. They are: 1) not making an additional deployment of Terminal High Altitude Area Defense (THAAD); 2) not joining the United States-led missile defense; and 3) not developing Japan-U.S.-ROK security cooperation into a military alliance.[39]

With regard to Japan, Lee Jae-myung said he would continue to uphold the Moon Jae-in administration's two-track strategy of dealing resolutely with "historical issues, territorial sovereignty issues, and issues concerning the life and safety of the people," while promoting exchange and cooperation in the economic, social, and diplomatic fields.[40] Lee believes Japan is taking steps to become a military power and promote the resurgence of militarism, in sharp contrast to the reality in Japan. He has in fact called Japan an "enemy state,"[41] and it cannot be ruled out that he would take a tougher stance on Japan than the Moon administration.

In contrast, Yoon Suk-yeol contends that the Japan-ROK Partnership Declaration issued by Prime Minister Obuchi Keizo and President Kim Dae-jung in October 1998 already presents a "comprehensive vision" of the Japan-ROK relationship in the future. His stance is to cooperate with Japan based on this declaration, while "upholding a firm position on matters concerning territory, sovereignty, and past history." He further proposed to harmonize Japan-U.S.-ROK security cooperation and Japan-China-ROK functional cooperation.[42] It remains to be seen how a rational approach to Japan will be received by the South Korean people.

On defense policy, both candidates agree to strengthen the capabilities of the ROK Armed Forces by introducing advanced technologies, such as artificial intelligence and unmanned systems. Lee Jae-myung prioritizes independent defense, albeit premised on the U.S.-ROK alliance, and pledges to realize an early OPCON transition as mentioned above.[43] Yoon Suk-yeol, conversely, prioritizes U.S.-ROK cooperation. His position is that OPCON should be transferred when the ROK Armed Forces have reconnaissance capabilities to lead the U.S.-ROK combined defense posture, coupled with capabilities to deal with North Korea's nuclear weapons and missiles, as well as when the security situation has simmered down to a certain degree (conditions-based OPCON transition).[44] Regarding conscription, Lee proposes to increase the number of non-commissioned officers who volunteer for "medium-term" service and shorten the service period of conscripted soldiers. In contrast, Yoon proposes to enhance support for the college education, employment, and start-ups of soldiers while maintaining the conscription system.[45]

(2) "End-of-War Declaration" Aspirations

In 2021, President Moon Jae-in continued to take a conciliatory stance toward North Korea, seeking to break the deadlock of inter-Korean relations and U.S.-North Korea relations. As part of this effort, President Moon proposed the Korean War "end-of-war declaration" again at the UN General Assembly on September 22, as mentioned in the previous section. It calls for three parties (South Korea, North Korea, and the United States) or four parties (the three parties plus China) to declare an end to the Korean War, which has remained in a state of armistice since 1953, and advance to the next stage of signing a peace treaty. The North and the South had already agreed to "work together to advance" the "end-of-war declaration," both during the October 2007 summit meeting between then President Roh Moo-hyun and then National Defense Commission Chairman Kim Jong Il and during the April 2018 summit meeting between President Moon and State Affairs Commission Chairman Kim Jong Un. However, neither of these agreements materialized in concrete form amid the breakdown of inter-Korean and U.S.-North Korea dialogues. President Moon Jae-in hoped that reiterating calls for an "end-of-war declaration" would create momentum for resuming the stalled U.S.-North Korea denuclearization negotiations.[46]

Speaking to South Korean reporters after his speech at the UN General Assembly, President Moon Jae-in commented that the "end-of-war declaration" is a political declaration and will therefore maintain the armistice regime under the existing armistice agreement and will not affect the stationing of U.S. forces in the ROK.[47] As observed in the previous section, however, North Korea's seeming interest in the "end-of-war declaration" is coupled with preconditions, namely, demands on South Korea and the United States to retract their hostile policy and "double standards" against North Korea. These demands may refer to the lifting of economic sanctions, the withdrawal (or at least downsizing) of U.S. Forces Korea (USFK), and de facto U.S. and ROK acceptance of North Korea's development and possession of nuclear weapons and ballistic missiles (e.g., those with a range that cannot reach the U.S. mainland). It thus cannot be denied that the result will be contrary to President Moon's explanation or expectation.

To set the scene for North Korea's return to dialogue, the Moon Jae-in administration explored the options of resuming aid to North Korea and easing economic sanctions. On July 30, 2021, Lee In-young, minister of unification, announced the resumption of humanitarian assistance to North Korea, which had been suspended since September 2020 over North Korean forces' shooting and killing of a South Korean civil servant. Following this announcement, the Ministry of Unification, which oversees inter-Korean relations, approved small-scale assistance by civilian organizations. On September 24, the ROK government decided to disburse a total of 10 billion won from its fund to ROK civilian organizations, with aid for nutrition and health in North Korea capped at 500 million won (approximately 47 million yen) per project.[48] However, because of North Korea's continued rejection of ROK assistance and the closure of the China-North Korea border due to COVID-19, it appears that such ROK support has not been realized.

Senior officials in the Moon administration urged for sanctions relief on numerous occasions. For instance, when Chung Eui-yong, minister of foreign affairs, spoke at the Council on Foreign Relations (CFR) in the United States on September 22, he proposed that Washington consider easing sanctions as an incentive (to bring North Korea to the negotiating table), noting North Korea had not launched a long-range missile since November 2017.[49] While not formally announced, Minister Chung is thought to have made the same proposal to the U.S. government. As of the end of December 2021, the United States has not endorsed these proposals, and sanctions relief has not been realized along with the "end-of-war declaration."

The mode and scale of the annual U.S.-ROK combined military exercises were another area to which the Moon Jae-in administration sought to circumvent North Korean opposition as much as possible. Every year, the U.S. and ROK forces conducted a large-scale field training exercise in March and a large-scale command post exercise in August. Since August 2018, however, the field training exercise had been suspended and the command post exercise had been reduced in scale based on the progress in inter-Korean and U.S.-North Korea relations. During his New Year's press conference on January 18, 2021, President Moon emphasized that U.S.-ROK exercises were for defensive purposes. At the same time, he expressed the view that "This is a matter we can discuss [with North Korea]," saying "(North Korea) gets very nervous and sensitive [about the exercises] every time."[50] Some in the Moon administration even called for the postponement (de facto cancellation) of the combined U.S.-ROK exercises.[51] Although the U.S. Department of Defense did not directly object to this ROK stance, it likely has concerns that not holding large-scale field training exercises would adversely affect the readiness of the U.S. and

ROK forces. In the end, the March and August exercises were conducted as a command post exercise on a reduced scale without field training.

As for ROK-U.S. relations, President Moon Jae-in held his first summit meeting with President Biden in Washington, D.C. on May 22, 2021. The two leaders reaffirmed their commitments under the U.S.-ROK alliance, including the United States' provision of extended deterrence to the ROK as well as denuclearization of the Korean Peninsula and establishment of permanent peace through dialogue with North Korea. New developments included positive evaluation of the Quad, albeit without declaring the ROK's participation, and mentioning the importance of preserving peace and stability in the Taiwan Strait.[52] In the past, the ROK avoided involvement in such matters out of concern for China. The summit meeting, meanwhile, led to the termination of the U.S.-ROK Missile Guidelines, which had limited the range of South Korea's ballistic missiles to 800 kilometers. Taken together, some in South Korea interpret that the Biden administration sought to equip the ROK with deterrent mechanisms against China in exchange for not forcing South Korea to join the Quad.[53]

On December 2, 2021, a ROK-U.S. Security Consultative Meeting (SCM) was held in Seoul, attended by Defense Minister Suh Wook and Secretary of Defense Lloyd J. Austin III. At this SCM, it was agreed that a full operational capability (FOC) assessment necessary for OPCON transition would be conducted during the 2022 U.S.-ROK combined command post exercise.[54] What this means is President Moon Jae-in failed to deliver on his pledge to achieve OPCON transition during his term in office as part of efforts to realize independent defense. Due to COVID-19 and other factors, the FOC assessment could not be conducted during the 2021 U.S.-ROK command post exercise. Incidentally, if a war were to occur under the existing structure, OPCON for ROK combat forces is exercised by the ROK-U.S. Combined Forces Command (CFC), whose commander and deputy commander are a U.S. Army four-star general and ROK Army four-star general, respectively. Following the transition, the Future Combined Forces Command (F-CFC), whose commander is a ROK four-star general and whose deputy commander is a U.S. four-star general, will have OPCON.[55]

As to relations with Japan, ROK courts have rendered a series of judgments ordering the Japanese government and Japanese companies to pay compensation in connection with the issue of former civilian workers from the Korean Peninsula and the issue of former comfort women. The judgments neglect the principle of state immunity under international law and the 1965 Japan-ROK Agreement on the Settlement of Problems concerning Property and Claims and on Economic Co-operation. The Moon Jae-in administration has not taken any measures to correct this violation of international law, and Japan-ROK relations thus continue to be in "an extremely difficult situation."[56] Meanwhile, Japan-U.S.-ROK trilateral cooperation continued on the North Korean nuclear and missile issues. Furthermore, although the Moon administration notified Japan in August 2019 that the Japan-ROK Agreement on the Protection of Classified Military Information (GSOMIA) would be terminated in order to counter the enhancement of Japanese export controls,[57] the administration continued the agreement under the official pretext that it "suspended the effect of the notice."

Amid intensifying competition between the United States and China, the Moon administration has struggled to reconcile the U.S.-ROK alliance with the ROK-PRC strategic cooperative partnership. China is the largest trading partner for the ROK and a partner with which it hopes to cooperate toward the denuclearization of North Korea and the establishment of a peace regime on the Korean Peninsula. Militarily, however, the ROK is also wary of stepped-up activities by China's naval and air forces in the waters around the ROK, as the next section will examine. The ROK is increasingly demanded by the U.S. government to "stand together in confronting China's ambitions and authoritarianism."[58] These are expected to become serious issues for the new South Korean president who will take office in May 2022.

(3) Strike Capability Diversification by the ROK Armed Forces

The Moon Jae-in administration has implemented the "Defense Reform 2.0" plan since 2018, a year after the administration came to power. Namely, it has sought to reduce the number of ROK Armed Forces personnel from 599,000 in 2018 to 500,000 in 2022 (all reductions in the Army), while increasing strength through equipment modernization of the Army, Navy, and Air Force. This trend was institutionalized in 2005 during the Roh Moo-hyun administration as "Defense Reform" and was carried over to subsequent conservative administrations. The factors behind this shift were the issue of coping with the declining birthrate, i.e., decreases in the draft-eligible population, and the need to improve the capabilities of the ROK Armed Forces for OPCON transition.

Until the Park Geun-hye administration, force development was premised on the North Korea threat, especially its nuclear and missile threats. This was followed by potential threats, which are considered to refer mainly to neighboring countries although specific countries were not mentioned. After the Moon Jae-in administration took office, however, terms such as "threats from all directions," which are thought to include both North Korea and neighboring countries, came into increasing usage.[59] The Moon administration may have wished to avoid mentioning North Korea by name in order to pursue dialogue with North Korea. Another reason, as will be discussed below, may have been to signal the ROK's growing consciousness of developments in neighboring countries, including China.

The force buildup is designed to deal with mainly three areas of threat: 1) North Korea's nuclear weapons and missiles; 2) "threats from all directions," such as China; and 3) North Korea's conventional forces. Of course, as examined below, the forces in the first area, for example, can also be used in other areas in some cases.

The Moon Jae-in administration vows that a system to counter nuclear and WMD threats will deter and deal with the first threat of North Korea's nuclear weapons and missiles.[60] This system consists of a "strategic strike system" and KAMD. The strategic strike system combines the Park Geun-hye administration's "Kill Chain" and "Korea Massive Punishment and Retaliation" (KMPR) plans. Under the Park administration's strategies, if signs of North

Korea's use of nuclear missiles are detected, the ROK's ballistic and cruise missiles or other weapons would be used to destroy North Korean launch pads (Kill Chain). If North Korean nuclear weapons caused damage to South Korea, then its missiles and special operations forces would be used for retaliation to eliminate the North Korean leadership (KMPR).[61] These plans are no longer explicitly explained by the Moon administration, probably to avoid provocative actions against North Korea. In practice, however, the ROK continues to build up forces along the lines of this doctrine.

Long-range precision strike capabilities constitute the core of the strategic strike system. The ROK Armed Forces are already capable of projecting a variety of warheads from land, sea, and air platforms. In order to destroy protected missile launch sites and command posts in North Korea, the ROK has striven to develop longer-range missiles and precision guidance and to increase their power, including more warhead weight.[62] On September 15, 2021, South Korea announced it successfully developed a high-powered ballistic missile, which has "dramatically" increased the warhead weight and is capable of penetrating concrete buildings and underground tunnels with precision.[63] According to South Korean reports, this missile, known as "Hyunmoo-4," has a range of 800 kilometers, long enough to target all of North Korea, and has a load capacity of 2 tons.[64] Incidentally, the deployed ballistic missile Hyunmoo-2C has the same range but a load capacity of only 500 kilograms. As was stated in the previous section, the U.S.-ROK Missile Guidelines that limited the range of South Korean ballistic missiles to 800 kilometers were terminated in May 2021. As a result, missiles with even longer ranges and more weight are expected to be developed in the future.

KAMD—an abbreviation which the Moon administration tends not to use—refers to a system that deploys the indigenous missiles Cheongung-II (M-SAM, intercept altitude 20–25 kilometers) and PAC-3 (intercept altitude 30–40 kilometers) for lower-tier defense. In the future, the middle tier will be covered by L-SAM (intercept altitude 40–60 kilometers) currently under domestic development. The ROK has sought to strengthen KAMD's detection and surveillance capabilities, such as improving the capabilities of ground-based early warning radars and planning the launch of reconnaissance satellites. Yet the system relies heavily on the U.S. forces for intelligence, and the ROK's upper-tier defense is covered by the USFK Army's THAAD system (40–150 kilometers). Nonetheless, South Korea has underscored that KAMD is a separate system from the United States-led ballistic missile defense. Its main motivation is to avoid a backlash from China. For this reason, while the ROK Navy has three Aegis destroyers and plans to build three more by 2028 (construction of one of them began in February 2021), the destroyers are not fitted with SM-3s for ballistic missile interception and the ROK has been unable to announce their installation as a future plan.[65] As North Korean missiles gain the ability to take lofted trajectories, conduct gliding flights with an irregular trajectory, and fly at hypersonic speeds and at low altitudes, some have voiced concern that KAMD lacks the capabilities to provide sufficient defense.[66]

Capabilities that were developed highly mindful of the "threats from all directions" include SLBMs and their submarine platforms, along with light aircraft carriers (LAC). On September 15, 2021, the ROK Ministry of National Defense announced that a submarine successfully launched an SLBM underwater.[67] The submarine is believed to be the 3,000-ton class *Dosan Ahn Changho*, just commissioned in August, and is reportedly equipped with six Vertical Launching Systems (VLSs). The SLBM launched was an improved variant of the Hyunmoo-2B ground-launched ballistic missile (range 500 kilometers), and reportedly flew more than 400 kilometers and hit its target.[68] This would imply that the ROK Armed Forces have acquired a new means to accurately strike ground targets from underwater, which is difficult to detect in advance. While this, of course, gives the ROK with more means to strike North Korea, Cheong Wa Dae (office of the president) has emphasized rather the significance of "securing deterrence capabilities against threats from all directions."[69]

By 2033, the ROK Navy intends to construct and operationally deploy an LAC that is 265 meters long and 43 meters wide, weighs approximately

30,000 tons, and can carry over ten short takeoff and vertical landing fighters (presumably F-35B). The Navy explains the LAC's utility as a strike capability in the event of a contingency with North Korea and for protecting sea lines of communication. It also cites the LAC's usefulness

ROK Navy's *Dosan Ahn Changho* submarine that is thought to have successfully launched an SLBM (Yonhap News Agency/ Kyodo News Images)

for disputes that could occur over maritime interests with neighboring countries, namely, China and Japan. The Navy particularly stresses China's stepped-up activities of aircraft carriers and maritime patrol aircraft in the Yellow Sea near South Korea's territorial waters,[70] suggesting the ROK takes the Chinese threat seriously. The South Korean media has similarly expressed concern over the Chinese aim to turn the Yellow Sea into an inland sea.[71]

The LAC was included in the budget for the first time in FY2021 (the ROK's fiscal year is the calendar year). That said, whereas the government requested 10.1 billion won for this fiscal year, the National Assembly approved only 100 million won for commissioned research on the grounds that the appropriateness of the request had not been sufficiently examined. Likewise, in the FY2022 budget deliberations, whereas the government requested 7.2 billion won, ruling and opposition party members of the National Defense Committee of the National Assembly agreed to approve only 500 million won for data collection, reasoning that public understanding was inadequate. President Moon Jae-in expressed dissatisfaction with this proposed reduction internally, and on December 3, 2021, the ruling DPK passed a budget bill which restored the initial 7.2 billion won in its entirety, overriding objections of opposition parties. In this manner, the South Korean LAC moved from the conceptual stage to the design stage.[72]

The third area of force buildup is improving capabilities for warning, monitoring, and countering North Korean conventional forces. As was touched upon earlier, significant troop cuts will be made in the ROK Army. Accordingly, the number of Army corps will be reduced from eight as of 2017 to six by 2026, while the number of divisions will decrease from 39 to 33 over the same period. Therefore, the operational area of each corps and division is being expanded. Specifically, the firepower, armored capabilities, and air power of the corps will be strengthened. The mobile power of general divisions (infantry divisions) will be enhanced by introducing wheeled armored vehicles, wheeled self-propelled howitzers, and other equipment. One Quick Response Division capable of air assault was established in January 2021.[73] In addition, reconnaissance drones and robots (e.g., for reconnaissance, hazardous material disposal, and delivery) are being introduced at a rapid pace.[74] Separate from missile defense, the ROK is scheduled to develop the "Korean Iron Dome," or long-range artillery interception system, for protecting the metropolitan area and other areas from North Korean rocket artillery.[75]

South Korea has also put efforts into the use of space as a base for supporting the modernized forces. In July 2020, it launched the first dedicated military communications satellite (using SpaceX, Falcon 9). In addition to the aforementioned reconnaissance satellite program, plans are underway to develop the Korean Positioning System (KPS), which will launch dozens of microsatellites to monitor North Korea and other countries at all times, and enable access to location information to the nearest centimeter on the Korean Peninsula and its periphery (by the target year of 2035).[76] The ROK also established a Space Center in the Air Force in September 2021 and indicated it would further strengthen space operations capabilities, such as space situational awareness.[77]

As was touched upon earlier, the FY2022 defense budget was approved at a plenary session of the ROK National Assembly in December 2021. It amounts to 54.611 trillion won, up 3.4% from the previous fiscal year.[78] The budget has grown by 3.3 times since 20 years ago. Moreover, the allocations for procuring new equipment and developing new technologies (force enhancement budget) account for approximately 30% of the budget. This budget financially supports the vigorous force modernization efforts described above. The ROK's defense budget for FY2022 is equivalent to $46.28 billion (1,180 won per dollar). If the budget continues to grow at this rate (6.3% per year on average during the Moon Jae-in administration), it will soon surpass Japan's defense budget ($48.49 billion in FY2022; 5.480 trillion yen budget request converted at 113 yen to the dollar), giving the ROK the second largest defense budget in East Asia after China.

Figure 4.1. The ROK's defense budget (2002–2022)

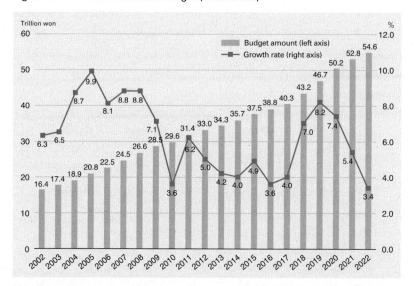

Note: The budget amount is the initial budget amount for each fiscal year and does not include supplementary budget amounts.

Sources: Compiled by the author based on ROK Ministry of National Defense (MND), *2020 Defense White Paper* (Korean version) (Seoul: MND, 2021); ROK MND press release, December 3, 2021.

NOTES

1) KCNA, January 9, 2021.

2) KCNA, March 26, 2021.

3) Jonathan McLaughlin, "North Korea Missile Milestones – 1969-2017," Wisconsin Project (January 23, 2018); "Notable Missile Tests," Missile Defense Advocacy Alliance (April 2019).

4) KCNA, February 7, 2015.

5) KCNA, June 15, 2015.

6) KCNA, June 9, 2017.

7) KCNA, June 9, 2017.

8) KCNA, September 16, 2021.

9) Radio Free Asia, August 30, 2016.

10) KCNA, September 20, 2021.

11) KCNA, September 29, 2021.

12) Ibid.

13) Vann H. Van Diepen, "Six Takeaways from North Korea's 'Hypersonic Missile' Announcement," *38 North* (October 13, 2021).

14) *Joongang Ilbo*, September 30, 2021.

15) KCNA, October 1, 2021.

16) KCNA, October 20, 2021.

17) [Japan] Ministry of Defense, "Kitachosen no misairu to kanren joho (zokuho)" [Information related to North Korea's missile activities (follow-up)], Ministry of Defense website, October 19, 2021.

18) *Yomiuri Shimbun*, October 21, 2021.

19) JIJI.COM, June 14, 2021.

20) International Atomic Energy Agency, Atoms for Peace and Development, Board of Governors General Conference, The Director General, *Application of Safeguards in the Democratic People's Republic of Korea* (August 27, 2021).

21) *Dong-A Ilbo*, October 7, 2021.

22) *Rodong Sinmun*, October 12, 2021.

23) *Rodong Sinmun*, October 12, 2021.

24) KCNA, September 24, 2021.

25) KCNA, September 24, 2021.

26) *Rodong Sinmun*, September 30, 2021.

27) KCNA, July 11, 2021.

28) *Yomiuri Shimbun*, July 11, 2021.

29) *Mainichi Shimbun*, December 27, 2021.

30) Gallup Korea Research Institute, "Daily Opinion," Gallup Korea website, September 30, 2021.

31) Ibid.; *Seoul Shinmun*, October 1, 2021.

32) ROK National Assembly, "Seat Number Status," National Assembly website.

33) Gallup Korea Research Institute, "Daily Opinion," Gallup Korea website, December 2, 2021.

34) Gallup Korea Research Institute, "Daily Opinion," Gallup Korea website, January 6, 2022.

35) Lee Jae-myung, "Unification and Diplomatic Initiative in the Era of Great Transformation," Lee Jae-myung blog, August 22, 2021.

36) Yonhap News, November 12, 2021.

37) Lee Jae-myung, "Unification and Diplomatic Initiative in the Era of Great Transformation."

38) Lee Jae-myung, "Smart Independent Defense with the People," Lee Jae-myung blog, October 1, 2021.

39) Yoon Suk-yeol, "Foreign and Security Policy Pledges," Yoon Suk-yeol blog, September 22, 2021; Yoon Suk-yeol, "Yoon Suk-yeol's Vision (5) Foreign Affairs and Security," Yoon Suk-yeol blog, October 30, 2021; Yonhap News, November 12, 2021; ROK National Assembly, *Foreign Affairs and Unification Committee Record*, Audit Session, October 30, 2017, 6-7; Watanabe Takeshi, "The Korean Peninsula: Wavering North-South Relations," in *East Asian Strategic Review 2021*, English edition, ed. National Institute for Defense Studies (NIDS) (Tokyo: NIDS, 2021), 103.

40) Lee Jae-myung, "Unification and Diplomatic Initiative in the Era of Great Transformation."

41) Newsis, November 25, 2021; Yonhap News, December 14, 2016.

42) Yoon Suk-yeol, "Foreign and Security Policy Pledges"; Yonhap News, November 12, 2021.

43) Lee Jae-myung, "Smart Independent Defense with the People."

44) Newsis, December 2, 2021.

45) Yoon Suk-yeol, "Foreign and Security Policy Pledges."

46) ROK Ministry of Foreign Affairs, "Address by President Moon Jae-in at 76th Session of United Nations General Assembly" (September 24, 2021); Watanabe Takeshi, "The Korean Peninsula: Wavering North-South Relations," 95.

47) Cheong Wa Dae, "President Moon Jae-in's Press Occasion Inside Code One on September 22 (Wed.) (Full Text)," Cheong Wa Dae website, September 24, 2021.

48) Yonhap News, July 30 and September 24, 2021.

49) "A Conversation with Foreign Minister Chung Eui-yong of the Republic of Korea,"

Council on Foreign Relations (September 22, 2021).

50) Cheong Wa Dae, "2021 New Year's Press Conference," Cheong Wa Dae website, January 18, 2021.

51) *Chosun Ilbo*, February 1, 2021.

52) Embassy of the Republic of Korea in the USA, "U.S.-ROK Leaders' Joint Statement" (May 22, 2021).

53) *Hankyoreh*, May 23, 2021.

54) [U.S.] Department of Defense (DOD), "Secretary of Defense Lloyd J. Austin III and South Korean Defense Minister Suh Wook Hold a Press Conference following the 53rd U.S.-Republic of Korea Security Consultative Meeting in Seoul" (December 2, 2021).

55) [U.S.] DOD, "Joint Communique of the 50th U.S.-ROK Security Consultative Meeting" (October 31, 2018); Murooka Tetsuo and Akutsu Hiroyasu, "The Korean Peninsula: North Korea's Advanced Nuclear and Missile Capabilities, and South Korea's Response," in *East Asian Strategic Review 2016*, English edition, ed. NIDS (Tokyo: NIDS, 2016), 103.

56) [Japan] Ministry of Foreign Affairs (MOFA), "Daikan Minkoku kiso deta" [Republic of Korea: Basic data], MOFA website, July 20, 2021.

57) Watanabe Takeshi and Koike Osamu, "The Korean Peninsula: Diplomacy and Politics of Reintroducing a State of Nuclear-Missile Crisis," in *East Asian Strategic Review 2020*, English edition, ed. NIDS (Tokyo: NIDS, 2020), 66.

58) VOA Korean Program, November 24, 2021; Newsis, November 24, 2021.

59) ROK Ministry of National Defense (MND), *2020 Defense White Paper* (Korean version) (Seoul: MND, 2020), 38, 48; Watanabe Takeshi and Koike Osamu, "The Korean Peninsula: Prospects of the 'Denuclearization' Negotiations," in *East Asian Strategic Review 2019*, English edition, ed. NIDS (Tokyo: NIDS, 2019), 95; Watanabe and Koike, "The Korean Peninsula: Diplomacy and Politics of Reintroducing a State of Nuclear-Missile Crisis," 90.

60) ROK MND, *2020 Defense White Paper* (Korean version), 61-62.

61) Murooka Tetsuo and Akutsu Hiroyasu, "The Korean Peninsula: North Korea's Growing Nuclear and Missile Threat and South Korea's Anguish," in *East Asian Strategic Review 2017*, English edition, ed. NIDS (Tokyo: NIDS, 2017), 121-125; Watanabe Takeshi and Koike Osamu, "The Korean Peninsula: ICBMs and the New South Korean Government's Alliance Politics," in *East Asian Strategic Review 2018*, English edition, ed. NIDS (Tokyo: NIDS, 2018), 94-95; Watanabe and Koike, "The Korean Peninsula: Prospects of the 'Denuclearization' Negotiations," 94-95.

62) Murooka and Akutsu, "The Korean Peninsula: North Korea's Growing Nuclear and

Missile Threat and South Korea's Anguish," 121-123.

63) ROK MND, press release, September 15, 2021.

64) Watanabe, "The Korean Peninsula: Wavering North-South Relations," 106; *Chosun Ilbo*, May 31 and September 16, 2021.

65) Watanabe, "The Korean Peninsula: Wavering North-South Relations," 101-104; *Kookbang Ilbo*, March 31, 2021.

66) Newsis, October 2, 2021.

67) ROK MND, press release, September 15, 2021.

68) *Chosun Ilbo*, September 16, 2021; *Joongang Ilbo*, September 29, 2021.

69) Yonhap News, September 15, 2021.

70) ROK Navy, "Light Aircraft Carrier Specifications" and "Light Aircraft Carrier Card News," ROK Navy website, May 6, 2021; *Kookbang Ilbo*, June 11, 2021.

71) *Munhwa Ilbo*, October 5, 2021; KBS, October 16, 2021.

72) Yonhap News, December 3, 2020 and November 6, 2021; Newsis, November 18 and December 5, 2021.

73) Yonhap News, January 1, 2021.

74) ROK MND, press release, September 2, 2021.

75) Watanabe, "The Korean Peninsula: Wavering North-South Relations," 99, 104-105; ROK MND, press release, MND website, September 2, 2021.

76) *Kookbang Ilbo*, July 21, 2020; ROK MND, press release, September 2, 2021; Korea Aerospace Research Institute, "Korean Positioning System (KPS)," Korea Aerospace Research Institute website, June 25, 2021.

77) *Kookbang Ilbo*, July 8, 2015 and September 30, 2021; Murooka and Akutsu, "The Korean Peninsula: North Korea's Advanced Nuclear and Missile Capabilities, and South Korea's Response," 100.

78) ROK MND, press release, December 3, 2021.

Chapter 5

Southeast Asia

The Post-Coup State of Affairs in Myanmar and Regional Security

MATSUURA Yoshihide (Lead author, Sections 1 and 2 (1))
TOMIKAWA Hideo (Sections 2 (2) and (3) and 3)

Myanmar was absent from the October ASEAN Summit held virtually (Xinhua/Kyodo News Images)

Summary

On February 1, 2021, the Armed Forces of Myanmar, known as the Tatmadaw, detained Aung San Suu Kyi, state counsellor, and other senior members of the government and ruling party in objection to the general election process the previous year. Following this, the State Administrative Council (SAC) took complete control of the country. The Provisional Government, established in August and led by Senior General Min Aung Hlaing, the commander-in-chief of the Defence Services, serving as prime minister, insists that they will end the State of Emergency by August 2023 and hold a general election thereafter. In April, democratic groups who oppose the coup d'état formed the National Unity Government (NUG) and civil resistance throughout the country has resulted in more than 1,300 deaths due to crackdowns by security forces. As the NUG calls for fighting against the Tatmadaw and armed clashes between ethnic armed organizations (EAOs) and the military have rekindled, the state of affairs in the country demonstrates a revival of national military rule with the possibility that the situation may escalate into a civil war. With United Nations diplomacy stalled due to opposition from China and Russia, the dispatch of a special envoy of the Association of Southeast Asian Nations (ASEAN), who was expected to mediate, did not materialize since he was not allowed to meet with State Counsellor Aung San Suu Kyi under detainment. The association refused to invite Senior General Min Aung Hlaing to the ASEAN Summit in response, taking measures to apply increased pressure.

In the South China Sea, ASEAN and China came to a tentative agreement in August on the Preamble for the Code of Conduct (COC) in the South China Sea they are negotiating surrounding security in the region, but progress on the remainder of the document remains unclear. The United Kingdom and France, both of which hold interests in the Indo-Pacific, have dispatched naval vessels on long-distance missions to increase their involvement in the region, calling at ports in numerous Southeast Asian countries and engaging in joint training exercises. In the Philippines, the Rodrigo Duterte administration has adjusted its stance toward the United States and China based on changes in both domestic and international circumstances, including the situation in the South China Sea and the supply of novel coronavirus disease (COVID-19) vaccines.

A number of Southeast Asian countries are also working to promote their domestic defense industries. Thailand is providing support for joint ventures with the private sector as well as export schemes, and Indonesia is moving forward with plans to establish a holding company to consolidate defense-related state-owned enterprises. Malaysia has added the development of local small- and medium-sized vendors as one of its offset policies to strengthen the foundation of its national economy, and the Philippines is going forward with measures to convert military reservations into ecozones to make effective use of them for the defense industry and other economic activity.

Keywords

Myanmar | coup d'état | ASEAN | South China Sea | defense industry

1. Issues surrounding Myanmar's Political Upheaval

(1) Execution of the Coup d'État and Establishment of the Provisional Government: The Logic of the Tatmadaw

The February 2021 coup d'état in Myanmar revived military rule and reduced to ashes the democratization process that had transitioned the country from a military to a civilian government over the course of nearly three decades. The path toward normalization is extremely uncertain, and the issue has serious implications for not only the country itself but also the Association of Southeast Asian Nations (ASEAN) and regional security.

In the November 8, 2020 general election held in Myanmar, the ruling National League for Democracy (NLD) won 396 of the 476 seats in the lower and upper houses of the Pyidaungsu Hluttaw (Assembly of the Union), the country's Parliament, securing a victory even greater than their prior win. Meanwhile, the Union Solidarity and Development Party (USDP), an opposition party close to the Tatmadaw, won only 33 seats. Election observer missions affirmed that the election was held in a fair manner, including the mission dispatched from Japan.[1] Some opposition parties as well as the Tatmadaw had cited voter list errors and other problems prior to the election, and the USDP among others announced that they would not accept the results even after it was held. The Union Election Commission (UEC), however, refused to recognize these objections.

Before the new Parliament convened on February 1, 2021, the Tatmadaw pursued the issue of electoral fraud with greater intensity, though to no avail. Then, on January 31, it issued a statement citing over 10.5 million cases of potential fraudulent conduct, stating that such an electoral process was unacceptable and made clear its stance that "the Tatmadaw will do everything possible to adhere to the democratic norms of free and fair elections, as set out by the 2008 Constitution."[2]

On the morning of February 1, the Tatmadaw detained (and later criminally prosecuted) State Counsellor Aung San Suu Kyi, President Win Myint, and other senior members of the government and the ruling party. Vice President Myint Swe, former member of the Tatmadaw who became acting president in President Win Myint's absence, conferred authority over the three branches of government on Senior General Min Aung Hlaing, the commander-in-chief of the Defence Services. The Tatmadaw then declared a nationwide State of Emergency that same day. The Presidential Order transferring power to the military explained that the UEC "had not only failed to properly perform their duties but also neglected to ensure [a] free, fair and transparent election," which affects the sovereignty of a nation which "must be derived from the citizens." It stated that refusal to address the concerns and calling Parliament were in violation of Article 417 of the Constitution, which provides that acts or attempts to take over the sovereignty by insurgency, violence, and "wrongful forcible means" shall cause the loss of the sovereignty of Myanmar and the unity of the of the ethnic nationalities in Myanmar. The Tatmadaw declared the State of Emergency on this basis, and the president "decided to utilize Article 418 (a) of the Constitution [...] which mandates the transferring of 'Legislative, Judicial and Executive Powers' to the Commander-in-Chief of the Defence Services."[3]

That same day, Senior General Min Aung Hlaing gave notice of his policy priorities, later referred to as the Five-Point Road Map: 1) reconstituting the UEC and implementing its tasks, including the scrutiny of voter lists; 2) taking measures to prevent and manage the COVID-19 pandemic; 3) taking action to ensure the recovery of businesses from the impact of COVID-19; 4) restoring peace in line with the agreements set out in the Nationwide Ceasefire Agreement (NCA); and 5) holding free and fair multiparty democratic elections after which State duties will be handed over to the winning party in accordance with democratic norms and standards.[4] On February 2, the following day, he formed the State Administrative Council (SAC) as the new governing body under the State of Emergency in accordance with Article 419 of the Constitution and assumed the role of chair himself.[5] Wunna Maung Lwin, a former member of the military who had served as minister of foreign affairs during the Thein Sein administration, was appointed as minister of foreign affairs once again (hereinafter, "SAC foreign minister").

The newly appointed UEC Chairman Thein Soe, a former general, moved forward with an investigation into the issue of electoral fraud, and on July 26, said in a statement that the results were annulled as the vote was held in violation of country's constitution and electoral laws, resulting in an election that was not free and fair. The UEC claimed to have found over 11.3 million intentional irregularities in the voter lists, including voters without national ID cards as well as duplicate votes in which the same ID card numbers appeared on multiple ballots and further accused the NLD government of attempting to fraudulently "grab State power" by using pandemic-related restrictions on movement to limit opposition candidates' campaign activities.[6]

On August 1, the SAC reconstituted its Management Committee comprised of Chairman Min Aung Hlaing and cabinet ministers into the Provisional Government "with the aim of easily, promptly and more effectively performing the State duties in accord with the adopted Five-Point Road Map," and with the SAC chairman as its prime minister.[7] In a speech, Chairman Min Aung Hlaing pointed out that it would take time to "create conditions to hold a free and fair multiparty general election," the final objective of the State of Emergency. He explained that "according to Subsection (b) of Section 421, if one cannot accomplish the duties within one year of the emergency period," which began in February 2021, the Constitution "permits only two extensions of the prescribed duration for a term of six months for each extension [...]. Then, we will take six months to prepare for the election according to the law. We will accomplish the provisions of the state of emergency by August 2023," suggesting that the general election would be held thereafter. He raised the need to rectify systemic limitations causing delays in the time it takes to issue Citizenship Scrutiny Cards (CSCs) for those who have the right to cast votes but lack the requisite identification for voter registration as an example of one such condition for holding an election.[8]

In a speech on December 23, 2021, the chairman stated that the Tatmadaw would strive to hold a general election in August 2023 if possible, depending on the state of peace and stability in the country. At the same time, he asked for the public's cooperation as CSCs had only been issued for 25% of eligible voters. He neglected, however, to provide an overview of the conditions for the election or an overall timetable. The threat of "the loss of the sovereignty of Myanmar" through "wrongful forcible means," the grounds upon which the State of Emergency was declared, would be eradicated should the new conditions for holding a general election be put in place, but it is conceivable that a State of Emergency could be reinstated based on other items from the Five-Point Road Map, including measures against COVID-19 or failure to achieve peace with ethnic armed organizations (EAOs). It is thus unclear whether a general election will be held in a punctual manner in or after August 2023 as per the timeframe presented.

In this way, the Tatmadaw has sought to justify itself by insisting that electoral fraud is a national crisis threatening loss of sovereignty and that its actions were unavoidable, as well as by emphasizing that the transfer of power is temporary and was done lawfully pursuant to the provisions of the Constitution. In contrast, President Win Myint, facing prosecution, testified at his own trial that two generals who came to his residence on the morning of February 1 demanded he resign on the grounds of poor health, threatening him further harm if he were to refuse, casting doubt on the validity of the Tatmadaw's claims.

(2) Establishment of a Rival Government by Democratic Groups

These actions by the Tatmadaw provoked strong opposition domestically from democratic groups, ordinary citizens, and EAOs that have long faced off against the military, leading them to form a rival government. The Tatmadaw, meanwhile, has been using increasingly harsh force to crack down against this resistance.

On February 1, 2021, a message was posted on the NLD Facebook account thought to have been prepared by Suu Kyi prior to her detainment saying the "actions of the military are actions to put the country back under a dictatorship," calling on people "not to accept this, to respond and wholeheartedly to protest against the coup by the military."[9] NLD representatives elected in the general election took their own oath of office on February 4 and announced the establishment of the Committee Representing Pyidaungsu Hluttaw (CRPH) the following

Protestors confronting the police holding shields with the word "people" written on them (Yangon, March 8, 2021) (©Aung Kyaw Htet/SOPA Images via ZUMA Wire/ Kyodo News Images)

day. The CRPH gave a statement saying that they "will not recognise any institutions [...] and the cabinet appointed by the military who seized power through an illegitimate coup," insisting that as elected representatives they are duly mandated to select the presidents and appoint the new cabinet members in accordance with the Constitution, announcing to the international community that "only the government led by President U Win Myint is the official Government of the Republic of the Union of Myanmar," and calling for "the unconditional release of those detained including the President of the Republic of the Union of Myanmar and the State Counsellor."[10]

Civilians have demonstrated defiance against the Tatmadaw through the Civil Disobedience Movement (CDM), abandoning their workplaces and refusing to pay taxes, while also protesting in the streets in support of the NLD and CRPH and calling for the release of Suu Kyi and others being detained. The number of people participating in the protests being held daily around the country grew rapidly, with millions reported to have taken part in protests and general strikes on February 22.[11] Then, on February 28, the Office of the United Nations High Commissioner for Human Rights announced that at least 18 people had been killed across the country as a result of gunfire and other wounds caused by security forces, shocking the world and prompting ASEAN and the United Nations (UN) to hold a series of discussions on how to respond. Large-scale protests continued on the streets through mid-April. Since then, they are said to have shifted to shorter guerrilla-style outbreaks due in part to the increase in casualties.[12] However, the death toll resulting from security force crackdowns has continued to grow, reaching 1,384 as of the end of 2021 according to research by a local NGO.[13]

Democratic groups proceeded to organize throughout March,[14] and on March 31, the CRPH announced the enactment of the Federal Democracy Charter. The charter set forth the goals of eradicating dictatorship, abolishing the 2008 Constitution, building a Federal Democracy Union, and establishing a public government, with elected parliamentarian representatives, political parties, Civil Society Organizations (CSOs) including those involved in the resistance, and EAOs to collaborate to establish an interim government alongside legislative and judiciary institutions, draft a new constitution in a Constitutional Convention, and hold a national referendum.[15] Then, on April 16, the CRPH formed the National Unity Government (NUG) as said interim government, comprised of President Win Myint and State Counsellor Suu Kyi, who remain incarcerated, Vice President Duwa Lashi La, an ethnic Kachin, as well as Prime Minister Mahn Win Khaing Than, an ethnic Karen who served as speaker of the upper house until the coup, with 11 Union ministers and 12 deputy ministers serving under him.[16]

The Tatmadaw has taken measures to prohibit any moves by democratic groups to form a rival government. In a statement issued on March 5, the SAC gave repeated warnings not to conspire with the CRPH in any fashion. The SAC said that the CRPH violated the constitution in forming a government and illegal public administrative organizations, an act which constitutes high treason under the Penal Code and carries a statutory penalty of death, life imprisonment, or 22 years of imprisonment, noting that the act of indirectly supporting the CRPH can also equate to 7 years' imprisonment.[17] Dr. Sasa, who was appointed as special envoy to the UN by the CRPH and is serving as its external spokesperson outside of the country, was then actually charged with high treason on March 15, followed by then Active Vice President Mahn Win Khaing Than and Kyaw Moe Tun, permanent representative to the UN.[18] On March 21, the Home Affairs Ministry further declared the CRPH and its related organizations "unlawful associations" under the Unlawful Associations Act, claiming that they pose harm to the peace, tranquility, and rule of law of Myanmar.[19] The NUG was also designated as an unlawful association and its ministers indicted on charges of high treason in a similar fashion.[20]

On May 5, the NUG proclaimed it had established an armed organization known as the People's Defence Force (PDF) as the forerunner to the future Federal Democratic Armed Forces envisioned by the Federal Democracy Charter. The NUG stated that SAC is committing war crimes through its "violent torture and killings, arbitrary arrest and detention of the people resisting the military dictatorship" as well as its use of "extreme force including air strikes and bombing of ethnic armed [...] organizations and people working on federal democracy." It noted that the NUG "has the responsibility to end...the violent actions, military aggression and hostilities of [the] military council."[21] In response, the government's Anti-Terrorism Central Committee identified the CRPH, NUG, and PDF as terrorist organizations under the Anti-Terrorism Act with agreement from the SAC.[22] Yee Mon, NUG defence minister, said that more than 8,000 PDF soldiers were to have completed training by the end of July.[23] In addition to its own recruitment efforts, the PDF appears to be incorporating affiliate groups that have spontaneously emerged across different parts of the country as it gradually consolidates its structure, and is conducting military operations against the Tatmadaw as well as attacks against the police and other security force personnel and facilities in cooperation with EAOs.[24] In a video address posted to Facebook on September 7, NUG Vice President Duwa Lashi La announced that the NUG had launched a people's defensive war against the military junta, urged all of Myanmar's citizens to revolt, and called for armed groups and EAOs across the country to attack the military. In an interview, the vice president emphasized that such actions are in self-defense to protect Myanmar's citizens from massacre.[25] The NUG claims that attacks by the PDF and EAOs caused the Tatmadaw to suffer at least 2,478 causalities from June through September and a further 1,300 in October, suggesting that military clashes are progressively intensifying, though the losses on the NUG's side are unclear. In November, large-scale

Tatmadaw reinforcements were reportedly deployed to Chin State, prompting warnings of heightened military tensions in the state as well as the neighboring Magway and Sagaing regions.[26] The increase in clashes has also had an impact on civilians, causing casualties among the general population and resulting in a large number of refugees and internally displaced persons.[27] On December 24, at least 35 civilians were reported to have been killed in an attack by the Tatmadaw in Kayah State, including international NGO staff and children, with over 5,000 refugees fleeing to Thailand as a result of the fighting in Kayin State that same month.[28] The United Nations High Commissioner for Refugees says the political upheaval has resulted in approximately 200,000 more internally displaced persons on top of the 370,000 that had been displaced prior, and that they, alongside nearly 1.1 million refugees and asylum seekers (including the Rohingya people), are in need of assistance.[29]

Since February 3, Suu Kyi has been indicted on more than 10 charges including violations of the Anti-Corruption Law and the Official Secrets Act, which reportedly carry a total maximum sentence of more than 100 years of imprisonment.[30] The first verdict handed down on December 6 sentenced her to four years' imprisonment on charges of incitement for the message posted when she was detained in February, for which she received a "pardon" from Chairman Min Aung Hlaing reducing her sentence to two years. While Suu Kyi and others do have attorneys, they have been prohibited from speaking about the case since October, and as such no information has been available to assess the condition of Suu Kyi and others or whether their trials are being conducted in a proper manner. Though the NLD has not been deemed an unlawful association as of the time of writing, the official decision to invalidate the election found the NLD to be responsible, leading to Suu Kyi and other NLD officials being charged with electoral fraud. Should the NLD be legally found to have engaged in fraud, the party could be subject to dissolution, suspended operation, or other punishment in the future. In this way, these symbols of modern Burmese history in the country's democratization process have had their activities stifled, and democratic groups appear to be turning course down the path of armed struggle alongside ethnic minority groups and other forces.

(3) Background behind the Tatmadaw's Actions and Prospects for a Transition to a Civil Government

The direct cause behind this recent political upheaval has been the confrontation between the government and its ruling party and the Tatmadaw over claims of electoral fraud. But if the Tatmadaw's actions were targeted at avoiding the formation of a new NLD administration, then it is likely that the military's own political standing was a major underlying factor. In multi-ethnic Myanmar, the military's identity lies in its self-perception as the guardian of national unity, the reverse of this being its sense of distrust in civilian politics which can potentially lead the country into division, a notion that stems from historical circumstances. The 2008 Constitution of Myanmar accordingly grants the military strong rights particularly in the executive and legislative branches, ensuring that the military is able to operate as an independent actor separate from the country's civilian government (see *East Asian Strategic Review 2019*, Chapter 4, Section 2).[31]

A National Convention was called in 1993 following the 1988 military coup to draft a new constitution, and it took until 2008 to draft one that would not threaten that military's status. The new constitution was ratified by a nation-wide referendum that year, though the first general election held under it was boycotted by the NLD, and the USDP, a party comprised mainly of former military officers, took power. When the NLD proceeded to win the 2015 general election, the military accepted the results and the transfer of power the following year went smoothly. State Counsellor Suu Kyi, de facto leader of the NLD government, established a non-hostile relationship with the military while raising issue with the non-elected seats allocated to it and other issues in Parliament and sought constitutional reform.

The amendments driven by the NLD included reductions to the number of seats reserved for the military and the number of Parliament members needed to approve constitutional amendments. Although these were debated by Parliament's Constitutional Amendment Committee beginning in 2019, they were ultimately rejected in March 2020. Under the current Constitution, no amendments can be passed without support from military members of parliament, and as such, the move was generally regarded as self-promotion by the NLD ahead of the next election. The military, however, may have taken it as a warning and viewed it as a potential threat to its own political standing should a future civilian government gain more popular support and intensify efforts to amend the Constitution. The UEC reportedly supports replacing the electoral system with one of proportional representation, which may be aimed at making it difficult for a party that has won a sole majority to implement systemic change. Some reports also note that the military's moves may be intended to protect the economic interests of organizations, including companies affiliated with the military, and individual military officers.[32]

The ramifications of this political upheaval have spread in all directions, not only in terms of the number of resistance movement victims and detainees, refugees, and internally displaced persons, but also in the form of marked delays in responding to COVID-19 and the healthcare crisis, interruptions to all forms of learning from primary and secondary schools through higher education, rising prices, and declines in production, employment, and investment due to the suspension of social and economic functions and the resulting stagnation caused by the resistance movement and subsequent crackdowns (including dismissal from employment, detainment, and prosecution of those engaged in the CDM). Above all, the deteriorating humanitarian situation is a pressing issue that underscores the critical need to stop the violence and ensure access to humanitarian assistance.[33]

However, there is no sign of the conflict between the military and democratic groups easing, meaning there is a strong possibility that the military will maintain dominance for the foreseeable future. Only able to operate underground or outside the country if not via the internet, the NUG has virtually no means to implement its policies domestically on its own, so the military is unlikely to view it as a potential partner for political dialogue to begin with even with a high level of domestic and international support. It is believed that the SAC's Provisional

Government intends to continue preparations for a new election and exclude the NLD, and hold a general election between pro-military and centrist parties at an appropriate time, thereby achieving a "transition to a civilian government." However, should the extensive cooperation, including military cooperation, between the NUG and ethnic minority forces advance further, it would put a certain amount of pressure on the military. The help of ethnic minority forces which possess areas of substantial control may also increase the NUG's level of influence by enabling it to implement its policies as well as supply and support the PDF and other cooperating forces across various regions.

Foreign pressure is another factor capable of altering the situation. While the SAC does not seem to give much weight to Western criticism and sanctions by such countries and regions against Myanmar have been limited as of the end of 2021, the SAC may stage dialogue with democratic groups and could potentially release Suu Kyi and other officials should it come to anticipate a situation that would hinder the state's economic management. The fact that Suu Kyi received a pardon in December halving her sentence can be taken as a sign that the SAC is not completely indifferent to international scrutiny. However, given that loss is certain for the military junta should free political activity be allowed, compromise may be sought contingent on the Constitution remaining untouched and military officials going unprosecuted.

(4) Divided Reactions by the International Community

The international community's reaction to the post-coup state of affairs in Myanmar has been split, with no concerted effort seen to remedy the situation.

Many Western countries have condemned and placed pressure on the military for seizing authority and using force to crack down on democratic groups, resulting in heavy casualties. On February 1, U.S. President Joseph R. Biden, Jr. issued a statement in which he described the military's takeover of power, the detainment of Suu Kyi and other public officials, and the declaration of the State of Emergency as a direct attack on Myanmar's transition to democracy and the rule of law, calling for the international community to apply concerted pressure on the military to relinquish its control and release those being held.[34] The following day, the U.S. State Department asserted that "the Burmese military's actions [...] having deposed the duly elected head of government, constituted a military coup d'état."[35]

On February 1, Japan expressed "grave concern" over the erosion of the democratic process in Myanmar and called for the release of senior government officials being detained. On February 3, the G7 foreign ministers and the high representative of the EU condemned the coup and called on the military to immediately lift the State of Emergency, restore the democratically elected government to power, release those unjustly detained, and to respect human rights and the rule of law, further stressing that the results of the previous year's election must be respected and Parliament convened at the earliest possible opportunity.[36] On February 18, the foreign ministers of the Quad, a strategic security dialogue between Japan, the United States, Australia, and India, held a teleconference during which they expressed "grave concern" regarding the situation in the country.[37] On March 28, the Chiefs of Defense of Australia, Canada, Germany, Greece, Italy, Japan, Denmark, the Netherlands, New Zealand, South Korea, the United Kingdom, and the United States, including General Yamazaki Koji, chief of staff of the JSDF Joint Staff, issued a joint statement condemning the use of force against unarmed people by the Myanmar Armed Forces and associated security forces, and at the ASEAN Defence Ministers' Meeting (ADMM)-Plus held virtually on June 16, Defense Minister Kishi Nobuo urged the Myanmar military to put an immediate stop to its violence against civilians, release those being detained, and swiftly restore the country's democratic political system.[38]

Since February 10, the U.S. government has issued sanctions against military personnel and military-affiliated companies, imposed restrictions on exports to Myanmar's Ministry of Defence and Ministry of Home Affairs, and suspended development aid, expanding the scope of said measures as crackdowns on the resistance movement have intensified. The United Kingdom, Canada, the EU, and New Zealand, among others, have also imposed sanctions and travel restrictions on the military as well as other figures and companies tied to the junta.[39] On May

21, Japan's Foreign Minister Motegi Toshimitsu mentioned the possibility that Japan may be compelled to review its Official Development Assistance (ODA) to Myanmar,[40] and Australia and South Korea have also suspended defense cooperation programs and exchanges with the country.[41]

Meanwhile, China and Russia have avoided criticizing the military's power grab. At a press conference on February 1, Wang Wenbin, China's Foreign Ministry spokesperson, expressed hope that "all parties in Myanmar will properly handle their differences under the constitutional and legal framework and maintain political and social stability," but neglected to address the military's actions.[42] China's stance remained unchanged at the UN, with the Security Council Press Statement on Situation in Myanmar issued February 4 following an informal meeting of the UN Security Council on February 2 expressing "deep concern at the declaration of the state of emergency [...] and the arbitrary detention of members of the Government, including State Counsellor Aung San Suu Kyi," but failing to recognize the situation as an illegitimate coup.[43] In the Statement by the President of the Security Council on Myanmar issued March 10 following a meeting on March 5 in response to the sharp increase in deaths resulting from crackdowns on protests, the Security Council again condemned the violence against peaceful protesters and called on the military "to exercise utmost constraint," but lines condemning the coup and suggesting sanctions in the original draft were reportedly removed at China and Russia's disapproval.[44] In April, Josep Borrell, EU high representative for foreign affairs and security policy, criticized China and Russia for hindering a concerted international response to the situation in Myanmar. On June 18, the UN General Assembly further adopted a resolution calling on Member States to prevent arms from flowing into the country, but China, Russia, and India, among others, abstained from the vote.[45]

Amid such circumstances, Myanmar's military has been deepening ties with Russia and China. On March 27, representatives from Russia, China, India, Pakistan, Bangladesh, Vietnam, Laos, and Thailand reportedly attended the Armed Forces Day ceremony held in Naypyidaw.[46] Russia in particular was represented by Deputy Defense Minister Alexander Fomin, who met with Chairman Min Aung Hlaing the previous day. The chairman also visited Moscow and met with Security Council Secretary Nikolai Patrushev on June 21, where they reportedly discussed bilateral cooperation on security measures, the state of affairs in Myanmar, and the continuation of good relations between the two country's militaries.[47]

SAC Foreign Minister Wunna Maung Lwin attended a Special ASEAN-China Foreign Ministers' Meeting held in Chongqing, China on June 7 to celebrate the 30th anniversary of ASEAN-China Dialogue Relations where he also held bilateral talks with Wang Yi, state councilor and foreign minister the following day. The Chinese delegation stated that "China's friendly policy toward Myanmar is not affected by changes to Myanmar's domestic and external situation," and "stressed that China supports all parties of Myanmar in resolving differences through political dialogue, implementing the Five-Point Consensus reached with ASEAN [described below], preventing future recurrence of violence, [and] restoring social stability of the country."[48] China is also reported to have initially considered inviting Chairman Min Aung Hlaing to the ASEAN-China Special Summit in November, but abandoned the idea due to opposition from ASEAN Member States.[49]

As China and Russia move to effectively allow the SAC to run the government, U.S. Deputy Secretary of State Wendy R. Sherman spoke with NUG Foreign Minister Zin Mar Aung on August 4 on a virtual call during which they "discussed ongoing efforts to return Burma to a path to democracy, including continued U.S. support for the pro-democracy movement,"[50] believed to be the first publicized contact between a top U.S. government official and a democratic group.[51] On October 25, Jake Sullivan, national security advisor, then met virtually with Vice President Duwa Lashi La, the highest ranking NUG official outside of those detained, during which National Security Advisor Sullivan stressed the United States' continued support for the pro-democracy movement in Myanmar. At the UN, the General Assembly agreed in December to defer its decision on the credentials of representative Kyaw Moe Tun, who was notified that he had been dismissed from his position after delivering a speech at the Assembly on February 26 criticizing the coup and calling for a return to civilian rule.[52] While the NUG has maintained channels of communication in the international community, other countries have not recognized the NUG administration as a legitimate national delegate except at the parliamentary or representative level.

(5) ASEAN Diplomacy and the Limits of Regional Solutions

The international community has pinned high hopes on ASEAN to help stabilize the situation in Myanmar. On February 1, the day of the political upheaval, 2021 ASEAN Chair Brunei issued the ASEAN Chairman's Statement on the Developments in the Republic of the Union of Myanmar, recalling "the principles enshrined in the ASEAN Charter, including, the adherence to the principles of democracy, the rule of law and good governance, respect for and protection of human rights and fundamental freedoms" and encouraging "the pursuance of dialogue, reconciliation and the return to normalcy in accordance with the will and interests of the people of Myanmar."[53] In conjunction with this, the UN Security Council issued a statement on February 4 in which its members expressed their strong support for regional organizations, ASEAN in particular, and welcomed the ASEAN Chairman's Statement. Thai Prime Minister Prayut Chan-o-cha met with SAC Foreign Minister Wunna Maung Lwin on February 24, marking the first official interaction between a Southeast Asian country and a senior SAC official, and a meeting between the foreign ministers of Myanmar, Thailand, and Indonesia was also held the same day.

The SAC foreign minister also attended the Informal ASEAN Ministerial Meeting held virtually on March 2. The Chair's Statement expressed concern over the situation in Myanmar, prefaced by mention that ASEAN is a "family" and that "the political stability in any and all ASEAN Member States is essential to achieving a collective peaceful, stable and prosperous ASEAN Community." The chair then called on all parties to "refrain from instigating further violence," "exercise utmost restraint as well as flexibility," and "seek a peaceful solution, through constructive dialogue," expressing "ASEAN's readiness to assist

Myanmar in a positive, peaceful and constructive manner."[54] Following the meeting, the foreign ministers of Malaysia, Singapore, and Indonesia clarified that they had each called for the release of the political detainees, but Hishammuddin Hussein, Malaysian foreign minister, opposed any sanctions against the country.[55] In an interview with the BBC published that day, Singapore's Prime Minister Lee Hsien Loong described the military's takeover of power as a "tragic step back" from the gradual steps that had been made in the process of democratization since the previous military regime, condemning the military's violence and calling for the immediate release of political leaders but expressing disapproval of sanctions, noting that they would hurt Myanmar's population and not the military.[56]

ASEAN's basic stance has thus been that while it would not endorse the military's power grab, it would nevertheless accept representatives from the military as a point of contact for dialogue and provide support to promote dialogue amongst concerned parties while calling for restraint in the use of violence, though it would not use sanctions to enforce its position. The ASEAN Leaders' Meeting on April 24, which took place in person at the ASEAN Secretariat in Jakarta and was attended by SAC Chairman Min Aung Hlaing demonstrates the results of that line of thinking. The Chairman's Statement released after the meeting indicated that the leaders had "expressed deep concern on the situation in the country, including reports of fatalities and escalation of violence," "acknowledged ASEAN's positive and constructive role in facilitating a peaceful solution," and "agreed to the 'Five-Point Consensus'": 1) the immediate cessation of violence and the exercise of utmost restraint by all parties; 2) the pursuit of constructive dialogue among all parties concerned to seek a peaceful solution in the interests of the people; 3) the mediation of the dialogue process by a special envoy of the ASEAN chair with the assistance of the secretary-general of ASEAN; 4) the provision of humanitarian assistance through the ASEAN Coordinating Centre for Humanitarian Assistance on disaster management (AHA Centre); and 5) a visit to Myanmar by the special envoy and delegation and meetings with all parties concerned.[57]

Some criticized the Leaders' Meeting for inviting the head of the military and instigator of the coup as a "leader," but on the other hand, getting the country's effective top authority to agree to ASEAN's demands could be considered an accomplishment. The items agreed to at the meeting, however, have not yet been implemented. As of the end of 2021, the post-coup death toll has nearly doubled, and with democratic groups being detained, going underground, and fleeing the country, there has been no meaningful progress in terms of dialogue.

In addition, the ASEAN special envoy meant to help facilitate dialogue between the parties has also faced significant problems. It is reported that Thailand, Malaysia, and Indonesia each submitted candidates and competed over the position,[58] but it was not until the ASEAN Foreign Ministers' Meeting in August, more than three months after the Leaders' Meeting, that Brunei's Second Minister of Foreign Affairs Erywan Yusof was selected as envoy. The appointment was welcomed by the United States, China, the UN, and other countries,[59] but Erywan, demanding access to "all parties concerned," canceled his first visit scheduled for October claiming that his request to meet Suu Kyi, among others, was not granted. To this, the military's spokesman released a statement explaining that the envoy cannot meet with Suu Kyi as she is facing criminal prosecution.[60]

Discontent with the position Myanmar had taken, ASEAN decided at the emergency ASEAN Foreign Ministers' Meeting held virtually on October 15 not to invite representatives from the military to the series of summits set to begin on October 26, including the ASEAN Summit. The Statement of the Chair pointed out that "there had been insufficient progress in the implementation of the Five-Point Consensus," in particular refusal to allow the envoy access to State Counsellor Suu Kyi, President Win Myint, and others undergoing legal proceedings, as well as the CRPH, NUG, PDF, and other organizations declared as illegal, expressing "concerns over Myanmar's commitment [...] on establishing constructive dialogue among all concerned parties." On top of this, it noted, "some ASEAN Member States had received correspondence from the NUG requesting to be invited to [...] ASEAN Summits and Related Summits. Following extensive discussions, there was no consensus reached for a political representative from

Myanmar to attend," but "the Meeting accepted the decision to invite a non-political representative."[61] In a speech given on October 18, Chairman Min Aung Hlaing said it is the NUG that is provoking violence, calling it a terrorist group and criticizing ASEAN for not addressing its violence.[62] Myanmar's Ministry of Foreign Affairs also refused to accept the decision, claiming on October 22 that the decision "was not in line with the procedures [of the ASEAN Charter] and beyond the mandate of the Chair," finding the decision in breach of the Charter's principles of sovereignty, equality, and non-interference in the internal affairs of Member States.[63]

Myanmar failed to attend the October 26 ASEAN Summit (held virtually). In the Chairman's Statement, ASEAN "expressed concern of the situation in the country, including reports of fatalities and violence," calling on Myanmar to "fulfil its commitment to the Five-Point Consensus" and comply with its "timely and complete implementation."[64] After the summit, Myanmar continued to deny the ASEAN special envoy a meeting with Suu Kyi and criticized ASEAN for excluding it from the summit.[65] Meanwhile, ASEAN opposed China inviting Chairman Min Aung Hlaing to the ASEAN-China Special Summit (held virtually) on November 22, agreeing instead to invite Myanmar's ambassador to China though Myanmar was absent once again. Representatives from the country also failed to participate in the Asia-Europe Meeting (ASEM) Summit held November 25 and 26, as well as the meeting between the G7 Foreign and Development Ministers and ASEAN Member States on December 12 (both held virtually).

It is highly unusual in ASEAN diplomacy for a particular member state to continuously fail to participate. The ASEAN Charter enacted in 2007 is a constitution-like document that defines ASEAN's legal standing and systems, and although Chapter VIII includes provisions regarding the settlement of disputes amongst Member States, it makes no reference to disqualification, expulsion, or sanctions, and "when a dispute remains unsolved [...] this dispute shall be referred to the ASEAN summit, for its decision" (Article 26).[66] Myanmar has objected to the decision to exclude it from summit meetings on this basis, and claims that the aftermath of the political upheaval is a domestic issue and that only Myanmar is facing unequal treatment, contradicting the principle of non-interference in internal affairs which has stood since ASEAN's establishment. In fact, even looking exclusively at similar examples that have taken place since the Charter's enactment, Thailand faced no restrictions on its participation following the May 2014 coup, and General Prayut Chan-o-cha, commander-in-chief of the Royal Thai Army, participated in the November 2014 ASEAN Summit hosted by Myanmar in Naypyidaw after assuming the role of prime minister of the military junta that August.[67] Tied with this, Chairman Min Aung Hlaing's participation at the Leaders' Meeting in April 2021 as previously mentioned would also seem to suggest that the means itself of obtaining power is not what constitutes an issue.

The unprecedented measures taken in October were, in effect, a criticism of Myanmar's failure to abide by the agreement and a way to pressure the country into compliance. Nevertheless, while the ASEAN countries are in agreement on stopping the violence and finding a peaceful resolution, they are divided into two camps: those that have taken a strong stance emphasizing the principles of democracy, human rights, and the rule of law enshrined in the Charter, and those that seek restraint in ASEAN's involvement seeing it as an internal affair as Myanmar insists. Indonesia, Malaysia, and Singapore are among the former, with Indonesian Foreign Minister Retno Marsudi tweeting that "Indonesia propose [sic] the participation of Myanmar at the Summits should not be represented at the political level until Myanmar restore [sic] its democracy through an inclusive process," and Malaysian Foreign Minister Saifuddin Abdullah stating that "we cannot use the principle of non-interference as a shield to avoid issues being addressed."[68] Vietnam, Cambodia, and Thailand fall under the latter camp, seemingly concerned that regional intervention over political situations and human rights issues particularly in countries with institutional or de facto single-party rule as well as strong military influence will extend to their own countries as well. Thailand's Ministry of Foreign Affairs expressed its "full support for Myanmar-led efforts to promote a peaceful resolution" and has reportedly curbed moves to put pressure on the SAC.[69]

On December 7, 2021, SAC Foreign Minister Wunna Maung Lwin visited Cambodia, set to serve as the 2022 ASEAN chair, where he met with Prime Minister Hun Sen, who agreed to pay visit to Myanmar from January 7. The day before the meeting, Prime Minister Hun Sen said that he would meet with Chairman Min Aung Hlaing to find a solution to Myanmar's crisis and bring ASEAN's summit meetings back to full attendance, with Myanmar included, noting that a solution can only be found through dialogue with those currently in power.[70] On December 8, the chairman also met virtually with General Vong Pisen, commander-in-chief of Royal Cambodian Armed Forces. During the meeting, they reportedly discussed Myanmar's full cooperation with Cambodia as ASEAN chair, the need for all ASEAN Member States to abide by the ASEAN Charter, and the possible impacts some countries violating the Charter may have on all members countries.[71] In this way, Myanmar expects ASEAN's approach to change with its new chair, but if a compromise is reached without improvements to the situation that are to other member countries' satisfaction, it could further widen the fissures between the different camps.

The problems surrounding ASEAN's response to the political upheaval in Myanmar can be considered a consequence of the yet unaddressed contradiction between the principles and goals set forth in the Charter and the realities of its member countries as the association has sought to become a united regional community. The current situation serves as a test of ASEAN Member States' ability to transcend their differences of opinion and take effective steps to protect the lives and security of all of Myanmar's people, including the Rohingya, and support a peaceful resolution. ASEAN's effectiveness as a community and its trustworthiness in the eyes of the international community depend on it.

2. Regional and Domestic Security Trends

(1) Moves toward Finalizing the South China Sea Code of Conduct

The situation in the South China Sea remained far from stable in 2021. While some progress is said to have been made on the text for the Code of Conduct (COC) in the South China Sea between ASEAN and China, the initial goal of finalizing it during the year was left unachieved, and overall progress on the document is still unclear. Meanwhile, China continues to unilaterally engage in activity in the region, and European countries have also moved to strengthen their involvement alongside the United States.

Regarding the developments surrounding the issue of the South China Sea and the COC, on January 21, 2021, the ASEAN Foreign Ministers' Retreat was held in an online format led by Brunei, ASEAN chair for the year. It is clear that the wording of the statements on the South China Sea and the COC in the Press Release by the Chairman released thereafter largely follows that of the Joint Communiqué from the ASEAN Foreign Ministers' Meeting and the Chair's Statement from the ASEAN Summit the previous year. The press release stated, "We discussed the situation in the South China Sea, during which concerns were expressed by some Ministers on the land reclamations, activities, and serious incidents in the area, which have eroded trust and confidence, increased tensions, and may undermine peace, security, and stability in the region."[72] (Underlines by author.) The underlined wording has been used since the June 2020 summit, and while the phrase "recent developments" is missing, it can be said that ASEAN's perception of the situation remains largely unchanged, with China engaging in demonstrative behavior based upon its unilateral assertion of its rights and confrontation amongst related parties repeatedly resulting from it.

The same wording was used in the Joint Communiqué from the ASEAN Foreign Ministers' Meeting held virtually on August 2 despite incidents in which Chinese fishing vessels gathered in disputed waters near the Philippines from March and Malaysia scrambled jets to intercept Chinese military aircraft in May (see next section). That being said, the phrase "including damage to the marine environment" was appended to the "serious incidents" used in the January Press Release by the Chairman,[73] which is thought to have been in response to July reports that Chinese fishing vessels operating in the area's waters were pumping out sewage and damaging coral reefs while anchored.[74] The same language was used again in the Chairman's Statement from the ASEAN Summits held on October 26 via videoconference.[75]

It should be noted that with Brunei as ASEAN chair, the statement reaffirming that the United Nations Convention on the Law of the Sea (UNCLOS) is "the basis for determining maritime entitlements, sovereign rights, jurisdiction and legitimate interests over maritime zones" and "sets out the legal framework within which all activities in the oceans and seas must be carried out" from the previous year's Chairman's Statements of the ASEAN Summits chaired by Vietnam was removed.[76] The reference to the "universally recognised principles of international law, including the 1982 UNCLOS" was left unchanged and the language returned to that used through 2019, though this could be seen as a weaker assertion than the 2020 version which placed emphasis on legal principles. This suggests that Brunei and Vietnam hold different positions and stances both as countries involved in territorial claims over the South China Sea.

While ASEAN as a whole has maintained a continued understanding of the issue, statements from the East Asia Summit (EAS), in which major countries outside the region also participate, have shown a change in wording. The Chairman's Statement of the EAS Foreign Ministers' Meeting held virtually on August 4 retained the language from aforementioned the ASEAN Foreign Ministers' Meeting, but in another paragraph stated, "The Meeting reaffirmed the importance of maintaining and promoting peace, security, stability, prosperity, safety, and freedom of navigation in and overflight above the South China Sea and pursue peaceful resolution of disputes, without coercion, in accordance with universally recognised principles of international law, including the 1982 UNCLOS."[77] (Underline by author.) This represents a firmer message considering that the underlined portion replaced "[...] and recognised the benefits of having the South China Sea as a sea of peace, stability, and prosperity" from the previous year's Chairman's Statement of the EAS.

However, this language may have been included out of necessity following a tense dispute between the United States and China at the meeting, as official statements from both sides made it apparent that they each view the other's actions as "coercion": Antony J. Blinken, U.S. secretary of state "underscored the U.S. rejection of the PRC's unlawful maritime claims in the South China Sea, in line with the July 12, 2016 Arbitral Tribunal Award," while China's Wang Yi, state councilor and foreign minister, stated that "some countries outside the region desired to stir up trouble and have willfully launched a large number of advanced warships and warcraft into the South China Sea, deliberately inducing other countries outside the region to 'show their powers' in the South China Sea and openly sowing discord among countries in the region, especially countries concerned."[78] In light of its diplomatic stance not to "choose sides" in the conflict, ASEAN is unable to express clear opposition to China and take the United States' side even though China is the one directly confronting ASEAN in the South China Sea, and as such it is possible that the language was worded in a way that could be interpreted as taking into account both countries' claims.

At the October 27 EAS (held virtually), President Biden, attending for the first time, "reiterated the U.S. commitment to the international rules-based order and expressed concern over threats to that order," and while Chinese Premier of the State Council Li Keqiang made reference to cooperation between China and the ASEAN countries in the South China Sea, there was no exchange of direct criticism directed at either side as far as official communications indicate. In the Chairman's Statement, the phrase "without coercion" from August was replaced with "without resorting to the threat or use of force."[79]

To put this in context with regards to U.S.-ASEAN relations that year, the press release from the ASEAN Foreign Ministers' Retreat in January had congratulated President Biden and Vice President Kamala Harris who had taken office just the day before and stated that ASEAN looks forward to working with the new administration to further strengthen their strategic partnership. In contrast to former President Donald J. Trump's stance, who never attended a single EAS meeting and was extremely passive in his diplomacy with ASEAN leaders, this statement reveals the association's strong expectations for increased engagement from the Biden administration. As though to live up to this, Secretary of State Blinken reiterated the United States' rejection of China's unlawful claims and that it stands with the Southeast Asian claimants during the Special ASEAN-U.S. Foreign Ministerial Meeting on July 13 (held virtually).[80] Later that month, Defense Secretary Lloyd Austin visited Singapore, Vietnam, and the Philippines, which was followed by visits to Singapore and Vietnam by Vice President Harris in late August, reiterating the United States' commitment to the Southeast Asia region. On September 23, the first in-person (though partly virtual) ASEAN-U.S. Foreign Ministers' Meeting since the start of the pandemic was held in New York City on the margins of the UN General assembly, and in December, U.S. Secretary of State Blinken paid visit to Indonesia and Malaysia (Thailand was included on the original itinerary, but the trip was cancelled due to COVID-19). On December 15, Secretary Blinken gave an address on the United States' commitment to the security and prosperity of the Indo-Pacific in which he expressed the country's determination to defend the freedom of the seas in the South China Sea. He declared ASEAN centrality the foundation of the region's architecture, and stated that the United States will continue expanding its strategic partnership with the association as a strong and independent ASEAN is crucial for tackling pressing crises and long-term challenges.[81]

China is heavily cautious of these moves by the United States. At the ASEAN-China Ministerial Meeting held virtually the day before the EAS Foreign Ministers' Meeting, State Councilor and Foreign Minister Wang Yi stated that "China's sovereign rights and interests in the South China Sea conform to international laws," including UNCLOS, and that "[w]ith the joint efforts of China and ASEAN, the South China Sea has maintained a stable situation in general," but that "we should be vigilant that some countries outside the region have become the biggest disruptors of peace and stability" in the area.[82] He had also referred to the Quad as an "Indo-Pacific NATO" the previous year, stating that the framework would severely undermine the region's security.[83] In a comment on the *Defense of Japan 2021* white paper published in July 2021, China's Foreign Ministry spokesperson stated that the Indo-Pacific Strategy "aims to stoke bloc confrontation and create cliques for geopolitical game," "marks the comeback of Cold War mentality," and "should be tossed into the dustbin of history."[84]

Such Chinese discourse could be called an attempt to place China in the same group as ASEAN countries and create an image that "our" order is being undermined by unjustified intervention from the United States and other countries outside the region, though it is hard to believe that ASEAN would readily buy into such rhetoric. That being said, given that ASEAN member countries each have different relationships with China and differing interests in the South China Sea, China's intent to make resolving the issue an "intra-regional" problem and exclude the United States and other countries outside the region from involvement will surely have no small impact when the association attempts to establish a concerted stance toward countries outside of the region.

Negotiations on the COC stagnated again in 2021 due to the COVID-19 pandemic, making China's previously reported goal of reaching an agreement during the year impossible. The Co-Chairs' Statement on the Special ASEAN-China Foreign Ministers' Meeting (Chongqing) held June 7 marking the 30th anniversary of ASEAN-China Dialogue Relations stressed that they have maintained momentum in resuming negotiations step-by-step through several virtual meetings, and while physical meetings are to remain the primary mode of negotiation, they would pursue the possibility of resuming textual discussions on the COC through virtual platforms.[85] The Chairman's Statement of the ASEAN Post Ministerial Conference announced that textual negotiations on the Single Draft COC Negotiating Text had resumed and that a provisional agreement was reached on the Preamble at the ASEAN-China Ministerial Meeting in August, but it has been reported that there is still a wide divergence of opinion regarding the remainder of the content.[86] The Chairman's Statement of the ASEAN Summits in October subsequently stated that there had been progress in the negotiations on the Objectives section of the General Provisions,[87] and in November, Cambodian Prime Minister Hun Sen said he hopes to be able to finalize the COC in 2022 when Cambodia assumes the ASEAN Chairmanship, but it is unclear whether this can be achieved.

(2) Strengthened European Presence

The United Kingdom and France, both of which hold interests in the Indo-Pacific, have indicated policies of increased engagement in the Indo-Pacific including Southeast Asia in recent years. In 2016, the new regional British Defence Staff (BDS) Asia Pacific was set up in Singapore, along with BDS Gulf and BDS West Africa, and the policy paper *Global Britain in a Competitive Age: the Integrated Review of Security, Defence, Development and Foreign Policy* that was published in March 2021 confirmed the United Kingdom would place greater focus on its defense efforts in the region.[88] At the ASEAN Foreign Ministers' Meeting in August that year, the United Kingdom became one of ASEAN's Dialogue Partners.[89] Meanwhile, France, which holds overseas territories in the South Pacific, also released its Defence Strategy in the Indo-Pacific in 2019, updated its Indo-Pacific Strategy in 2021, and has called for international order based on the rule of law at sea.[90] Both countries have dispatched naval vessels to the Indo-Pacific under such policies for some time, and starting from 2021, the Netherlands and Germany have also begun sending naval vessels to more actively demonstrate their presence in the region.

In November 2020, the French Navy's SSN *Émeraude* and support vessel *Seine* conducted a joint training with a Royal Australian Navy frigate, submarine, and maritime patrol aircraft, after which they called at the RAN base HMAS *Stirling* for refueling and maintenance and called at the U.S. Naval Base Guam for another joint training exercise at the end of that month. Then, in February 2021, Florence Parly, minister for the armed forces of France, announced that the two vessels had sailed through the South China Sea, after which it was reported that they had conducted a passing exercise (PASSEX) with three Indonesian naval vessels in the Sunda Strait. That same month, LHD *Tonnerre* and frigate *Surcouf* departed Toulon on the mission Jeanne D'Arc 2021.[91] The vessels completed a multilateral joint training in the Bay of Bengal in April,[92] and later sailed through the South China Sea with two Australian naval vessels, calling at a port in Vietnam before heading to Japan. On the return trip, *Tonnerre* conducted a PASSEX with a Singaporean naval vessel off of Changi and *Surcouf* with a Malaysian vessel off

Figure 5.1. Deployments of European naval fleets to the Indo-Pacific

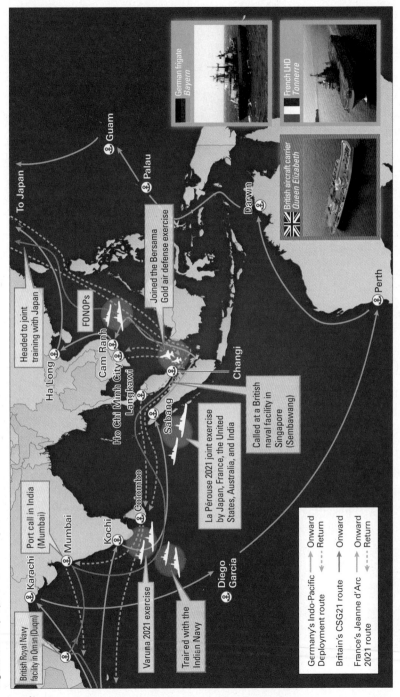

German frigate *Bayern*

French LHD *Tonnerre*

British aircraft carrier *Queen Elizabeth*

To Japan

Guam

Palau

Darwin

Perth

Headed to joint training with Japan

FONOPs

Joined the Bersama Gold air defense exercise

Ha Long

Cam Ranh

Ho Chi Minh City

Langkawi

Sabang

Changi

Called at a British naval facility in Singapore (Sembawang)

La Pérouse 2021 joint exercise by Japan, France, the United States, Australia, and India

Colombo

Kochi

Mumbai

Karachi

Port call in India (Mumbai)

British Royal Navy facility in Oman (Duqm)

Varuna 2021 exercise

Trained with the Indian Navy

Diego Garcia

Germany's Indo-Pacific Deployment route — Onward ---- Return

Britain's CSG21 route — Onward

France's Jeanne d'Arc 2021 route — Onward ---- Return

Sources: Compiled by the author based on French Ministry for the Armed Forces, British Royal Navy, and German Bundeswehr websites; ©Wesley Timm/U.S. Navy, 2018; © Mike Banzhaf/U.S. Navy, 2008

Photos: Japan Maritime Self-Defense Force official Twitter account; ©Wesley Timm/U.S. Navy, 2018; © Mike Banzhaf/U.S. Navy, 2008

of Langkawi, thereby affirming France's relationship of cooperation with coastal countries in the region which is crucial for distant voyages.

In 2020, British Prime Minister Boris Johnson expressed plans to dispatch an aircraft carrier to the Indo-Pacific. It was then announced in April 2021 that Carrier Strike Group 21 (CSG21) would be formed as a far-sea operation set to engage with 40 countries, and the group departed from Portsmouth led by the aircraft carrier *Queen Elizabeth* in the latter half of the following month.[93] The fleet consisted of a total of nine ships, including two Royal Navy destroyers, two frigates, and two supply ships alongside a U.S. navy destroyer and a Royal Netherlands Navy frigate, with the aircraft aboard the aircraft carrier also joined by U.S. Marine Corps F-35Bs. CSG-21 conducted exercises including PASSEXes with the Thai, Malaysian, and Singaporean navies as the group passed through the Andaman Sea, the Strait of Malacca, and the Singapore Strait. The British frigate *Richmond* also made a port call in Vietnam on the return trip, working to strengthen relations with Southeast Asian countries. In September, as CSG-21 was on deployment in the Indo-Pacific, the British Ministry of Defence announced plans for a new operation to deploy two patrol vessels to the region for a five-year period.

The member countries to the Five Power Defense Arrangements (FPDA), a security framework comprised of the Commonwealth states in the region, conducted the annual command post exercise Bersama Shield in April virtually for the first time due to the global COVID-19 pandemic, and the air defense exercise Bersama Lima was renamed Bersama Gold to commemorate the FDPA's 50th anniversary with field trainings conducted in the airspace and waters around Singapore and Malaysia in October. CSG21's *Richmond* and vessels from Australia's regional engagement activity, Indo-Pacific Endeavour, also participated in the exercise.[94]

Germany also released its policy guidelines for the Indo-Pacific in 2020,[95] and announced its intent to contribute to stability in the region that December when it participated in a joint session celebrating the 10th anniversary of the founding of the ASEAN Defence Ministers' Meeting (ADMM)-Plus as a guest of the chair alongside the United Kingdom and France, among others.[96] In 2021, Germany then dispatched a naval vessel to the region. The frigate *Bayern* departed Wilhelmshaven that August,[97] supporting various operations across numerous locations as it headed for the Indo-Pacific and later stopped in Japan. On its return trip, Berlin is reported to have approached China about the vessel calling at Shanghai before passing through the South China Sea, but was rejected. After stopping in Japan, *Bayern* engaged in monitoring and surveillance activities against illicit maritime activities, including ship-to-ship transfers with North Korean-flagged vessels, and participated in the Japan-led ANNUALEX naval exercise alongside the United States, Australia, and Canada. Both marked the first time Germany has engaged in such initiatives.

(3) Philippine Foreign Policy

President Rodrigo Duterte has adjusted his stance toward both the United States and China in response to changes in domestic and international circumstances depending on the prevailing situation at the time. In terms of U.S. relations, 2021 saw a solution to the Visiting Forces Agreement (VFA) issue, a problem which has been pending since February 2020 when President Duterte unilaterally announced he would terminate the agreement.

The VFA stipulates the legal status of visiting U.S. military units in joint exercises and various other activities, including humanitarian assistance and disaster relief. Together with the Enhanced Defense Cooperation Agreement (EDCA), which outlines the use of Philippine military facilities made available to U.S. forces, the VFA upholds the effectiveness of the Mutual Defense Treaty between the Republic of the Philippines and the United States of America, which celebrated 70 years in 2021. The VFA has been automatically extended since it went into effect in 1999, with one party to give 180 days' notice to the other should it wish to abrogate said extension. While the reason behind the move to terminate the agreement has not been made public, it is believed to be a rebuke of the United States' critical assessment of the Duterte administration's war on drugs. The decision on whether to terminate the agreement following President Duterte's announcement was postponed three times, however, in June 2020, November 2020, and June 2021. It was then reported that June that the Duterte administration intended to suspend its consideration of the termination, which was then conveyed to U.S. Defense Secretary Austin on his visit to the Philippines the following month.

Changes to the Philippines' domestic and international circumstances, including developments in the South China Sea and the spread of COVID-19, are thought to have been contributing factors in the reversal on terminating the VFA. President Duterte has sought to strengthen bilateral ties with China, particularly on the economic front, by not addressing the Arbitral Tribunal Award for the time being.[98] China, meanwhile, has continuously made illegal claims regarding in the Nansha (Spratly) Islands, among others, and taken demonstrative action. This posturing continued into 2021, and amidst growing concerns from neighboring countries over China's Coast Guard Law, a multitude of Chinese ships in excess of 200 vessels were observed gathered around the Whitsun (Julian Felipe) Reef in March of that year. The Philippine Coast Guard and Bureau of Fisheries and Aqua Resources maintained a continued response, with the Air Force also conducting surveillance activities. The Philippine government lodged a diplomatic protest at the same time, asking China to evacuate the area, but the latter persisted in asserting its own claims.

The following month, the Philippines intensified its response by conducting coast guard drills in the exclusive economic zone (EEZ) it claims and by expanding patrols by the Area Task Force-West, which includes naval vessels. It also lobbied the international community for cooperation, with National Security Advisor Hermogenes Esperon holding a teleconference with U.S. National Security

Chinese fishing vessels tightly anchored around the Whitsun Reef as photographed by the Philippine government in March 2021 (Photo courtesy of the Philippine government/Kyodo)

Advisor Jake Sullivan during which they confirmed that the two countries would work together to address the issue.[99]

China expanded its area of activities in May,[100] making the Philippines' on-the-ground response more difficult. In June, the United States then decided to allow arms sales to the Philippines despite opposition from some members of Congress, and in July, which marked the fifth anniversary of the aforementioned arbitral award, Secretary of State Blinken issued a statement upholding the U.S. Position on Maritime Claims in the South China Sea press statement originally released in July 2020, demonstrating that the United States has taken a position of shared interest with the Philippines.[101]

However, there has been no change to the Duterte administration's basic stance of seeking a peaceful resolution to the South China Sea issue through diplomatic means. In May, following Secretary of Foreign Affairs Teodoro L. Locsin Jr.'s vilification of China over social media and out of concern for an unintended spread of anti-Chinese sentiment, President Duterte prohibited members of his cabinet from making any independent remarks on the situation in the South China Sea. Then, in the last administrative policy speech of his term to Congress that July, he reiterated the legitimacy of his administration's stance of not taking hard-line measures against China in light of the gap in military capacity. Meanwhile, President Duterte expressed his support for the arbitral award in his speech to the UN General Assembly that September as he had done the previous year, maintaining his position that there would be no compromise on the issue.[102]

Although China has been exacerbating tensions in the South China Sea, it has also been conducting so-called "vaccine diplomacy" targeted at Southeast Asian nations, including the Philippines, to which the United States has responded by also providing more active support through supplies of additional vaccines. While international cooperation on vaccine supply was underway via the COVAX Facility in 2020 amidst COVID-19's global spread, developing countries, including the Philippines, were not poised to be able to secure sufficient quantities of the vaccines developed by Western companies. Under these circumstances, China announced plans to provide its own vaccine, later known as the Sinovac vaccine, and the Philippines began supply discussions with China at the end of the year.[103] The Philippine Food and Drug Administration (FDA) then authorized Sinovac among other COVID-19 vaccines for emergency use under an Executive Order with vaccinations using Sinovac beginning in the country thereafter. Meanwhile, the United States pledged that May to supply countries in need, including its allies, with additional vaccines, and announced that it would provide nearly one million doses to the Philippines.[104]

Just as the reasons behind the Philippines' decision to terminate the VFA have not been made public, neither have the reasons behind the reversal, though in August of that year, President Duterte did state, for example, that the reversal on the decision was in return for the supply of vaccines. As such, the reversal is thought to have resulted from a pragmatic judgement regarding the effectiveness of U.S. support as an ally, including on the situation in the South China Sea.

With the pending issue surrounding the VFA resolved, there has been increased correspondence between U.S. and Philippine government and military officials. Defense Secretary Austin visited the Philippines in July as part of his previously mentioned tour of Southeast Asia, Philippine Secretary of Foreign Affairs Locsin visited the United States in September where he met with Secretary of State Blinken, and that same month, General David H. Berger, commandant of the Marine Corps, visited the Philippines to meet with senior military officials. In October, it was further reported that President Duterte also wished to pay a visit to the United States.[105]

3. Southeast Asian Countries Driving Defense Industry Investment: Equipment Development and Economic Promotion

(1) Thailand

Countries across Southeast Asia are promoting their domestic defense industries through a variety of measures, such as by encouraging investment and increasing their rates of domestic production.

Thailand has traditionally engaged in joint ventures when procuring armaments from abroad on a case-by-case basis in an aim to transfer technology and increase its rate of domestic production as part of its offset policy. In January 2021, however, the Thai Defence Technology Institute (DTI) unveiled a plan to improve the technological capabilities of Thailand's domestic defense industry and improve its export competitiveness by promoting joint ventures with private sector companies both domestic and foreign, developing domestically produced armaments, and providing cooperation to export businesses. DTI selected four priority areas of investment focused on the capabilities needed by the country's armed forces: unmanned aerial vehicles (UAVs), personal firearms, offshore patrol vessels (OPVs), and light tactical vehicles.[106] Until then, DTI had only been involved in the development of national military armaments up to the prototyping stage due to legal and financial constraints. With the enactment of the Defence Technology Act BE 2562 (2019), however, DTI is now able to collaborate with the private sector and thus can participate in equipment development through to the mass production phase.

The investment plan is seen as consistent with Thailand's national strategy of enhancing its domestic industry. Aerospace and defense has been designated as one of the 12 industrial sectors to receive preferential treatment in attracting investment for Thailand's Eastern Economic Corridor, aimed at advancing the structure of the country's industry, and various incentives have been prepared to promote direct foreign investment into the applicable sectors, including a relaxation of the existing 49% cap on said foreign investment.[107] In addition, a plan to create a new industrial park for the defense industry was announced in 2020, and the government is reportedly conducting a preliminary study on relocating a number of military and Ministry of Defence-related facilities to it. It is conceivable that the industrial park may also be linked to the investment plan by DTI.[108]

Of the four priority areas indicated by DTI, investment will be made into UAVs and personal firearms through a newly established corporation that will form joint ventures with both domestic and foreign private sector companies, and DTI will offer OPV and light tactical vehicle manufacturers its support and cooperation. The aforementioned corporation was set to be established and commence joint venture operations in FY2021.

In June, the Royal Thai Armed Forces reached an agreement with DTI to develop the new D-Eyes 04 UAV based on the CY-9 by the Beijing University of Aeronautics and Astronautics (Beihang) to replace the Israel Aerospace Industries (IAI) Searcher Mk.2 UAVs currently in operation. Beihang has been collaborating with DTI on UAV research and development since 2018, and signed a contract with the institute in June 2020 to provide Thailand's armed forces with UAV training systems.

In terms of personal firearms, DTI is reportedly developing the DTI-7 automatic rifle in collaboration with KHT Firearms.[109] According to reports, the Ministry of Defence worked with Narac Arms Industry and other companies to develop the AR-15 style MOD963 rifle for domestic production which has been deployed by some national army and police units, but the DTI-7 is said to be a lighter, shorter-barreled design that is more suited to soldiers' physiques and operational specifications.

In February 2020, DTI, the Royal Thai Navy, and the state enterprise Bangkok Dock Company agreed to collaborate on the Philippine Navy's OPV requirements, promoting exports to the country. The Philippines has plans to procure six OPVs, and in doing so is expected to seek support in shifting to domestic production as part of an offset agreement. In anticipation of this, Thailand signed an intergovernmental memorandum of understanding with the Philippines in March 2021 on expanding defense industry cooperation. However, Australia-based Austal, which operates a shipyard on the island of Cebu, is reported to be the frontrunner in negotiations for the program.[110]

The Philippine Army also plans to procure at least 200 light tactical vehicles as part of its military modernization program, and the First Win 2 developed by Thailand's Chaiseri is reported to be one of the strongest candidates. The procurement program is expected to involve an intergovernmental contract instead of going through a public tender, and DTI is likely to provide Chaiseri, a private company, with technical assistance in the export process and other related matters.

(2) Indonesia

In June 2021, Indonesia's Ministry of State-Owned Enterprises announced an initiative to establish a holding firm to integrate the country's defense-related state-owned companies, consolidating the management of ship manufacturer PAL, land-based military systems manufacturer Pindad, aerospace company PTDI, and ammunition and explosives provider Dahana under electronic equipment manufacturer Len Industri as the parent company. The scheme is thought to be aimed at expanding the scale of the country's defense-related businesses and promoting collaboration among companies in the field of arms development, an area that is growing more sophisticated and systematized technologically. As with the medium weight tank Harimau development program between Pindad and Turkish manufacturer FNSS, the initiative is expected to drive domestic production of major weapons platforms, though for the time being the management integration will reportedly proceed in stages with project management offices established to oversee seven management functions including finance, marketing, and R&D.[111] The transition to a holding firm-based system is not projected to result in any major changes to the government's control,[112] and private investment is still not permitted as before.[113] In July, Minister of State-Owned Enterprises Erick Thohir explained that he was awaiting agreement from the relevant ministries on the scheme. In December, however, the government regulations surrounding the establishment of state-owned electronics companies were amended which led to the plan to make Len Industri a de facto holding firm for defense-related companies being approved.

In May, speaking to the need to reinforce the foundation of Indonesia's defense industry, Minister of Defense Prabowo Subianto told the Defense Industrial Policy Committee that they must tighten regulations surrounding the rate of domestic production and promote investment into the country as part of its offset policy. RI Law number 16 of 2012 on the Defense Industry states that when procuring major defense equipment from abroad, at least 50% of the value must be paid via countertrade transaction and at least 35% of the value must be offset via offset agreements including domestic production and technology transfers in order to counteract the outflow of foreign currency, but application of the law is said to have lacked consistency thus far.[114]

In addition to promoting such measures to strengthen the foundation of its defense industry, Indonesia also undertook a review of its plan to modernize its military by procuring new armaments. At the end of 2020, the Ministry of Defense prepared a revision to its Strategic Plan, which will reportedly undergo consideration by the House of Representatives. The new Strategic Plan calls for a complete review of the military's tactics and capacities in line with the evolution of the so-called Fourth Industrial Revolution.[115] In June 2021, a document purported to be the draft Presidential Regulation on Fulfilling the Need for Defense and Security Equipment of the Ministry of Defense and the Indonesian National Army for 2020–2024 was leaked to the media.[116] The document is said to stipulate equipment acquisitions for the first phase (2020–2024) of a five-phase, 25-year long-term strategy to modernize Indonesia's military amounting to a total of 1,785 trillion rupiah in investments. The first phase also coincides with the final phase of the three-phase, 15-year Minimum Essential Force (MEF) program that began in 2010. The total breaks down to 1,130 trillion rupiah for defense equipment, 458 trillion for maintenance and improvements, and the remaining 186 trillion is earmarked for interest payments on external debt, meaning that over 10% of the investment budget is allocated to paying interest. This ties back to Indonesia's lasting dependency on foreign countries to procure equipment, and is thought to be a factor behind the country's efforts to strengthen the competitiveness of its domestic defense industry by integrating its management and promote domestic production through offset policies.[117]

In the final phase of the aforementioned MEF program, the Air Force has expected to see a significant budget increase that included the procurement of F-16Vs; the Navy has been projected to procure four OPVs and three dock landing ships; and the Army has expected to procure medium weight Harimau tanks described previously.[118] With such a large procurement program planned, Indonesia's defense budget for FY2021 came to a total of 136.99 trillion rupiah, a 16.2% increase year-over-year, with 42.6 trillion allocated to military modernization. Three consecutive years of budget cuts are planned for 2022 through 2024, however, and the defense budget for FY2022 finalized in August 2021 came to a total of 134.11 trillion, down approximately 2% over the previous year.[119]

(3) Malaysia

Malaysia is developing a policy of promoting its national economy by bolstering local venders, including small and medium enterprises, as it simultaneously improves its domestic defense industry's R&D capabilities. The country's Defence White Paper, released in December 2019, proposed five initiatives to promote the defense industry: 1) Enhancing the economic strategic framework for defense science, technology, and industry, focusing on niche sectors; 2) Restructuring organizations related to the defense industry; 3) Establishing a Defence and Security Investment Committee; 4) Stimulating R&D and innovation through sustainable funding; and 5) strengthening talent development programs.[120] The overall defense budget for FY2021 released in November 2020 came to 15.86 billion ringgit, growing roughly 1.8% over the previous year, with development spending seeing a substantial 46.1% year-over-year increase to 4.5 billion.[121] The FY2022 defense budget grew again by approximately 1.8% to a total of 16.14 billion ringgit with development spending going up by about 12% to 5.04 billion, showing a steady increase in funding.

In his budget presentation to Parliament at the end of 2020, Senior Minister (Security Cluster) Ismail Sabri Yaakob outlined his plan to utilize the Science & Technology Research Institute for Defence (STRIDE) to promote cooperation with the private sector on R&D in the defense and security sector. While STRIDE's budget is reported to have increased considerably year by year reaching 26.3 million ringgit in 2021 and 40.7 million in 2022,[122] the total budget set for investment over the five years starting from 2021 came to 192 million and is expected to primarily be used for relatively small-scale programs.[123] One example of STIDE's collaboration in the domestic defense industry is the development of Mildef Technologies' MRAP Tarantula unveiled in February 2021. Having passed the first round of assessment testing by the Malaysian Army the following month, the vehicle is expected to be officially procured and begin mass production moving forward.[124]

In March 2021, Senior Minister Ismail Sabri said that the government is considering developing guidelines for the defense and security industry.[125] The guidelines are to focus not only on meeting military requirements but also on promoting the national economy and creating jobs, with the Industrial Collaboration Program (ICP) in government procurements, which the Defence White Paper suggested needs revitalization, cited as a means of implementing the guidelines.[126] The ICP, approved in 2014, added a new Economic Enhancement Program (EEP) calling for cooperation in training Malaysia's local vendors on top of the existing offset provisions for government procurement. For example, Airbus, which manufactures the A400M transport aircraft procured by the Royal Malaysian Air Force, is one of the companies in the defense and aerospace sector participating in the program and has expressed its commitment to supporting Malaysia's plans to launch a multi-mission telecommunications satellite.[127] Started from September 2021, the Technology Depository Agency (TDA), which is in charge of implementing the ICP, has required contractors to raise the rate of domestic production from the previous 30% to 40% and involve local vendors in the supply chain as part of a series of economic recovery strategies in response to the downturn caused by the COVID-19 pandemic. This measure applies to not just defense equipment but all government procurement.

After becoming prime minister in August following period of political turmoil, Ismail Sabri announced the Twelfth Malaysia Plan, 2021–2025 in September, which serves as a national economic and industrial blueprint, and further reiterated that the guidelines for the defense and security industry would be developed over that term.[128] In addition, he announced that one of the programs planned for the period would include the construction of a new air base in Bintulu, Sarawak as a forward operating base.[129] China has continuously dispatched vessels to engage in activity in the EEZ claimed by Malaysia that Bintulu faces, causing incidents such as in May 2021 when 16 People's Liberation Army Air Force aircraft including Il-76 and Y-20 multipurpose airlifters flew near the airspace above waters claimed by Malaysia, prompting the Royal Malaysian Air Force to scramble jets in response. The plan to construct a base is thus expected to contribute to Malaysia's maritime domain awareness and help strengthen the air force's operational capabilities in an area key to air defense. The aforementioned Defence White Paper also calls for three new air defense radar sites to be built by 2025, and the Ministry of Defence issued a request for information on surveillance radars for the air force in June in connection with this.[130]

(4) Philippines

In his inaugural speech, Lt. Gen. Jose Faustino Jr., who was appointed chief of staff of the Armed Forces of the Philippines (AFP) at the end of July 2021, pushed for the creation of a Center for Self-Reliant Defense Posture (SRDP) and expressed his view that domestic defense manufacturing capabilities would serve as the foundation of the SRDP program.[131] The Philippines has attempted to produce defense equipment domestically since 1988 as part of the program, but with the exception of select munitions such as firearms, many of its efforts failed, an unavoidable outcome given budget limitations and the lack of a viable domestic market to support the industry.[132] Nevertheless, a certain technical base capable of equipping and supporting a military force is required for stable operations, and in March 2019, President Duterte issued an Executive Order transferring the Philippine Aerospace Development Corporation from the Department of Transportation's purview to the Department of National Defense (DND).[133] Later in November, Secretary of National Defense Delfin Lorenzana further stated at a ceremony commemorating the 80th anniversary of DND's founding that he hopes the country will possess a defense industry of reasonable size by the end of

President Duterte's term in 2022. A draft of the Defense Industry Development Act of 2019 was also submitted to Congress that year proposing to establish a regulatory agency to promote domestic production and technology transfers, but the bill did not pass.[134]

In order to overcome this predicament, the Philippines has been advancing efforts to strengthen its national defense posture in recent years by invoking existing measures that are aimed at achieving economic growth by converting military-held assets for commercial use.[135] In February 2021, the House of Representatives passed the House Bill on the Special Defense Economic Zone backing plans to ease restrictions on arms production, convert Camp General Antonio Luna in the Province of Bataan and other sites into special defense economic zones, and build defense industrial complexes in order to promote the defense industry.[136] Such economic zones are expected to offer incentives in terms of investment visas for foreign investors and the rates of domestic production required with respect to government procurement. Two South Korean munitions manufacturers began operations at the Government Arsenal at Camp General Antonio Luna in July 2019 and it was expected that the law, if passed, would proactively accept private sector investment both domestically and from abroad to develop industrial clusters, but the Senate is unlikely to vote on the law by the end of 2021.

In May 2021, Director General Charito Plaza of the Philippine Economic Zone Authority (PEZA), which falls under the jurisdiction of the Department of Trade and Industry (DTI), said that PEZA is aiming for the bill to pass during President Duterte's term of office and will proceed with plans to convert military reservation areas in Fort Bonifacio, partially developed as a business district in Metro Manila, Camp Evangelista, home to the 4th Infantry Division headquarters in Cagayan de Oro, the regional center of Northern Mindanao, and military reservations in the Province of Maguindanao for commercial use, with other military-owned sites also under consideration. In July, PEZA and the AFP then signed a memorandum of agreement guiding the effective utilization of these military reservations.[137]

Effective utilization under the plan includes not only arsenals, aircraft MRO and ship repair facilities, and other defense-related industries, but also information and food industry clusters as well as tourist and residential areas with the prospect of developing the reservations for an array of uses and purposes.[138] Meanwhile, in areas such as the Province of Maguindanao where anti-government terrorist organizations such as the Bangsamoro Islamic Freedom Fighters (BIFF) have been operating since the autonomous Bangsamoro government was established, causing delays in economic development and unstable security situations, the conversion of military reservations is believed to be aimed at creating jobs to indirectly facilitate regional stability more than promoting the defense industry.

Despite being growth drivers for the domestic defense industry, significant cuts were made to the defense budget and equipment spending in 2020 in order to fund the government's extraordinary budget for its stimulus package. This has made it unlikely that the equipment procurements planned for the second phase of the Philippine's military modernization plan (2018–2022) will be met. The FY2021 defense budget, though, allocated approximately 33 billion pesos for equipment spending, a 32% increase year-over-year, and in May the Department of Budget and Management approved an allotment of approximately 12 billion pesos for the second phase of the plan.[139] Major programs funded by the allotment included a ground-based air defense system and medium-lift transport aircraft based on the C295 for the Philippine Air Force as well as a light tank development program led by the Israeli defense manufacturer Elbit Systems. However, Secretary of National Defense Lorenzana has stated that plans to procure combat jets that were expected to begin during phase two are still currently underway, and as such the procurement of said jets may be postponed to the phase three (2023–2028) or thereafter.[140]

Having developed into middle-income countries as a result of economic growth, the nations described in this section are now aiming to develop their own locally produced armaments and promote their domestic defense industries in tandem with their military modernization efforts. This is seen as a response to their current dependence on foreign imports for much of their modern equipment, aiming to gradually increase both their technological capabilities and strategic autonomy at the same time by promoting import substitution.

NOTES

1) [Japan] Ministry of Foreign Affairs (MFA), "General Election Held in Myanmar (Statement by Foreign Press Secretary Yoshida Tomoyuki)" (November 9, 2020).

2) [Myanmar] Tatmadaw Information Team, "Myanmar Tatmadaw's Response" (January 31, 2021).

3) [Myanmar] The Office of the President, "Order No. 1/2021" (February 1, 2021).

4) [Myanmar] Commander-in-Chief of Defence Services (CCDS), "Notification No. 1/2021" (February 1, 2021).

5) [Myanmar] CCDS, "Notification No. 9/2021" (February 2, 2021).

6) *Irrawaddy* (online), July 27, 2021; *Straits Times* (online), July 26, 2021; Jiji Press, July 27, 2021.

7) [Myanmar] State Administrative Council (SAC), "Formation of Provisional Government of the Republic of the Union of Myanmar, Order No. 152/2021" (August 1, 2021).

8) *Global New Light of Myanmar*, August 2, 2021.

9) Reuters, February 1, 2021.

10) [Myanmar] Committee Representing Pyidaungsu Hluttaw (CRPH), "Statement by the Representatives of the Pyidaungsu Hluttaw (National League for Democracy) (2/2021)" (February 5, 2021).

11) *Irrawaddy* (online), February 22, 2021.

12) Jiji Press, May 11, 2021.

13) Assistance Association for Political Prisoners, "Daily Briefing in Relation to the Military Coup," December 31, 2021.

14) [Myanmar] CRPH, "Appointment of Acting Union Ministers, Announcement No. 11/2021" (March 2, 2021); Twitter, @CrphMyanmar, March 9, 2021.

15) [Myanmar] CRPH, "Federal Democracy Charter, Announcement No.19/2021" (March 31, 2021).

16) [Myanmar] CRPH, "Formation of the National Unity Government, Announcement No.23/2021 and 24/2021" (April 16, 2021).

17) [Myanmar] SAC, "Announcement for CRPH that Commits High Treason and its Organizations" (March 5, 2021).

18) *Irrawaddy* (online), March 18, 2021.

19) Eleven News, March 22, 2021.

20) Reuters, April 21, 2021; Jiji Press, April 23, 2021.

21) [Myanmar] National Unity Government, "Announcement of the Establishment of People's Defence Force, Notification 1/2021" (May 5, 2021).

22) Eleven News, May 9, 2021.

23) Radio Free Asia (RFA) (Burmese), July 13, 2021.

24) Jiji Press, July 1, 2021; RFA, May 25, 2021; RFA, September 1, 2021.

25) *Asahi Shimbun*, September 27, 2021.

26) United Nations Office for the Coordination of Humanitarian Affairs (UNOCHA), "Statement from ERC Martin Griffiths regarding the Increasing Violence and Humanitarian Need in Myanmar" (November 8, 2021).

27) Jiji Press, September 13, 2021; *Asahi Shimbun* (online), September 27, 2021.

28) *Bangkok Post* (online), December 26, 2021.

29) United Nations High Commissioner for Refugees, "Global Focus: Asia Pacific."

30) CNN, December 7, 2021.

31) Matsuura Yoshihide and Tomikawa Hideo, "Southeast Asia: Readjusting External Relations," in *East Asian Strategic Review 2019*, English edition, ed. National Institute for Defense Studies (NIDS) (Tokyo: NIDS, 2019), 117-120.

32) NHK, August 23, 2021.

33) UNOCHA, "Statement from ERC Martin Griffiths regarding the Increasing Violence and Humanitarian Need in Myanmar."

34) The White House, "Statement by President Joseph R. Biden, Jr. on the Situation in Burma" (February 1, 2021).

35) [U.S.] Department of State (DOS), "Briefing with Senior State Department Officials on the State Department's Assessment of Recent Events in Burma" (February 2, 2021).

36) [Japan] MFA, "G7 Foreign Ministers' Statement" (February 3, 2021).

37) Jiji Press, February 19, 2021.

38) [Japan] Joint Staff, "Joint Statement of Chiefs of Defense" (March 28, 2021); [Japan] Ministry of Defense, "Minister of Defense Kishi's Participation in the 8th ASEAN Defence Ministers' Meeting-Plus" (June 16, 2021).

39) Risk Advisory, "Myanmar Sanctions List," last updated on July 20, 2021.

40) [Japan] MFA, "Press Conference by Foreign Minister Motegi Toshimitsu" (May 21, 2021).

41) Reuters, March 12, 2021; *Guardian* (online), March 7, 2021.

42) [China] MFA, "Foreign Ministry Spokesperson Wang Wenbin's Regular Press Conference" (February 1, 2021).

43) United Nations Security Council, "Security Council Press Statement on Situation in

Myanmar" (February 4, 2021).

44) U.S. Mission to the United Nations, "Statement by the President of the Security Council on Myanmar" (March 10, 2021).

45) United Nations General Assembly, "General Assembly Reappoints Secretary-General to Second Five-Year Term, Adopting Resolution Condemning Lethal Violence by Myanmar's Armed Forces" (June 18, 2021).

46) *Nikkei Asia* (online), March 27, 2021.

47) Reuters, June 21, 2021.

48) [China] MFA, "Wang Yi Meets with Myanmar's Foreign Minister U Wunna Maung Lwin" (June 8, 2021).

49) *Irrawaddy* (online), November 22, 2021.

50) [U.S.] DOS, "Deputy Secretary Sherman's Call with Zin Mar Aung" (August 4, 2021).

51) Reuters, August 5, 2021.

52) UN News, "General Assembly Defers Decision on Afghanistan and Myanmar Seats," December 6, 2021.

53) ASEAN Secretariat, "ASEAN Chairman's Statement on the Developments in the Republic of the Union of Myanmar" (February 1, 2021).

54) ASEAN Secretariat, "Chair's Statement on the Informal ASEAN Ministerial Meeting (IAMM)" (March 2, 2021).

55) *Nikkei Shimbun* (online), March 2, 2021.

56) BBC, March 2, 2021; [Singapore] MFA, "PM Lee on the Situation in Myanmar at the Interview with BBC for Talking Business Asia" (March 2, 2021).

57) ASEAN Secretariat, "Chairman's Statement on the ASEAN Leaders' Meeting" (April 24, 2021).

58) Kyodo News, July 6, 2021; AP News, August 2, 2021.

59) Twitter, @SecBlinken, August 5, 2021; [China] MFA, "Wang Yi Speaks with Special Envoy of ASEAN to Myanmar and Bruneian Second Minister of Foreign Affairs Erywan bin Pehin Yusof on the Phone" (August 18, 2021); United Nations, "Secretary-General Welcomes ASEAN's Appointment of Special Envoy on Myanmar, Saying United Nations Expects Continuing Cooperation in Quest for Coherent Response" (August 4, 2021).

60) Reuters, October 14, 2021.

61) [Brunei] MFA, "Statement of the Chair of the ASEAN Foreign Ministers' Meeting" (October 16, 2021).

62) *Myawady News*, date unknown; Aljazeera, October 18, 2021.

63) [Myanmar] MFA, "Press Release" (October 22, 2021).

64) ASEAN Secretariat, "Chairman's Statement of the 38th and 39th ASEAN Summits"

(October 26, 2021).

65) Reuters, November 3, 2021.

66) ASEAN Secretariat, *Charter of the Association of Southeast Asian Nations* (November 2020).

67) [Thailand] MFA, "Prime Minister Prayut Chan-o-cha to Attend the 25th ASEAN Summit and Related Summits in Nay Pyi Taw, Republic of the Union of Myanmar" (November 4, 2014).

68) Twitter, @Menlu_RI, October 15, 2021; Reuters, October 21, 2021.

69) Jiji Press, October 20, 2021.

70) *Phnom Penh Post*, December 7, 2021.

71) *Global New Light of Myanmar*, December 9, 2021.

72) ASEAN Secretariat, "Press Release by the Chairman of the ASEAN Foreign Ministers' Retreat" (January 21, 2021).

73) ASEAN Secretariat, "Joint Communiqué of the 54th ASEAN Foreign Ministers' Meeting" (August 2, 2021).

74) *South China Morning Post (SCMP)*, July 13, 2021.

75) ASEAN Secretariat, "Chairman's Statement of the 38th and 39th ASEAN Summits."

76) ASEAN Secretariat, "Chairman's Statement of the 36th ASEAN Summit" (June 26, 2020); ASEAN Secretariat, "Chairman's Statement of the 37th ASEAN Summit" (November 12, 2020).

77) ASEAN Secretariat, "Chairman's Statement of the 11th East Asia Summit (EAS) Foreign Ministers' Meeting" (August 4, 2021).

78) [U.S.] DOS, "Secretary Blinken's Participation in the East Asia Summit Foreign Ministers' Meeting" (August 4, 2021); [China] MFA, "Wang Yi Stresses 'Four Respects' on South China Sea Issue" (August 5, 2021).

79) The White House, "Readout of President Biden's Participation in the East Asia Summit" (October 27, 2021); [China] MFA, "Li Keqiang Attends the 16th East Asia Summit" (October 28, 2021); ASEAN Secretariat, "Chairman's Statement of the 16th East Asia Summit" (October 27, 2021).

80) [U.S.] DOS, "Secretary Blinken's Meeting with ASEAN Foreign Ministers and the ASEAN Secretary General" (July 14, 2021).

81) [U.S.] DOS, "Secretary Blinken's Remarks on a Free and Open Indo-Pacific" (December 13, 2021).

82) [China] MFA, "Wang Yi Attends the ASEAN-China Ministerial Meeting" (August 3, 2021).

83) *SCMP* (online), October 13, 2020.

84) [China] MFA, "Foreign Ministry Spokesperson Zhao Lijian's Regular Press Conference on July 13, 2021" (July 13, 2021).

85) ASEAN Secretariat, "Co-Chairs' Statement on the Special ASEAN-China Foreign Ministers' Meeting in Celebration of the 30th Anniversary of the Dialogue Relations" (June 7, 2021).

86) ASEAN Secretariat, "Chairman's Statement of the ASEAN Post Ministerial Conference (PMC) 10+1 Sessions with the Dialogue Partners" (August 3-6, 2021).

87) ASEAN Secretariat, "Chairman's Statement of the 38th and 39th ASEAN Summits."

88) Government of the United Kingdom, "Britain Extends Global Defence Reach" (December 12, 2016); Government of the United Kingdom, *Global Britain in a Competitive Age: the Integrated Review of Security, Defence, Development and Foreign Policy* (March 16, 2021).

89) Government of the United Kingdom, "Press Release: UK Becomes Dialogue Partner of the Association of Southeast Asian Nations" (August 5, 2021).

90) [France] Ministry for the Armed Force (MAF), *France's Defence Strategy in the Indo-Pacific* (June 2019); [France] Ministry for Europe and Foreign Affairs, *France's Indo-Pacific Strategy* (July 2021).

91) [France] MAF, "Dossier de presse_Mission JEANNE D'ARC 2021" (March 22, 2021).

92) *Naval News*, April 6, 2021; Antara News, April 8, 2021.

93) [U.K.] Royal Navy, "Carrier Strike Group Deployment to Visit 40 Countries," April 26, 2021.

94) Asia Pacific Defence Reporter (online), July 10, 2021.

95) [Germany] Federal Government, *Progress report on the implementation of the German Government policy guidelines on the Indo-Pacific region* (September 6, 2021).

96) [Germany] Federal Ministry of Defence, "The EU and ASEAN Share an Interest in the Indo-Pacific Region" (December 9, 2020); *Vietnam Plus*, December 9, 2020.

97) *Defense News*, August 2, 2021.

98) [Japan] MFA, "Saikin no firipin josei to nichi-firipin kankei" [The recent situation in the Philippines and Japan-Philippines relations] (August 12, 2021).

99) U.S. Embassy Manila, "Statement by National Security Council Spokesperson Horne on National Security Advisor Sullivan Call with National Security Advisor Esperon" (April 5, 2021).

100) Bloomberg, May 12, 2021; *Philippine Star*, May 12, 2021.

101) [U.S.] DOS, "Press Statement: Fifth Anniversary of the Arbitral Tribunal Ruling on the South" (July 11, 2021).

102) Reuters, May 18, 2021.

Chapter 5

Southeast Asia

103) *Nikkei Asia* (online), March 1, 2021; *Manila Bulletin*, May 6, 2021.

104) *Rappler*, June 22, 2021.

105) PNA, October 1, 2021.

106) *Bangkok Post* (online), December 29, 2020.

107) *Bangkok Post* (online), June 24, 2020.

108) *New Straits Times* (online), February 22, 2020; *Jane's*, June 25, 2020.

109) *Jane's*, September 3, 2021; *Army Recognition*, March 9, 2021.

110) *Jane's*, March 4, 2021.

111) *Kompas* (online), May 6, 2021.

112) CNBC Indonesia, July 28, 2021.

113) *Jane's*, June 16, 2021.

114) *Jane's*, May 24, 2021.

115) *Tribun News*, November 9, 2020.

116) *Kontan*, June 1, 2021.

117) Voice of Indonesia, June 2, 2021.

118) *Jane's*, December 10, 2019.

119) *Jane's*, August 25, 2021.

120) [Malaysia] Ministry of Defence, "Defence White Paper: A Secure, Sovereign and Prosperous Malaysia" (February, 2020).

121) *Malay Mail* (online), November 7, 2020.

122) *Sinar Harian* (online), October 31, 2021.

123) *New Straits Times* (online), December 14, 2020.

124) *New Straits Times* (online), February 11, 2021.

125) *Malay Mail* (online), March 3, 2021.

126) *Jane's*, March 4, 2021.

127) *New Straits Times* (online), February 22, 2021.

128) Bernama, September 27, 2021.

129) Bernama, September 27, 2021.

130) *Jane's*, June 2, 2021.

131) *Manila Bulletin* (online), July 31, 2021.

132) Ava Patricia C. Avila, "Philippines' Defence Build-Up: Revival of the Self-Reliant Posture," S. Rajaratnam School of International Studies Commentaries 125/2012 (July 12, 2012).

133) *Philippine Daily Inquirer* (online), March 21, 2019.

134) *Philippine Daily Inquirer* (online), November 21, 2019.

135) PNA, December 9, 2017; PNA, July 7, 2018; *Philippine Star*, July 8, 2018.

136) ABS-CBN News, February 4, 2021.

137) Business Mirror (online), February 29, 2020.

138) PNA, July 30, 2021; *Manila Bulletin*, July 31, 2021.

139) *Jane's*, May 11, 2021.

140) PNA, September 16, 2021.

Chapter 5 Southeast Asia

Chapter 6

Russia

The New National Security Strategy and Development of Paramilitary Organizations

HASEGAWA Takeyuki (Lead author, Sections 1 and 2)
SAKAGUCHI Yoshiaki (Section 3)

Summary

On July 2, 2021, the National Security Strategy of the Russian Federation, the highest standing strategic document in modern Russia, was revised for the first time in approximately five and a half years. The document sees international order "at a turning point" and perceives Russia as being in a strategic environment in which "the strengthening positions of new global and regional leaders are changing the fabric of the world order." On top of this, it lays out the country's strategic priorities to ensure its position as one center in a multipolar world, i.e., as a bearer of the international order. Russia further shows a tendency toward augmenting the presence of not only the country's military but also Coast Guard vessels from the Border Service of the Federal Security Service (FSB) in the Arctic, a region of strategic focus for Russia in terms of climate security, liquified natural gas (LNG) development, and the establishment of sea routes. Section 1 will focus on Russia's paramilitary organizations operating across a broad spectrum, from security and rescue at sea to counter-terrorist special operations ashore, and will examine the country's efforts to enhance said capacities. Section 2 will provide an overview of new political developments following Russia's 2020 constitutional reforms with a particular focus on the State Duma elections in September 2021. While no major changes have been seen in the system of single-party dominance led by the United Russia party, noteworthy are movements by the political elite and opposition networks in the run-up to the next presidential election from the perspective of the "Post-Putin" issue.

Section 3 analyzes the principles of Russian military behavior, concentrating on policy documents, movements to modernize equipment, and military-technical cooperation. In December 2020, Russia formulated its New Defense Program that will further modernize the Russian military with strategic nuclear forces at its core. In response to the Russian military leadership's perception of increased U.S. and NATO military activity on the country's periphery, the Russian military has been putting effort into improving its response capabilities on each strategic front, and Pacific Fleet exercises have intensified. In addition, Russia is seeking to further strengthen military cooperation through the Collective Security Treaty Organization (CSTO) and the Shanghai Cooperation Organisation (SCO). This stems from Russia's concerns that instability in Afghanistan following the withdrawal of U.S. and NATO troops will have repercussions in the Central Asia region. Russian arms exports also remain high as the country is seen moving to further strengthen military-technical cooperation with Middle Eastern and Southeast Asian countries.

An ice-breaking LNG carrier entering Sabetta Port located on Russia's Yamal Peninsula (Reuters/ Kyodo)

Keywords

National Security Strategy   Border Service of the FSB   Joint Sea 2021
Zapad 2021   Shanghai Cooperation Organisation (SCO)

1. Approval of the New National Security Strategy

(1) Modern Russia's General Coordination Mechanism for Strategic Planning

On July 2, 2021, President Vladimir Putin approved an updated version of the National Security Strategy of the Russian Federation (NSS 2021), the first revision to the country's highest standing strategic document in approximately five and a half years.[1] The Security Strategy covers a wide range of policy areas, from military security and foreign policy to educational, social, and economic affairs, with policy documents including the Military Doctrine (revised December 2014), the Foreign Policy Concept (revised November 2016), and Fundamentals of the State Border Policy (revised April 2018) formulated on individual issues.[2] The federal law On Strategic Planning in the Russian Federation enacted in June 2014 mandates the National Security Strategy be revised every six years and legally defines the leadership role of the Security Council of the Russian Federation (hereinafter, "Security Council") in strategic planning.[3]

As a cross-disciplinary bureaucratic coordination mechanism is an essential element in revising the Security Strategy, the Security Council, which sits at the core of overall coordination, has established the Interdepartmental Commission on Strategic Planning (hereinafter, "Commission on Strategic Planning"). As shown in Table 6.1, the Commission on Strategic Planning is comprised of deputy ministers and deputy heads of various ministries and agencies, chaired by Secretary of the Security Council Nikolai Patrushev (President Putin's closest aide). It is responsible for assessing internal and external threats to national security that could impact social and/or economic development and offering proposals on the formulation of and amendments to the National Security Strategy and special federal (national) programs.[4] In addition, members of the subcommittees established in the Scientific Council of the Security Council,[5] such as the Strategic Planning Subcommittee, assist in formulating and evaluating policies from an academic perspective and legitimize those policies.

Table 6.1. Structure of the Interdepartmental Commission of the Security Council of the Russian Federation on Strategic Planning

Authorized by Presidential Decree No. 37 dated January 19, 2013 (revised November 10, 2018)		
Commission chair Secretary of the Security Council		
Vice chair Deputy secretary of the Security Council	**Secretary** Director general-level of the Security Council Secretariat	

<Commission Structure>

Federal executive bodies under jurisdiction of the president First deputy minister, Ministry of Internal Affairs; First deputy minister (deputy minister), Ministry of Civil Defense, Emergencies and Disaster Relief; Deputy minister, Ministry of Foreign Affairs; Deputy minister, Ministry of Justice; First deputy chief (deputy chief), General Staff of the Armed Forces; First deputy head (Deputy head), Foreign Intelligence Service (SVR); Deputy director, Federal Security Service (FSB); Deputy director, Federal National Guard Service (Rosgvardiya)

Federal executive bodies under jurisdiction of the chairman of the government (the prime minister) Deputy minister, Ministry of Science and Higher Education; Deputy minister, Ministry of Education; Deputy minister, Ministry of Finance; Deputy minister, Ministry of Economic Development

■ Deputy head, Presidential Control Directorate; Deputy chief, Presidential Domestic Policy Directorate; Deputy chief, Presidential Experts' Directorate of the Presidential Administration; Chief secretary-level, Security Council Secretariat

■ Deputy presidential plenipotentiary envoys to the Central, Northwestern, Southern, North Caucasian, Volga, Ural, Siberian, and Far Eastern Federal Districts

■ Deputy chief of staff, Federal Government

○ Vice president, Russian Academy of Sciences (by consent)

○ Auditor, Accounts Chamber of the Russian Federation

Source: Compiled by the author based on Указ Президента РФ от 19 января 2013г., № 37 (ред. от 10 ноября 2018г.), «Об утверждении состава Межведомственной комиссии Совета Безопасности Российской Федерации по проблемам стратегического планирования по должностям», *Собрание Законодательства Российской Федерации, 21 января 2013г., № 3, ст. 180.*

However, even under such a systematic design, a consistent and structured set of policy documents has by no means been developed. To this end, the Foundations of State Policy of the Russian Federation in the Field of Strategic Planning was approved by Presidential Decree on November 8, 2021, which laid out measures for codifying a set of policy documents, including on the interrelation between bodies of public power led by the president and the balance between ensuring military security and economic development.[6] As Moscow prepares to revise the Military Doctrine, the Foreign Policy Concept, and other policy documents that concern military security and foreign policy, attention will be paid to the overall coordinating function of the Kremlin, the symbol of Russia's "strong presidential system," amidst the political dynamics surrounding the interests of the military and security agencies supporting the Putin administration, so-called *siloviki* forces, and liberal forces adept at economic and fiscal policy.

(2) Russian Conservatism and Patriotism in Strategic Documents

The National Security Strategy was reportedly scheduled to be revised in 2020.[7] Yet the overall revision process is thought to have been delayed due to major changes in the strategic environment surrounding Russia, including the global spread of the novel coronavirus disease (COVID-19) and the advent of the Joseph Biden administration in the United States.

The 2021 NSS follows the basic structure of the 2015 version, comprised of Chapter I, General Provisions; Chapter II, Russia in the Modern World: Trends and Possibilities; Chapter III, National Interests and Strategic National Priorities; Chapter IV, Ensuring National Security; and Chapter V, Organizational Foundations and Mechanisms for Implementing this Strategy.

That said, Chapter III replaced "Culture" (2015 version) with "Defense of Traditional Russian Spiritual and Moral Values and Preservation of Culture and Historical Memory" (2021 version) as one of the nine strategic priorities presented. The 2021 NSS version of the chapter notes that "fundamental ethical and cultural norms, religious foundations, the institution of marriage, and family values have been subjected to increasingly devastating influences" (paragraph 85), then recognizing that "Russia's traditional spiritual, moral, cultural, and historic values are under active attack by the United States and its allies, multinational corporations, foreign NPOs and NGOs, religious organizations, extremist organizations, and terrorist organizations" (paragraph 87). From the perspective of defending Russia's traditional spiritual and moral values, this shows a firmer sense of caution toward Western values surrounding gender and diverse familial structures as compared to the 2015 NSS. Paragraph 88 also uses stronger language on the issue of historical perception than the 2015 version, evidenced by the description of increasing attempts to alter Russian and world history, distort historical truth, and subvert historical memory.

The establishment of new conservative and patriotic provisions as part of the large-scale constitutional reforms in 2020 was likely behind this policy direction. In addition to preserving Russia's traditional family model and the institution of marriage, the constitutional reforms stipulate that the state "honors the memory of defenders of the Fatherland and protects historical truth." With these new constitutional principles heavily reflected in strategic documents, Russia's future diplomacy will likely focus on the conflict over liberal values with advanced democracies, particularly in Western Europe, as well as the issue of historical perception between Russia and the countries that fought during World War II.[8]

(3) Russia's Perception of Its Strategic Environment

(i) Perspective on International Order

Chapter II, Russia in the Modern World: Trends and Possibilities (NSS 2021), presents Russia's perception of its strategic environment, noting that international order is "at a turning point" and that "the increasing number of centers (*tsenter*) of worldwide economic and political development and the strengthening positions of new global and regional leaders are changing the fabric of the world order, forming new architectures, rules, and principles for the international structure" (paragraph 6). While the 2015 NSS expressed that Russia is "shaping a multipolar world" regarding international order (paragraph 7), the 2021 NSS depicts a perspective on order stating that although "Western countries" are aiming to maintain hegemony,[9] the rise of emerging powers has brought about a "turning point" toward the multipolar world that Russia is pursuing.

At the same time, it emphasizes the rivalry between emerging and existing powers at said turning point, stating, "Increased geopolitical instability, rising conflicts, and intensifying tensions between nations have heightened the risk of use of military force […], and a series of countries have named Russia as a threat and even a military adversary. There is a growing danger that military conflicts will escalate into local or regional wars involving the participation of nuclear powers" (paragraph 17), while also referring to various aspects of military escalation in the era of competition amongst great powers, using the phrase "participation of nuclear powers." Chapter I, General Provisions of the Foundations of State Policy of the Russian Federation in the Area of Nuclear Deterrence approved on June 2, 2020 states that one of the state policies for nuclear deterrence is "the preclusion of the escalation of military actions" "in the event of an outbreak of a military conflict...and [their] cessation on conditions acceptable to the Russian Federation and [(or)] its allies."[10] (Brackets by author.) While careful consideration of Russia's so-called "escalate to de-escalate" (E2ED) policy[11] is needed based upon an examination of consistency across policy documents, including statements in the expected revision of the Military Doctrine as well as discussions by Russia's military leadership, the 2021 NSS

Table 6.2. Key points from the National Security Strategy of the Russian Federation (revised July 2, 2021)

National Security Strategy of the Russian Federation

- Modern Russia's perception of its strategic environment and perspective on international order
  ➡ World today at "a turning point"
- Strengthening positions of new global and regional leaders changing the fabric of the world order. New architectures, rules, and principles for the international structure being formed
- Traditional Russian spiritual and moral values emphasized following 2020 constitutional reforms
- Policy toward China
  ➡ Develop comprehensive partnership and relationship of strategic cooperation
- Policy toward India
  ➡ Develop highly privileged strategic partnership
- Build reliable mechanisms to ensure regional stability and security on a non-bloc basis in the Asia-Pacific region
- Growing concerns over climate change and the issue of environmental protection
  ➡ Used as pretext to establish control over transportation routes and obstruct Russia's development of the Arctic
- Focus on border protection and security, security of territorial waters, security of exclusive economic zones and the continental shelf, and modernization of border security infrastructure

Source: Compiled by the author based on Указ Президента РФ от 02 июля 2021г., № 400, «О Стратегии национальной безопасности Российской Федерации», *Собрание Законодательства Российской Федерации, 05 июл 2021г., № 27 (часть II), ст. 5351.*

demonstrates Russia's harsh perception of its strategic environment at this turning point in international order in which local and regional wars involving nuclear powers as actors may break out.

As with the 2015 NSS, the updated version of the document also expresses alarm toward interference in Russia's internal affairs with Western countries in mind, stating that "unfriendly countries are attempting to use Russia's social and economic problems to destroy Russia's domestic unity, incite and radicalize protest movements, and support fringe groups in Russian society" (paragraph 20).[12]

On the other hand, it refers to how "attempts to interfere in the internal affairs of the Russian Federation have been effectively thwarted" (paragraph 12) as a result of a series of military and social security policies by the current administration, further noting that "Russia has proven its ability to resist external pressure from sanctions" and that "the level of food and energy security has improved,"[13] exuding confidence in Russia's countermeasures (embargoes, etc.) against economic sanctions following the annexation of Crimea in 2014.

In fact, the emphasis of Russia's agricultural policy in recent years has shifted from import substitution policies and improving self-sufficiency to a policy of promoting exports in response to an overall increase in the country's self-sufficiency rate for commodities subject to import bans (meat and meat products, milk and dairy products, and vegetables).[14] Positioned as a fundamental national security strategic document,[15] the Food Security Doctrine was revised in January 2020,[16] taking an "aggressive stance" by setting forth policy to expand production in order to increase Russia's rate of self-sufficiency while developing its agricultural export potential.[17] Under Minister of Agriculture Dmitry Patrushev, eldest son of Secretary of the Security Council Patrushev, Russia's agricultural policy has been positioned as a strategic national priority with a view to securing Russia's status as one center in a multipolar world.

Overall, the document demonstrates Russia's perception that the international order has entered a new phase marking a turning point toward a multipolar world, and that in order for Russia to consolidate its influence as one such center, it is necessary to ensure not only military security but also economic security and enhance its national strength holistically as a sovereign state playing a leading role in said international order. On the other hand, Russia continues to be highly cautious of Western countries' political influence penetrating into Russia and the former Soviet bloc and has launched ideological countermeasures (conservative and patriotic policies) against interference in internal affairs, highlighting both its <u>confidence</u> and <u>concern</u> as a center of a multipolar world. (Underlines by author.)

(ii) Asia-Pacific Policy and Policies toward the United States, China, and India

With regard to its policy toward Asia, the 2021 NSS states that Russia will "develop a comprehensive partnership and relationship of strategic cooperation with the People's Republic of China alongside a highly privileged strategic partnership with the Republic of India, including the building in the Asia-Pacific region of reliable mechanisms to ensure regional stability and security on a non-bloc basis." It presents its direction for engaging in Asia-Pacific with policies toward China and India at the core, countries with which Russia has close military and economic ties. Since its inauguration in May 2012, the second Putin administration has advocated a policy of "shifting east" in its foreign economic relations and worked to strengthen ties with a wide range of Asian nations, a diplomatic stance that has been further reinforced by deteriorating relations with the United States and Europe in the wake of the annexation of Crimea in 2014. By bolstering bilateral economic and military ties with China and India and enhancing the function of multilateral frameworks such as the Shanghai Cooperation Organisation (SCO) while simultaneously engaging in active summit diplomacy with Turkey, a member of the North Atlantic Treaty Organization (NATO), the Putin administration has sought to build a multipolar international order in Eurasia.

From the perspective of strengthened trilateral relations between Russia, China, and India, and enhanced SCO coordination, this "shift east" in Russian diplomacy, i.e., its emphasis on the Asia-Pacific region, will have no minor impact on the foreign policies of Japan and the United States as well. While critical of the Free and Open Indo-Pacific (FOIP) vision,[18] Russia is expected to continue increasing its involvement in the Asia-Pacific/Indo-Pacific region as it seeks to build this multipolar international order in Eurasia on land and at sea.

In 2021, the 50th anniversary of the Indo-Soviet Treaty of Friendship and Cooperation, moves were seen toward strengthening Russia-India relations: in April, the leaders of both countries agreed to launch a 2+2 Dialogue between Foreign and Defense Ministers,[19] and at the Eastern Economic Forum held in Vladivostok that September, India's Prime Minister Narendra Modi delivered a video-address in which he pledged to strengthen cooperation in the areas of energy and transportation, including the Northern Sea Route.[20] India, a participant to the Quadrilateral Security Dialogue ("Quad") between Australia, India, Japan, and the United States, had already established 2+2 dialogues with the three countries, with Russia thus becoming its fourth 2+2 partner. In mid-November, Russia began supplying India with S-400 surface-to-air missile systems,[21] further increasing the momentum of military-technical cooperation between the two countries ahead of the Russia-India summit in December.

The summit, held in New Delhi, was President Putin's second foreign visit during the COVID-19 pandemic following the Russia-U.S. summit in Geneva that June. Russia and India signed 15 agreements as a result of their first 2+2 dialogue and the summit meeting, including a Long-Term Program for Military and Technical Cooperation for 2021 to 2031.[22] The agreements included local production of Russia-made AK-203 automatic rifles as part of the Make in India program to promote India's industry, and also laid out measures to strengthen Russia-India economic cooperation in the Russian

The Russia-India summit (©Press Information Bureau/Pib Pho/Planet Pix via ZUMA Press Wire/Kyodo News Images)

Far East.[23] (Underline by author.)

By attracting foreign investment in the Arctic LNG 2 project on the Gydan Peninsula in the Arctic, designing an LNG reloading terminal (floating LNG storage unit) on the Kamchatka Peninsula, and through the Vladivostok-Chennai Maritime Corridor, Russia is seeking to form its own order to tap into the expected future economic development of emerging Asian countries.

In the context, the U.S. Biden administration and European countries' involvement in the Indo-Pacific represents a national security concern for Russia. In September 2021, the EU announced the Joint Communication on the EU Strategy for Cooperation in the Indo-Pacific, noting that it "will seek to play a stronger role in the ASEAN security architecture and participate in the ASEAN Defence Ministers Meeting Plus (ADMM+) structure and the East Asia Summit."[24] The United Kingdom also deployed the Carrier Strike Group 21 (CSG21) led by HMS *Queen Elizabeth* to the Indo-Pacific, an example of how European countries are showing a heightened interest in Asia with China's growing presence in the international order in mind. On September 24, the second Leaders' Summit of the Quad was held in Washington, D.C., the first-ever done so in-person,[25] demonstrating the functional strengthening of multilateral frameworks in the Indo-Pacific region that include the United States.

As a new security pact between the United States, United Kingdom, and Australia, AUKUS in particular has the potential to bring about a major tectonic shift in the Indo-Pacific region. Russia along with China strongly opposes AUKUS, with President Putin expressing his displeasure by calling it a "closed alliance in the Pacific area that comprises the United States, United Kingdom, and Australia."[26] Russia has shown a strong sense of caution over Europe's logic surrounding international politics and is particularly concerned that the traditional pattern of confrontation between Russia and the United Kingdom will spread to Asia, a view it is coming into alignment with China in this regard.

Chinese-Russian cooperation on both the European and Asian fronts will be the subject of attention moving forward. Amid European countries' increasingly harsh perceptions of China, the Baltic state Lithuania saw the establishment of the Taiwanese Representative Office in Lithuania that serves as a local branch for Taiwanese authorities in the capital of Vilnius.[27] China strongly objected to the naming of the recently established entity and announced it would downgrade its diplomatic ties with Lithuania,[28] which has actually been distancing itself from China by withdrawing from the "17+1" cooperation forum between China and Central and Eastern European countries in May 2021. Alongside the Biden administration's Summit for Democracy held in December 2021, this series of events has offered a glimpse into the global regime contest between "authoritarian regimes" and "democratic regimes," and as China and Russia strengthen relations on political and military fronts, the perception of China by the three Baltic states, which have traditionally held a harsh view toward Russia, will likely be the object of focus as a new factor defining Russia-Europe relations.

The 2021 NSS also expressed alarm at the strengthened U.S. coalition network and military presence in Asia, noting in paragraph 36 that "the United States' planned deployment of short- and mid-range missiles in Europe and the Asia-Pacific region is a threat to strategic stability and international security." This caution is also evident in Russia's military activities in the Sea of Japan area. In July and October 2021, the Russian government gave notice that it would be conducting missile firing drills in the Sea of Japan around the Yamato Bank, with the Japan Coast Guard issuing marine safety navigational warnings on multiple occasions.[29] On October 6, the corvette *Gromkiy* conducted an anti-air combat drill in the Sea of Japan using the REDUT air defense missile system,[30] and on October 7, major vessels from the Pacific Fleet departed Vladivostok for a military exercise in the Sea of Japan.[31] On December 21, the state-of-the-art Borei-A class nuclear-powered ballistic missile submarine (SSBN) *Kynaz Oleg* and the multi-purpose nuclear-powered submarine *Novosibirsk* were delivered to the Russian Navy, both of which are scheduled to be deployed under the Pacific Fleet.[32] Russia is making steady progress in building its anti-access and area denial (A2/AD) capabilities while maintaining its second strike capabilities in the Sea of Okhotsk, further augmenting its naval capacity in the Russian Far East near Japan conscious of the United States and other countries' military presence in the Indo-Pacific.

From October 14 to 17, 2021, the 10th China-Russia joint naval exercise Joint Sea 2021 was held in the Sea of Japan for the first time in two years.[33] Following the exercise, Chinese and Russian vessels conducted their first joint maritime patrol by circling Japan, navigating through the Tsugaru Strait, the waters surrounding the Izu Islands, and the Osumi Strait,[34] demonstrating how joint China-Russia military operations in Japan's vicinity are intensifying.

Russian and Chinese strategic bombers further flew a joint patrol on November 19, 2021 (Figure 6.1).[35] While joint patrol flights between the two countries drew particular attention during the first such exercise in July 2019 when an A-50 early warning and control aircraft violated Japanese airspace over Takeshima in Shimane Prefecture on two occasions, this is now the third following a second exercise in December 2020 as they become institutionalized. During the recent patrol flight, Russian Tu-95 strategic bombers passing through Chinese airspace and Chinese H-6 strategic bombers that had taken off from Yanji Airport met over Mudanjiang in China, after which they crossed Russian airspace together and advanced to the Sea of Japan, showing a new development in the countries' military operations.

With Russian and Chinese naval vessels navigating through the Tsushima Strait on November 18, 2021, and a Chinese survey vessel intruding upon Japan's territorial waters (off the southern coast of Yakushima, Kagoshima Prefecture),[36] activity by both the Russian and Chinese militaries in Japan's vicinity is rapidly increasing. The China-Russia Joint Sea 2021

The China-Russia joint naval exercise Joint Sea 2021 (Xinhua/ Kyodo News Images)

Figure 6.1. The third China-Russia joint patrol flight (November 19, 2021)

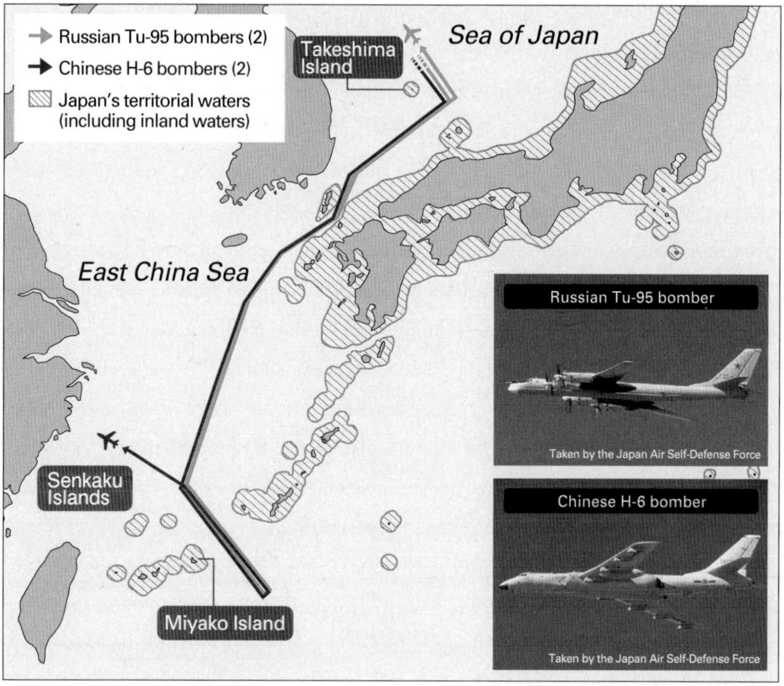

Source: Compiled by the author based on Press release by the Joint Staff of the Ministry of Defense of Japan.

exercise in the Sea of Japan, the joint maritime patrol that followed, and the third China-Russia joint patrol flight indicate that a framework for joint naval and aerial military exercises by China and Russia around Japan is being steadily developed.

Following the inauguration of the Biden administration, the United States and Russia agreed to a five-year extension of the New Strategic Arms Reductions Treaty (New START) in February 2021, and later in June held the first U.S.-Russia summit in three years in Geneva which resulted in the Joint Statement on Strategic Stability.[37] Two Strategic Stability Dialogues were convened pursuant to this statement, and at the second dialogue between Deputy Foreign Minister Sergey Ryabkov and Deputy Secretary of State Wendy Sherman, the two delegations agreed to establish two working groups: the Working Group on Principles and Objectives for Future Arms Control, and the Working Group on Capabilities and Actions with Strategic Effects.[38] Moreover, U.S.-Russia National Security Council (NSC) diplomatic engagements between National Security Advisor Jake Sullivan and Secretary of the Security Council Patrushev have seen rapid momentum since the Biden administration came to power. On January 25, 2021, the two sides held their first telephone discussion to discuss security issues between the two countries immediately following National Security Advisor Sullivan's appointment, which included the extension of New START.[39] Such U.S.-Russia NSC diplomatic discussions have already been held seven times under the new Biden administration on topics including both countries' strategic stability as well as the situation in Afghanistan,[40] and are being positioned as a mechanism for managing their overall bilateral relationship.

Amidst rapidly escalating tensions due to the large-scale deployment of Russian military troops near the Ukrainian border, Secretary Patrushev and National Security Advisor Sullivan held a telephone conversation on November 17, 2021,[41] followed by a series of online U.S.-Russia summit meetings on December 7 and 30.[42] Russia has taken a bullish stance, calling for NATO to refrain from any further eastern expansion and roll back its troop and equipment deployments to their pre-1997 position[43] in a draft treaty with the United States and draft agreement with NATO it released on December 17. Against these circumstances, a series of talks were held under various frameworks, with a U.S.-Russia Strategic Stability Dialogue on January 10, 2022, the first NATO-Russia Council (NRC) in approximately two and a half years on January 12, and an Organization for Security and Co-operation in Europe (OSCE) meeting on January 13, but saw no concrete results breaking the stalemate. In addition to the situation in Ukraine, the recent security climate in the former Soviet bloc suggests that the wavering hierarchy of international order in the post-Soviet space,[44] the sovereignty of states closely related to it, and issues surrounding

Russia's traditional security perspective will remain at the core of U.S.-Europe-Russia relations.

Regional organizations centered around Russia, China, India, and other countries are also advancing their activities in Eurasia, which includes the former Soviet bloc. The Shanghai Cooperation Organisation (SCO), marking its 20th anniversary in 2021, held a heads-of-state summit in Tajikistan that September where observer Iran was officially confirmed as a full member state. A leaders' summit of the Collective Security Treaty Organization (CSTO) also convened in parallel, with the first joint SCO-CSTO summit held on the situation in Afghanistan chaired by Tajikistan's President Emomali Rahmon.[45] The CSTO plans to establish programs to strengthen border arrangements between Tajikistan and Afghanistan,[46] and CSTO measures including the special counter-narcotic operation "Kanal" and multilateral "Nelegal" operation against illegal migration are seeing increased importance.[47] It is not only Russia's own ability to deal with this growing "threat from the south" that is being questioned, but also the actual operational capacities of multilateral frameworks in the Eurasia region that have repeatedly undertaken anti-terror military exercises and anti-drug trafficking trainings.

Russia is facing challenges on each of its strategic fronts that it must address simultaneously, including the situations in Ukraine and Belarus on the European front, relations with China and India on the Asian front, the establishment of new security frameworks by Western countries in the Asia-Pacific and Indo-Pacific, as well as the situation on the Tajikistan-Afghanistan border, the situation in Kazakhstan, and the power struggle over the Arctic. As such, it is worth keeping a close eye on movements within the Kremlin's strategic community to see how they will use their limited resources to address these issues.

(4) Improving Paramilitary Capacities: The Strengthening of the Border Service of the Federal Security Service

The Arctic is of increasing military and economic importance to modern Russia. The 2021 NSS shows that Russia sees "the international community's growing concern over climate change and the issue of environmental protection being used as a pretext to establish control over transportation routes" and "obstruct Russia's development of the Arctic."[48] Based on this, Russia declared "border protection and security, the security of territorial waters, the security of exclusive economic zones and the continental shelf, the modernization of border security infrastructure, and improvements to border controls, customs, disease prevention, and other control mechanisms" as matters of national and social security policy[49] and put forth a plan to further strengthen efforts related to maritime security policy, such as securing sea lanes. In addition, reinforced land border protection and security in the former Soviet bloc as a result of the situation in Afghanistan is a key national security issue for Russia as previously noted. This part will focus on the movements of Russian paramilitary organizations involved in land and maritime border security in light of these concerns.

Amidst growing debate over "hybrid warfare" as a new means of war following the March 2014 annexation of Crimea,[50] Russian paramilitary organizations along with both the Main Directorate of the General Staff of the Armed Forces (a foreign intelligence agency)[51] and the Special Operations Forces (SSO)[52] under the General Staff have drawn attention. Article 7 of the federal law On Defense (hereinafter, "Defense Act") stipulates that "the Russian Armed Forces, other armed forces, military units and agencies shall carry out their national defense duties in accordance with the Operational Plan of the Russian Armed Forces."[53] In this context, "other armed forces" refers to the National Guard, "military units" includes the Paramilitary Rescue Units of the Ministry of Civil Defence, Emergencies and Disaster Relief (hereinafter, "Emergencies Ministry"), and "agencies" includes the Foreign Intelligence Service, the Federal Security Service, the Federal Guard Service, military prosecutor's offices, the Military Investigations Departments of the Investigative Committee, and the Chief Directorate for Special Programmes of the Russian President.[54] The National Guard of the Russian Federation (Rosgvardiya) was newly established in April 2016, formed with the Interior Troops of the Ministry of Internal Affairs as its basis,[55] marking a large-scale paramilitary reorganization. Accompanying this, Russia's security operations units and special forces involved in crackdowns on protests and special operations against terrorism, chiefly the Special Rapid Response Unit (SOBR) and the Special Purpose Mobile Unit (OMON), were transferred from the Ministry of Internal Affairs to the Federal National Guard Service, further strengthening this auxiliary agency which serves as a "power resource" for President Putin.

In July 2021, the National Guard, alongside the Emergencies Ministry and other paramilitary organizations, held the Zaslon 2021 strategic maneuver exercise, the largest such exercise to date. It was positioned as a preparatory step ahead of the Zapad 2021 joint exercise between Russia and Belarus,[56] demonstrating an advance in strengthened operational cooperation between the Russian military and an array of paramilitary organizations.

Many of Russia's paramilitary organizations are successors to various units of the Committee for State Security (KGB), and the Border Service of the Federal Security Service (FSB), responsible for terrestrial and maritime border security, is no exception. The Border Service is the successor to the KGB Border Troops, which formed part of the Soviet Armed Forces, but held the status of a federal executive organ as the Federal Border Service (FPS) for roughly 10 years from August 1993. In March 2003, however, it was integrated into the FSB as one of its divisions as the Border Service, and came to have jurisdiction over the Coast Guard.[57] Led by Vladimir Kulishov, who also serves as first deputy director of the FSB, the Border Service is estimated to possess a total force of approximately 160,000 troops, making it second only to the National Guard (roughly 340,000 troops) amongst Russia's paramilitary groups.[58]

In November 2018, the FSB Coast Guard seized Ukrainian naval vessels in the waters surrounding the Kerch Strait in the Black Sea, causing an incident and prompting the G7 foreign ministers to issue a statement expressing their "utmost concern" about Russia's actions.[59] Moreover, in June 2021 the sailing of HMS *Defender*, a U.K. Royal Navy destroyer belonging to CSG21, near the Crimean Peninsula led to a diplomatic row between the United Kingdom and Russia,[60] drawing international attention to Russia's border security activities including operations by the FSB Coast Guard. Regional border guard directorates have been placed in waters near Japan in the Russian Far East in the eastern Arctic, Sakhalin Oblast, and Primorsky Krai. Security vessels are also being modernized to establish sea routes and for military security in the Sea of Okhotsk and the Bering Sea alongside the Barents Sea, the Baltic Sea, and the Black Sea, strategic points on the European front. For example, the first new Project 22100 (Okean-class) patrol ship was deployed to the western Arctic border guard based in Murmansk,[61] the second was deployed to the eastern Arctic border guard based in Petropavlovsk-Kamchatskiy alongside Taymyr, a Project 22120 (Purga-class) patrol vessel,[62] and the third, *Anadyr*, is in the sea trial phase.[63]

In addition, the interagency exercise Safe Arctic 2021, held for the first time in September 2021 led by the Emergencies Ministry, was conducted simultaneously in seven federal subjects of Russia centered around Norilsk and Dudinka. The main objectives of the exercise were to amass practical experience in emergency response and preserve Russia's territory in the Arctic.[64]

With the establishment of new patriotic and conservative provisions as part of the 2020 constitutional reforms and the diplomatic stance surrounding territory and sovereignty symbolized by the provision banning the cessation of territory, Russia can be expected to further intensify its border infrastructure improvements as well as its security and rescue operation structure, primarily led by the Border Service of the Federal Security Service and the Emergencies Ministry. Moreover, efforts to secure a sea lane from the Arctic to the Asia-Pacific region aimed at developing and improving operational performance along the Northern Sea Route, the eastbound route in particular, are likely to be strengthened.

In the context, the Russian Far East and Sea of Okhotsk are of increasingly strategic importance, a trend that can be discerned from regional visits by senior government officials and the movements of the Russian military. On July 26, 2021, Prime Minister Mikhail Mishustin visited Etorofu Island in the Northern Territories where he inspected a seafood processing factory and a hospital[65] and referred to a plan for tax reforms to improve the investment environment for foreign capital.[66] As will be discussed in detail in Section 3, the Russian military has been seen upgrading its equipment and increasing its activities in the Northern Territories in recent years with the deployment of Su-35S fighter jets and S-300V4 missile defense systems, and in addition, the development of social and economic infrastructure has been steadily progressing to support this. On September 28, Secretary of the Security Council Patrushev visited Sakhalin Oblast on a working trip for a meeting in the Far Eastern Federal District where he observed an S-400 surface-to-air missile regiment,[67] underscoring the Kremlin's increasingly direct command and supervision over military policy in the Russian Far East. That December, the Bastion anti-ship missile system was deployed to the island of Matua for operational use,[68] thereby enhancing Russia's A2/AD capabilities. This trend in steadily implementing its policy is indicative of the Kremlin's growing interest in the region.

2. New Developments in Russian Politics following the 2020 Constitutional Reforms

The major constitutional reforms implemented in July 2020 introduced a so-called "presidential terms reset provision," creating a system by which Putin could potentially retain the presidency until at most 2036. With 30 years having passed since the fall of the Soviet Union, the political history of its successor, the Russian Federation, has been characterized by the Pluralism by Default of the Boris Yeltsin administration in the 1990s, as well as the stabilization of the constitutional system and the establishment of "competitive authoritarianism" at the federal level during the Putin administration in the 2000s, with the 2014 Ukraine crisis subsequently considered to mark the turning point in the country's shift to "populist authoritarianism."[69] In the run-up to the presidential election scheduled for 2024, Russian political order remains unable to break free of its regime which is strongly dependent on Putin individually, thus making the post-Putin issue the greatest concern in domestic Russian affairs.

Elections for the State Duma, the lower house of the Federal Assembly, were held from September 17–19, 2021 and served as a prelude to the next presidential election. While the ruling United Russia lost 10 of its current seats (down 19 seats as compared to the prior election in 2016), it won 324 out of a total of 450 seats in the electoral contest, 225 seats elected through constituencies and 225 through party list proportional representation, securing a constitutional majority in assembly power. In terms of the main opposition forces, the Communist Party won 57 seats, an increase of 15, and the A Just Russia party won 27, an increase of 4, while the Liberal Democratic Party of Russia (LDPR) saw a significant loss, winning just 21 seats as compared to the 40 it held previously. In addition, the newly formed New People party, which made strides in the September 2020 local elections allowing it to participate in the lower house elections under federal law, won 5.32% of the vote, earning it 13 seats in proportional representation.[70] The New People party is an emerging political force led by Alexei Nechayev, head of a major cosmetics company, but with Nechayey being a participant to the All-Russia People's Front, a coalition formed at Putin's initiative, the party is considered close to the Kremlin.[71]

No significant change to Russia's political landscape was seen in this recent election, with United Russia maintaining its one-party dominance and restrictions imposed on opposition groups' activities. Alexei Navalny, target

of an assassination attempt in Tomsk, Siberia in 2020, has been imprisoned since he returned to Russia following medical treatment in Germany and his probation was revoked by court order. As this symbol of the opposition was imprisoned and groups' activities were lacking steam, it was announced on October 8, 2021 that Dmitry Muratov, editor-in-chief of the liberal Russian news organization Novaya Gazeta, had won the Nobel Peace Prize. Novaya

Dmitry Muratov, editor-in-chief of Novaya Gazeta and winner of the Nobel Peace Prize (UPI/Newscom/Kyodo News Images)

Gazeta is a paper that focuses on investigative reporting, including on human rights conditions in Chechnya, and is known as the former employer of journalist Anna Politkovskaya, who was shot dead in her apartment in Moscow in 2006.[72] At the award ceremony held in Oslo in December, Muratov stated that "journalism in Russia is going through a dark valley. Over a hundred journalists, media outlets, human rights defenders and NGOs have recently been branded as 'foreign agents,'"[73] addressing the international community on the dire plight surrounding journalism and human rights advocacy in modern Russia under the Putin administration.

Laws surrounding this designation as so-called "foreign agents" have been used to curtail the activities of independent media and journalists, including Novaya Gazeta, and social groups. A series of amendments to federal law in July 2012, the federal law On Noncommercial Organizations in particular, made it possible to designate nonprofit organizations receiving funding from foreign organizations or individuals and engaging in political activity in the Russian Federation as "foreign agents."[74] The scope of coverage was later expanded to include the media and individuals, and according to the Ministry of Justice, 113 foreign media organizations (and individuals) were registered on the list of foreign agents as of January 14, 2022.[75]

Upon receiving notice regarding the Nobel Peace Prize winner, President Putin made a remark on October 13, 2021 that Editor-in-Chief Muratov would not be put on the list of foreign agents provided he does not violate Russian law,[76] though it remains to be seen how the current administration, which advocates preventing "foreign interference in internal affairs," will administer said law. In November 2021, the Prosecutor General's Office filed a lawsuit with the Supreme Court seeking to dissolve the nonprofit organization Memorial, claiming repeated infractions of the law,[77] and the Supreme Court ultimately ruled in favor of the suit on December 28.[78] Memorial was a nonprofit organization that conducted research on political suppression during the Soviet era and the Great Purge under Stalin's rule in particular, documenting and publishing historical materials.[79] It was designated as a foreign agent in 2016, and the series of developments surrounding the administration and Memorial had been of serious concern among scholars of Soviet and Russian history around the world. This shows how Russian politics have been growing rapidly more conservative following the 2020 constitutional reforms, once again calling into question the fundamentals of the constitutional system and the rights of citizens ensured by Chapters I and II of the Constitution of the Russian Federation, freedom of speech (Article 29) and freedom of association (Article 30) in particular.

3. The Advancing Modernization of the Russian Armed Forces and Its Strengthened Military Posture

(1) The Establishment of the New Defense Program and the Modernization of the Russian Armed Forces

In November 2020, President Putin issued a presidential decree stating that a Defense Program for 2021-2025 (hereinafter, "New Defense Program") was to be put in place as of January 1, 2021. In response, Sergei Shoigu, defense minister, announced that the work on formulating this New Defense Program had been completed at an expanded meeting of Defense Ministry Board in December 2020, where President Putin was also in attendance.[80] Equipment upgrades and the modernization of the Russian Armed Forces were thus to proceed in accordance with the program. With regard to the development of national defense capabilities, President Putin made reference in his speech at the meeting to issues in need of concentrated efforts in order to improve the Russian military's combat skills so that it is able to effectively deal with both current and foreseeable threats to Russia's security.[81] The first of said issues was the development and high level of maintenance of a nuclear deterrent, namely, strengthening all of the nuclear forces that comprise Russia's nuclear triad. Second was the reinforcement of non-nuclear deterrence capabilities, high-precision weapons above all. Regarding this, President Putin stated that Russia has no intention of unilaterally deploying mid-range missiles, but that it is crucial for Russia to be prepared to respond in the event the West should deploy similar weapons near its borders. The third issue was further upgrading the Russian military with the latest equipment, and to this end, bolstering the defense industry to steadily fulfill state defense orders. Fourth was to spur the development of AI-enabled equipment to promote equipment automation and enhance robotic weaponry, unmanned aerial vehicles (UAVs), and automated command systems as the outcome of future warfare hinges on research and development into these weapons.

In response to the president's remarks, Defense Minister Shoigu reported that the Russian Armed Forces had reached a 70.1% possession rate of the latest armaments as of the end of 2020, and that this figure is expected to rise to 75.9% by the end of 2024 should equipment procurement proceed as planned, which is within the term of the New Defense Program.[82] The current status of equipment upgrades for each military and independent army branch included in Defense Minister Shoigu's report, the equipment upgrade plans as per the New Defense Program, as well as the priority issues and main trends in equipment procurement in 2021 are summarized below, demonstrating how Russia is steadily modernizing its equipment and improving its capabilities.

The Land Forces were supplied with more than 3,500 pieces of the latest armaments in 2020, including 220 tanks and armored fighting vehicles. In 2021, more than 800 T-72B3 and T-72B3M tanks, T-80BVM tanks, T-90M tanks, BMP-2 and BMP-3 infantry fighting vehicles, as well as BTR-82A and BTR-82AM armored transport vehicles were supplied in total.[83]

The Navy saw a total of 29 submarines and surface vessels commissioned in 2020. In addition, a total of 41 combat vessels are under construction or undergoing modernization and refurbishment as per current state defense orders. Construction of Borei-A class nuclear submarines (Project 955A) armed with Bulava ballistic missiles continues, with the fourth vessel, *Knyaz Vladimir*, commissioned in 2020 and another Borei-A class nuclear submarine deployed in 2021. In addition, the first multi-purpose submarine (Project 949A) *Irkutsk* has been commissioned, with the second scheduled for commission in 2022. Important developments have also been seen in the development of hypersonic missiles, an area of focus for Russia. In 2020, the Project 22350 frigate *Admiral Gorshkov* successfully conducted a test launch of Russia's latest "Tsirkon" hypersonic missile, and another successful launch was made in July 2021.[84] Progress has also been seen in the deployment of surface-to-ship missiles such as the Bal and Bastion missile systems in conjunction with reinforcements to coastal missile forces.

The Aerospace Forces were supplied with 147 aircraft and more than 150 air defense weapons including S-400 and Pantsir-S surface-to-air missile systems in 2020, and the latest Inokhodzets and Forpost mid-range reconnaissance and unmanned combat aerial vehicles saw their first introduction. Further, five Tu-95MS long-range strategic bombers completed their modernization and refurbishment. According to the New Defense Program, the Aerospace Forces are set to bring 94 planes and helicopters into service by 2025, including 22 Su-57 fifth-generation fighters, and one of the program's priority tasks for 2021 was to complete the modernization and refurbishment of its Tu-160 long-range strategic bombers with two Tu-160Ms scheduled for deployment in 2022.[85]

The Strategic Missile Forces' rate of possession of the latest armaments was at 81% as of the end of 2020, one of the highest rates among the various military and independent army branches. This increase in the possession rate was brought by developments in converting the intercontinental ballistic missiles (ICBMs) for three regiments to the latest Yars ICBM and the adoption of the Avangard ICBM by another. The Strategic Missile Forces' priorities for 2021 were to have 13 Yars and Avangard missiles combat ready, and complete construction on five facilities for them. By the end of 2021, the possession rate of the latest armaments had risen to 83.0%,[86] and Sergei Karakayev, commander of Strategic Missile Forces, has stated that it is likely to reach 100% in 2024.[87]

For the Airborne Troops, one priority is expediting deployment of the latest BMD-4M armored fighting vehicles and BTR-MDM armored transport vehicles. The Novorosiisk airborne assault regiment deployed these vehicles at the end of 2020, and the Stavropol airborne assault regiment together with three other units were armed with this same equipment as of the end of 2021. It is said that this will enhance their ability to carry out any operation under any conditions.

(2) Russia's Growing Threat Awareness and Increased Military Exercises

Russia currently perceives there to be a growing military threat from increased military activity by the United States and NATO on Russia's periphery. At the

Figure 6.2. The Zapad 2021 exercise centered on the Western Military District

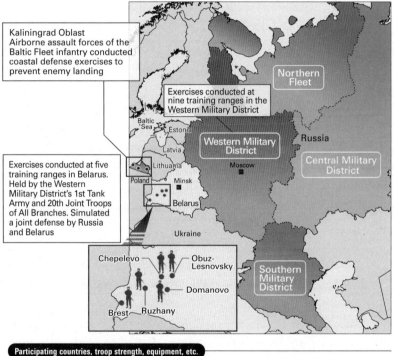

Source: Compiled by the author based on *Красная звезда*, от 17 сентября 2021г.; от 20 сентября 2021г.

June 2021 meeting of the Defense Ministry Board, Defense Minister Shoigu touched upon the growing military threat to Russia, noting factors such as intensified surveillance flights by U.S. strategic bombers near Russia's borders, increased activity by missile-bearing NATO vessels in neighboring waters, and a marked increase in military exercises.[88] The updated version of the National Security Strategy revised in July 2021 also recognizes that NATO's military infrastructure expansions near Russia's borders and its attempt to exert pressure on Russia through force pose a military threat to the country.[89] Russia sees this military threat by the United States and NATO growing on three fronts. The first is the threat faced by the Western Military District in the western strategic direction related to the defense of Russia's borders in the Baltic Sea and with the Baltic states. A further issue on this front is how to Russia will strengthen military cooperation with its ally, Belarus. Second is the threat faced by the Southern Military District in the south-western strategic direction, namely increased military activity by U.S. and NATO forces in Ukraine and the Black Sea region. Third is the increase in NATO military activity in the Arctic Ocean faced by the Northern Fleet chiefly in the Barents Sea, the ocean's western part. In response to such threats, Russia is strengthening its military posture on all fronts and more actively conducting exercises to improve its operational capabilities.

In the Western Military District, 20 new units were formed and approximately 2,000 pieces of the latest equipment brought into service by the end of 2021. Over 200 different exercises were held during winter in the first half of 2021, with the Baltic Fleet seeing a 30% increase in exercises over the previous season.[90] The most extensive of the year was Zapad 2021, a large-scale joint exercise between Russia and Belarus that took place in September. It was conducted across nine training ranges in Russia, five in Belarus, and in the Baltic Sea, mobilizing as many as 200,000 troops, approximately 80 aircraft, roughly 760 vehicles including 290 tanks, and as many as 15 naval vessels. Armenia, Kazakhstan, Kyrgyzstan, Mongolia, and India sent troops; Pakistan, Uzbekistan, and Sri Lanka dispatched officers to the General Staff; and China, Vietnam, and Myanmar participated as observers.

One of the main missions of the exercise was to execute a military operation meant to retake territory temporarily occupied by an enemy, and to this end Russia deployed the Western Military District's 1st Tank Army and 20th Joint Troops of All Branches to Belarus. According to Belarus' Defense Minister Viktor Khrenin, the exercise resulted in practical experience in planning joint operations to ensure the security of the Russia-Belarus union state.[91] Moreover, a coastal defense exercise was held by airborne assault forces of the Baltic Fleet infantry to prevent an enemy landing at the Dobrovolskiy training range in Kaliningrad Oblast, which faces the Baltic Sea.[92]

For the Southern Military District, their task was to respond to two major exercises conducted by U.S. and NATO forces in Ukraine and the Black Sea region: Defender Europe 2021, held from May to June 2021, and Sea Breeze 2021, held from June to July. Russia considers these exercises to have been the largest provocative anti-Russian exercises held in the past 30 years, and sees them as having been aimed at undermining its defensive position in Crimea and on the southwestern borders of Russia in addition to carrying out tactical landings on Russian territory and offensive operations against logistical military facilities.[93] The Russian military countered Defender Europe 2021 with a large-scale exercise by the Southern Military District and airborne forces, which included the 22nd Infantry Corps of the Black Sea Fleet, the 58th Joint Troops of All Branches, the Caspian Flotilla, air force and air defense units of the Southern Military District, and the Airborne Troops. In response to Sea Breeze 2021, the Navy's permanent operational force and Aerospace Force units conducted defense drills guarding the Khmeimim air base and the Tartus navy base near Cyprus in the Eastern Mediterranean. Coastal defense exercises were also held in the Black Sea region utilizing the Bal and Bastion anti-ship missile systems as well as the S-400 surface-to-air missile system.[94]

The Northern Fleet perceives activity by NATO forces in the Arctic Ocean to be increasing, notably in the Barents Sea. Alexander Moiseyev, commander of the Northern Fleet, has acknowledged that this increased NATO activity in the region must be addressed to uphold Russia's security and national interests in the

Arctic.[95] According to him, the Northern Fleet's equipment upgrades have been progressing and their rate of possession of the latest armaments was likely to reach 62.3% by the end of 2021, estimating that 245 pieces of modern equipment were to be brought into service by the fleet during the year. He further revealed that a frigate (Project 22350) will be commissioned in 2022. The fleet currently has a 97% ratio of contract service personnel, with this figure expected to reach 99.2% as of the end of 2021.[96] Exercises by the Northern Fleet are also intensifying, with a large-scale drill held in April 2021 under Nikolai Evmenov, commander in chief of the Navy, and there are plans for each fleet to conduct exercises on a similar scale annually hereinafter on a rotating basis. Tactical exercises have also been frequent, with one conducted in June 2021 in the Barents Sea to test and validate anti-submarine, anti-air attack, and anti-naval fleet operations.[97]

An increase in military exercises has also been seen in the Eastern Military District, primarily by the Pacific Fleet. In its exercises, the fleet has been focusing on improving its ships' operational capabilities in the deep sea and its coastal defense capacities on remote islands, as well as strengthening cooperation between its naval groups and the coastal defense forces on said islands. Behind Russia's increased military activities and moves to reinforce its military presence in the Pacific region is its objective of defending Russia's maritime interests in the region in response to the United States and other countries' Indo-Pacific strategies. In April 2021, five Tu-142M3 and Il-38 maritime patrol aircraft from the naval air force in Kamchatka conducted an anti-submarine patrol exercise during which they validated their coordination with naval search and strike groups.[98] In addition, the Pacific Fleet conducted a large-scale exercise in the central Pacific Ocean approximately 4,000 kilometers from base in June 2021 in which 20 combat ships, a number of submarines and supply ships, and roughly 20 aircraft were mobilized. Sergei Avakyants, commander of the Pacific Fleet, stated that the exercise was a test of the following operational objectives: 1) commanding forces remote from base, 2) executing anti-submarine operations, 3) organizing an air defense position, 4) executing security operations, 5) executing joint attacks against hypothetical enemy vessels and infrastructure, and 6) systemically replenishing all types of supplies.[99] Among the aircraft mobilized was the Kamchatka naval air forces' Tu-142M3 maritime patrol aircraft to validate its anti-submarine patrol capabilities in remote waters.[100]

The island of Sakhalin, the Kuril Islands, and the Northern Territories have seen increasingly frequent and active tactical exercises, but with a focus on improved coastal defense capacities given that the primarily function of island-based units is centered around defending against enemy landings.[101] In recent years, Russia has continuously moved to strengthen its military posture in the Northern Territories, deploying Bal and Bastion anti-ship missile systems from 2016 and T-72B3 tanks from 2018, followed by the revelation in 2020 that S-300V4 surface-to-air missile systems had also been deployed.[102]

The major tactical exercises conducted in the Northern Territories in 2021 are as follows. In February 2021, the Russian military held drills on Kunashiri Island and Etorofu Island involving more than 1,000 troops primarily from air force units of the Eastern Military District with the main objective of verifying their anti-air defense capabilities. That June, Russian forces conducted exercises on Kunashiri Island, Etorofu Island, Sakhalin, and in the Sea of Japan with over 10,000 troops, mobilizing approximately 500 military vehicles, 32 aircraft, and 12 naval vessels as a test of landing and anti-landing operations by the Eastern Military District's marine forces.[103] Subsequently, intermittent firing drills were held in the waters surrounding the Northern Territories from July through the end of August,[104] with a further exercise conducted in September in the Northern Territories and on the Kuril Islands. Involving more than 500 troops, this exercise included reconnaissance drills using UAVs and attack drills against hypothetical enemies at sea.[105]

(3) Arms Exports to Strengthen and Expand Foreign Military Cooperation

As U.S. and NATO forces accelerated their withdrawal from Afghanistan in 2021 and moves to revive the Taliban regime became apparent, concerns emerged that the country's destabilization could spread to other parts of the Central Asia region. For Russia, this meant an imperative need to strengthen defenses along

Central Asia's external borders, notably those of Tajikistan and Uzbekistan which neighbor Afghanistan. In other words, enhancing military cooperation with these two countries as well as multilateral military cooperation through the CSTO and SCO turned into a pressing issue. In April 2021, Defense Minister Shoigu met with the defense ministers of Tajikistan and Uzbekistan in succession to discuss this strengthened military cooperation. In his meeting with Sherali Mirzo, minister of defense of Tajikistan, the two sides agreed to enhance mutual cooperation through exercises to collectively eliminate threats from Afghanistan. In his meeting with Bahodir Kurbanov, minister of defense of Uzbekistan, both countries came to agreement on the Strategic Partnership Program for 2021-2025 under which they would strengthen their military cooperation.[106] In August 2021, in response to the worsening situation in Afghanistan, the three countries held a joint exercise at the Harb-Maidon training range in Tajikistan to assess their execution of combat operations when carried out as a joint military group.[107]

At a meeting of defense ministers held in July 2021, it was noted that the Peace Mission joint counter-terrorism drills conducted through the SCO must be made more effective, bringing up the need to examine issues such as countermeasures against new tactical methods utilized by international terrorist organizations, combat using UAVs, ensuring information security, and the prevention of terrorist attacks using chemical and biological weapons.[108] In September 2021, Peace Mission 2021 was conducted at the Donguz training range in Orenburg Oblast in Russia with the participation of Russia, China, Kazakhstan, Kyrgyzstan, Uzbekistan, India, and Pakistan. The exercise took into consideration the content of the discussions at the July 2021 defense ministers' meeting, with testing done for some of the issues raised including new methods of combat using UAVs and the prevention of chemical and biological terrorist attacks.[109]

In terms of military cooperation through the CSTO, three significant plans were adopted at a meeting of defense ministers held in September in response to the deteriorating situation in Afghanistan. First was a procurement plan to equip the Collective Operational Reaction Forces with the latest armaments. Second was an operational plan for the various CSTO collective forces in the Central

Asia region, which also concerned the structure and composition of the Collective Operational Reaction Forces' Special Task Force. Third was a plan to improve the joint training system for CSTO member military personnel through 2025.[110] That same month, the Rubezh ("border") 2021 joint exercise by the CSTO Collective Rapid Reaction Forces was held at the Edelweiss training range in Kyrgyzstan with the participation of Russia, Kazakhstan, Kyrgyzstan, and Tajikistan. The drill was conducted based on a scenario in which the forces worked to prevent illegal armed group forces from crossing the border into a CSTO member country, destroying them if they did.[111] Held almost simultaneously with Zapad 2021, the large-scale joint exercise between Russia and Belarus, Rubezh 2021 is thought to have also been an attempt to verify Russia's ability to execute a conflict response in the European theater and a counterterrorism response in Central Asia concurrently. In January 2022, the CSTO dispatched its Peacekeeping Forces comprised of nearly 4,000 troops, primarily from Russia's Airborne Troops, to Kazakhstan in response to domestic unrest. This marked the first time a CSTO force has been deployed in a CSTO member country for a domestic issue, and is noteworthy from the standpoint of the CSTO joint forces' enhanced capacity to respond to situations.[112]

According to Dmitriy Shugayev, director of the Federal Service for Military-Technical Cooperation, Russia's arms exports grew 2% year-on-year to reach approximately $15 billion in 2020, maintaining a high rate. The total value of orders also reached roughly $50 billion as of the same year, with the number of countries being supplied with Russian-made weapons amounting to 51.[113]

The International Military-Technical Forum "Army" held by Russia every August is the country's largest military technology trade fair and a venue for the development of new arms export markets. Delegations from a number of countries were present at "Army-2021" held in August 2021, 22 of which were led by defense ministers.[114] Moves were seen by Russia that year to strengthen military-technical cooperation in the Middle East and Southeast Asia, arms export markets that Russia wishes to maintain and expand. In April 2021, Alexander Fomin, Russia's deputy defense minister in charge of international military cooperation, met with Falih al-Fayyadh, Chairman of the Iraqi Popular Mobilization Forces, to discuss the future evolution of military and military-technical cooperation between the two countries.[115] Later in June, Defense Minister Shoigu further met with Senior General Min Aung Hlaing, Myanmar's commander-in-chief of defense services who was visiting Russia at the time to attend the Moscow Conference on International Security (organized by Russia's Ministry of Defense), to similarly discuss the two countries' future developments in military and military-technical cooperation.[116]

Steady progress has been made in upgrading equipment and modernizing the Russian army, and coupled with more vigorous exercises, definite improvements have been seen in its ability to carry out military operations. This is clearly evident not only in the Western Military District, the Northern Fleet, and the Southern Military District, which perceive increased threats from the United States and NATO, but also in the Eastern Military District with the modernization of the Pacific Fleet and the expanded scale and range of its exercises. Both bilateral and multilateral foreign military cooperation is being strengthened and joint forces are improving their ability to deal with contingencies, as demonstrated by the execution of multiple joint exercises simultaneously. Russia has also been seeking to expand its arms exports across various regions through enhanced military-technical cooperation, and in its relations with select Middle Eastern and Southeast Asian countries has achieved a level of success.

NOTES

1) Указ Президента РФ от 2 июля 2021г., № 400, «О Стратегии национальной безопасности Российской Федерации», *Собрание Законодательства Российской Федерации(далее - СЗРФ),5 июля 2021г., № 27 (часть II), ст. 5351*; Указ Президента РФ от 31 декабря 2015г., № 683, «О Стратегии национальной безопасности Российской Федерации», *СЗРФ, 4 января 2016г., № 1 (часть II), ст. 212*; In this chapter, the National Security Strategy of the Russian Federation, which is subject to revision every six years per the federal law On Strategic Planning, is abbreviated as the "Security Strategy" where appropriate. Further, the document authorized by Presidential Decree No. 400 dated July 2, 2021 is referred to as "NSS 2021,"

and the document authorized by Presidential Decree No. 683 dated December 31, 2015 is referred to as "NSS 2015" to distinguish between the two.

2) «Военная доктрина Российской Федерации», (утв. Президентом РФ 25 декабря 2014г., № Пр-2976), *Российская газета*, от 30 декабря 2014г.; Указ Президента РФ от 30 ноября 2016г., № 640, «Об утверждении Концепции внешней политики Российской Федерации», *СЗРФ, 5 декабря 2016г., № 49, ст. 6886*; Указ Президента РФ от 25 апреля 2018г., № 174, «Об утверждении Основ государственной пограничной политики Российской Федерации», *СЗРФ, 30 апреля 2018г., № 18, ст. 2614.*

3) Пункт 4, Статьи 10 и Пункт 1, Статьи 18, Федеральный закон от 28 июня 2014г., № 172-ФЗ (ред. от 31 июля 2020г.), «О стратегическом планировании в Российской Федерации», *СЗРФ, 30 июня 2014г., № 26 (часть I), ст. 3378.*

4) «б» и «г», пункта 3, «Положения о Межведомственной комиссии Совета Безопасности Российской Федерации по проблемам стратегического планирования», Указ Президента РФ от 6 мая 2011г., № 590 (ред. от 07 марта 2020г.), «Вопросы Совета Безопасности Российской Федерации», *СЗРФ, 9 мая 2011г., № 19, ст. 2721.*

5) Пункт 3, «Положения о научном совете при Совете Безопасности Российской Федерации», Указ Президента РФ от 6 мая 2011г., № 590 (ред. от 7 марта 2020г.), «Вопросы Совета Безопасности Российской Федерации», *СЗРФ, 9 мая 2011г., № 19, ст. 2721.*

6) Президент России, 27 сентября 2021г., Комментарий Секретаря Совета Безопасности Николая Патрушева по итогам заседания Совета Безопасности; Указ Президента РФ от 8 ноября 2021г., № 633, «Об утверждении Основ государственной политики в сфере стратегического планирования в Российской Федерации», *СЗРФ, 15 ноября 2021г., № 46, ст. 7676.*

7) *Российская газета*, от 18 июля 2019г.; *Известия*, от 10 февраля 2020г.

8) Hasegawa Takeyuki, "Dai niji puuchin seiken ni okeru kenpo kaikaku – seido henko ni miru daitoryo kenryoku" [Russia's constitutional reform in the second Putin administration: Presidential power in the Russian political system], *Security & Strategy* 2, no. 1 (2021): 8.

9) Пункт 7, Стратегии национальной безопасности Российской Федерации, Указ Президента РФ от 2 июля 2021г., № 400.

10) Пункт 4, Указ Президента РФ от 2 июня 2020г., № 355, «Об Основах государственной политики Российской Федерации в области ядерного сдерживания», *СЗРФ, 8 июня 2020г., № 23, ст. 3623.*

11) Paul Dibb, "Russia's New Strategy for Nuclear War," Arms Control Association (July/ August 2020); Petr Topychkanov, "Russia's Nuclear Doctrine Moves the Focus from non-Western Threats," Stockholm International Peace Research Institute (October 2020); Koizumi Yu, "'Kaku yokushi no bunya ni okeru roshia renpo kokka seisaku no kiso' ni miru roshia no kaku senryaku" [The nuclear strategy of Russia as seen in the Foundations of State Policy of the Russian Federation in the Area of Nuclear Deterrence], Japan Institute of International Affairs (JIIA) (August 24, 2020).

12) Пункт 17, 26 и 43, Стратегии национальной безопасности Российской Федерации, Указ Президента РФ от 31 декабря 2015г., № 683; Пункт 20 и 21, Стратегии национальной безопасности Российской Федерации, Указ Президента РФ от 2 июля 2021г., № 400.

13) Пункт 13, Стратегии национальной безопасности Российской Федерации, Указ Президента РФ от 2 июля 2021г., № 400.

14) Nagatomo Kenji, "Dai hassho – Roshia: Yunyu daitai kara yushutsu sokushin e" [Chapter 8 – Russia: From import substitution to promoting exports], in *Heisei 30 nendo kantorii repooto: Beikoku, kanada, EU (Joken furi chiiki ni okeru nogyo seisaku, kyotsu nogyo seisaku (CAP) no hensen ni okeru seijiteki yoin to no kento, doitsu, furansu, eikoku), roshia* [FY 2018 country report: United States, Canada, EU (Agricultural policy in conditionally disadvantaged areas, examination of political and other factors in the transition in common agricultural policy (CAP), Germany, France, United Kingdom), Russia] ("Purojekuto kenkyu [Shuyokoku nogyo senryaku odan/sogo] kenkyu shiryo dai 10 go" [Project Research [Cross Section and Comprehensive Overview of Agricultural Strategies in Major Countries] Research Materials no. 10]) (Tokyo: Policy Research Institute, Ministry of Agriculture, Forestry and Fisheries, 2019), 11. Note that introduction of export controls by the Russian government during emergency situations such as the COVID-19 pandemic is an important point of discussion from the perspective of Russia's credibility as an exporter, and the following literature should also be consulted: Nagatomo Kenji, "Roshia no kokumotsu yushutsu kisei" [Russia's crop export controls], in *PRIMAFF Review*, no. 102 (2021): 6-7.

15) *Российская газета*, от 27 декабря 2019г.

16) Указ Президента РФ от 21 января 2020г., № 20, «Об утверждении Доктрины продовольственной безопасности Российской Федерации», *СЗРФ, 27 января 2020г., № 4, ст. 345.*

17) «г» пункт 22, «Доктрины продовольственной безопасности Российской Федерации»; *Российская газета*, от 22 января 2021г., «Доктрина на экспорт Утверждена новая доктрина продовольственной безопасности».

18) *Взгляд*, от 13 января 2020г.

19) *Ведомости*, от 28 апреля 2021г.

20) *Российская газета*, от 2 сентября 2021г.; от 3 сентября 2021г.

21) *Известия*, от 14 ноября 2021г.

22) Президент России, 6 декабря 2021г., Российско-индийские документы, подписанные к встрече Президента Российской Федерации В.В.Путина с Премьер-министром Республики Индии Н.Моди.

23) Президент России, 6 декабря 2021г., Совместное заявление по итогам XXI российско-индийского саммита «Россия – Индия: партнёрство во имя мира, прогресса и процветания»; *Парламентская Газета*, от 6 декабря 2021г., Россия и Индия подписали соглашение о военно-техническом сотрудничестве до 2031 года; *Газета.Ру*, от 6 декабря 2021г., Нью-Дели опасается, что Вашингтон устроит войну с Пекином «до последнего индуса»; *Коммерсантъ*, от 6 декабря 2021г..

24) European External Action Service, *Joint Communication on the Indo-Pacific* (September 16, 2021).

25) [Japan] Prime Minister's Office, "Beikoku homon" [Visit to the United States] (September 25, 2021); [Japan] Ministry of Foreign Affairs (MOFA), "The Second Japan-Australia-India-U.S. Summit Meeting" (September 24, 2021); *Mainichi Shimbun*, September 24, 2021.

26) Президент России, 30 ноября 2021г., Инвестиционный форум «Россия зовёт!».

27) *РБК*, от 21 ноября 2021г.

28) *Guardian*, November 21, 2021; Higashino Atsuko, "EU-chugoku-taiwan kankei no shin tenkai (zenpen, chuhen, kohen)" [New developments in EU-China-Taiwan relations (Part I, Part II, Part III)], JIIA (October 7, 8, and 11, 2021).

29) Hydrographic and Oceanographic Department of the Japan Coast Guard, "Navigational Warning"; Japan Coast Guard, "Kinkyu joho: Shageki kunren (Nihonkai)" [Emergency information: Firing drill (Sea of Japan)] (October 5, 2021).

30) *Известия*, от 5 октября 2021г.

31) Минобороны РФ, 7 октября 2021г., Ракетный крейсер «Варяг» Тихоокеанского флота и БПК «Адмирал Трибуц» вышли в Японское море для проведения ракетных стрельб.

32) Президент России, 21 декабря 2021г., Ракетоносцы «Князь Олег» и «Новосибирск» приняты в состав ВМФ России.

33) Минобороны РФ, 18 октября 2021г., В Японском море завершилось совместное российско-китайское военно-морское учение «Морское взаимодействие-2021».

34) [Japan] Joint Staff, "Chugoku oyobi roshia kaigun kantei no doko ni tsuite" [Regarding the movements of Chinese and Russian naval vessels] (October 21, 2021); "Chugoku oyobi roshia kaigun kantei no doko ni tsuite" [Regarding the movements of Chinese and Russian naval vessels] (October 23); "Roshia kaigun kantei no doko ni tsuite" [Regarding the movements of Russian naval vessels] (October 25).

35) *Известия*, от 19 ноября 2021г.

36) [Japan] Joint Staff, "Chugoku kaigun kantei no doko ni tsuite" [Regarding the movements of Chinese naval vessels] (November 19, 2021); "Roshia kaigun kantei no doko ni tsuite" [Regarding the movements of a Russian naval vessel] (November 19, 2021); [Japan] Ministry of Defense, "Chugoku kaigun kantei no doko ni tsuite" [Regarding the movements of a Chinese naval vessel] (November 19, 2021); JIJI.COM, November 20, 2021.

37) Президент России, 16 июня 2021г., Совместное заявление Президентов России и США по стратегической стабильности.

38) МИД России, 30 сентября 2021г., Совместное заявление по итогам встречи в рамках российско-американского диалога по стратегической стабильности в Женеве, 30 сентября 2021 г. (№ 1950-30-09-2021).

39) Совет Безопасности (далее - Совбез) РФ, 25 января 2021г.

40) Совбез РФ, «Новости и информация».

41) Совбез РФ, 17 ноября 2021г.

42) Президент России, 7 декабря 2021г.; 31 декабря 2021г.

43) *Guardian*, December 17, 2021.

44) Yuasa Takeshi, *Gendai chuo ajia no kokusai seiji: Roshia, beiou, chugoku no kainyu to shin dokuritsukoku no jiritsu* [International politics in modern Central Asia: Russian, U.S., European, and Chinese intervention and the independence of newly independent states] (Tokyo: Akashi Shoten, 2015).

45) ТАСС, от 13 сентября 2021г.

46) *Известия*, от 15 сентября 2021г.

47) *Коммерсантъ*, от 15 сентября 2021г.

48) Пункт 16, Стратегии национальной безопасности Российской Федерации, Указ Президента РФ от 2 июля 2021г., № 400.

49) (3) пункт 47, Стратегии национальной безопасности Российской Федерации, Указ Президента РФ от 2 июля 2021г., № 400.

50) Hirose Yoko, *Haiburiddo sen: Roshia no atarashi kokka senryaku* [Hybrid warfare: Russia's new national strategy] (Tokyo: Kodansha, 2021); Koizumi Yu, *Gendai roshia no gunji senryaku* [Modern Russia's military strategy] (Tokyo: Chikuma Shobo, 2021).

51) Минобороны РФ, Главное управление Генерального штаба Вооруженных Сил Российской Федерации.

52) *Известия*, от 27 февраля 2021г.

53) Статья 7, Федеральный закон от 31 мая 1996г., № 61-ФЗ (ред. от 11 июня 2021г.), «Об обороне», *СЗРФ, 3 июня 1996г., № 23, ст. 2750.*

54) Статья 5 и 6, Федеральный закон от 31 мая 1996г., № 61-ФЗ (ред. от 11 июня 2021г.), «Об обороне».

55) Указ Президента РФ от 5 апреля 2016г., № 157 (ред. от 17 июня 2019г.), «Вопросы Федеральной службы войск национальной гвардии Российской Федерации», *СЗРФ, 11 апреля 2016г., № 15, ст. 2072.*

56) Росгвардия, Учение «Заслон 2021»; Российская газета, от 2 июля 2021г.; от 29 июля 2021г.; *Коммерсантъ*, от 2 июля 2021г.

57) Г. Н. Симаков, К. Н. Малов, В. В. Терещенко и др., 2008, *Пограничная служба России – Энциклопедия. Биографии,* М.: Ассоциация «Военная книга», с. 436-439.

58) The International Institute for Strategic Studies, "Chapter Five: Russia and Eurasia," *The Military Balance 2021* 121, issue 1 (2021): 204-205.

59) [Japan] MOFA, "G7 foreign ministers' statement on recent events near the Kerch Strait" (November 30, 2018).

60) *Guardian*, June 23, 2021.

61) *Российская газета*, от 29 января 2017г.

62) Интерфакс, от 28 сентября 2020г.; РИА Новости, 25 февраля 2020г.

63) Наука и техника, 17 июля 2021г., Испытания пограничных сторожевых кораблей «Анадырь» и «Расул Гамзатов».

64) МЧС России, 18 августа 2021г., Безопасная Арктика: Масштабные учения МЧС России пройдут в сентябре в Арктической зоне Российской Федерации.

65) Правительство РФ, 26 июля 2021г., Михаил Мишустин посетил рыбоперерабатывающий комплекс «Ясный»; 26 июля 2021г., Михаил Мишустин посетил поликлинику Курильской центральной районной больницы.

66) *Коммерсантъ*, от 26 июля 2021г.

67) Совбез РФ, 28 сентября 2021г., «Секретарь Совета Безопасности Российской Федерации Николай Патрушев посетил зенитный ракетный полк, дислоцированный в Сахалинской области».

68) *Российская газета*, от 2 декабря 2021г.

69) Ogushi Atsushi, "Jusoteki mashin seiji kara popyurisuto taisei e no henyo ka: Roshia ni okeru ken'i shugi taisei no seiritsu to tenkai" [Transformation from multi-tiered machine

politics to a populist regime: The formation and development of the authoritarian regime in Russia], in *Kotai suru minshu shugi, kyoka sareru ken'i shugi: Sairyo no seiji seido to wa nani ka* [Regressing democracy, strengthened authoritarianism: What is the optimal political system?], ed. Kawanaka Takeshi (Kyoto: Minerva Shobo, 2018), 159-188; Lucan A. Way, *Pluralism by Default: Weak Autocrats and the Rise of Competitive Politics* (Baltimore: Johns Hopkins University Press, 2015); Steven Levitsky and Lucan A. Way, "Elections Without Democracy: The Rise of Competitive Authoritarianism," *Journal of Democracy* 13, no. 2 (2002): 51-65.

70) Центральной избирательной комиссии Российской Федерации, Об установлении общих результатов выборов депутатов Государственной Думы Федерального Собрания Российской Федерации восьмого созыва; РИА Новости, «Итоги выборов в Госдуму — 2021».

71) Vadim Shtepa, "How New Are the 'New People' in Russia's Parliament?," *Eurasia Daily Monitor* 18, issue 152 (October 6, 2021).

72) Mano Shinsaku, *Posuto puuchin ron josetsu: "Chechen ka" suru roshia* [Introduction to post-Putinism: The "Chechenization" of Russia] (Tokyo: Toyo Shoten Shinsha, 2021).

73) *Новая газета*, от 10 декабря 2021г.

74) Госдума РФ, 21 июля 2021г., Как российское законодательство регулирует работу иноагентов.

75) Минюст России, 14 января 2022г., Реестр иностранных средств массовой информации, выполняющих функции иностранного агента.

76) *Новая газета*, от 13 октября 2021г.

77) *Guardian*, November 25, 2021.

78) *Коммерсантъ*, от 28 декабря 2021г.

79) International Memorial, What is International Memorial.

80) *Независимая газета*, от 21 декабря 2020г.

81) Президент России, 21 декабря 2020г.

82) *Независимое военное обозрение*, no. 47, 25 декабря 2020 - 14 января 2021.

83) *Красная звезда*, от 19 июля 2021г.; от 22 декабря 2021г.

84) Минобороны РФ, 19 июля 2021г., Фрегат «Адмирал Флота Советского Союза Горшков» успешно выполнил стрельбу гиперзвуковой ракетой «Циркон» по наземной цели.

85) *Красная звезда*, от 22 декабря 2021г.

86) *Красная звезда*, от 22 декабря 2021г.

87) *Независимое военное обозрение*, no. 47, 25 декабря 2020г.- 14 января 2021г.

88) *Красная звезда*, от 2 июня 2021г.

89) *Российская газета*, от 4 июля 2021г.

90) *Красная звезда*, от 2 июня 2021г.

91) *Независимая газета*, от 10 июня 2021г.; *Красная звезда*, от 20 сентября 2021г.

92) *Красная звезда*, от 17 сентября 2021г.

93) *Независимая газета*, от 30 июня 2021г.; *Красная звезда*, от 5 июля 2021г.

94) *Независимая газета*, от 30 июня 2021г.; *Красная звезда*, от 30 июня 2021г.

95) *Красная звезда*, от 17 мая 2021г.

96) *Красная звезда*, от 17 мая 2021г.

97) Минобороны РФ, 7 июня 2021г., В Баренцевом море началось учение разнородных сил Северного флота по защите морских рубежей России в Арктике.

98) *Российская газета*, от 30 апреля 2021г.

99) *Красная звезда*, от 9 июля 2021г.

100) *Российская газета*, от 15 июня 2021г.

101) *Красная звезда*, от 30 апреля 2021г.

102) *Известия*, от 28 октября 2020г.; *Независимая газета*, от 7 декабря 2020г.

103) *Красная звезда*, от 25 июня 2021г.

104) Минобороны РФ, 21 июля 2021г., Контрольные занятия начались с мотострелками армейского корпуса ВВО на Сахалине и Курильских островах.

105) Минобороны РФ, 8 сентября 2021г., Тактическое учение по противодесантной обороне с военнослужащими армейского корпуса ВВО стартовало на Курильских островах.

106) *Российская газета*, от 28 апреля 2021г.

107) *Российская газета*, от 19 июля 2021г.

108) Минобороны РФ, 28 июля 2021г., Глава российского военного ведомства принял участие в совещании министров обороны государств – членов ШОС.

109) *Независимая газета*, от 14 сентября 2021г.

110) *Красная звезда*, от 17 сентября 2021г.

111) *Независимая газета*, от 13 сентября 2021г.

112) *Независимая газета*, от 6 января 2022г.; *Российская газета*, от 7 января 2022г.

113) Президент России, 7 июня 2021г.

114) Минобороны РФ, 27 августа 2021г., Подведены итоги научно-деловой программы Международного военно-технического форума.

115) *Российская газета*, от 7 апреля 2021г.

116) Минобороны РФ, 22 июня 2021г., Министр обороны России провел переговоры с главкомом Вооружённых сил Мьянмы Мин Аунг Хлайном.

Chapter 7

The United States

"Strategic Competition" with China and the Restoration
of U.S. Leadership

KIKUCHI Shigeo

President Biden, appears on a press room screen at the NATO summit on June 14, 2021 (©Nicolas Landemard/Le Pictorium Agency via ZUMA Press/ Kyodo News Images)

Summary

The Joseph Biden administration took office following the January 6, 2021 attack on the U.S. Capitol—the nation's only political crisis comparable to the Civil War. Despite differing from the Donald Trump administration in many ways, including its background, and governing style, the Biden administration has followed in the footsteps of the previous administration in key areas of foreign and national security policies. The Biden administration upheld the agreement that the previous administration made with the Taliban to completely withdraw from Afghanistan, although it extended its deadline by more than four months. The Biden administration also identified as its first priority "new threats" created by China as the "distribution of power across the world is changing," and positioned China's relationship with the United States as one of "strategic competition." However, unlike the previous administration, the Biden administration believes that this "strategic competition" is a "complicated one" with "competitive," "collaborative," and "adversarial" aspects, and it has reemphasized the importance of engaging in diplomacy and in international organizations in order to secure the United States' position as a world leader. In addition, to maintain the international order in the Indo-Pacific region, the Biden administration has emphasized cooperation with concerned nations. This stance was reflected in a series of summit- and ministerial-level meetings held after the administration took power, as well as in President Biden's first overseas trip to Europe. Also notable was the administration's creation of the Australia-United Kingdom-United States trilateral security partnership (AUKUS), which was announced on September 15.

Due in part to the rapid progress of vaccination against novel coronavirus disease (COVID-19), in 2021, the Indo-Pacific saw a variety of large-scale exercises and active deployment of ships to the Western Pacific, including bilateral training with a British aircraft carrier. The Biden administration continued to deploy U.S. Navy ships in the South China Sea and conduct transits through the Taiwan Strait. As for the military posture in the Indo-Pacific, the administration launched a policy of strengthening the defense of Guam, which is a strategic hub for the United States, and has been promoting the distribution of base functions, reorganization of the Marine Corps, and the development of long-range strike capabilities by the Army.

Keywords

United States · Indo-Pacific · foreign policy · defense policy · Europe · Australia

1. The Biden Administration and Its Foreign Policy

(1) Afghanistan Drawdown

The Biden administration came into office after settling a political crisis not seen since the Civil War. On January 6, 2021, a mob of supporters claiming that President Donald Trump had been reelected broke through a barricade and stormed into the U.S. Capitol, where a Joint Session was in the process of certifying the electoral votes cast the previous year on December 14, and violently disrupted the proceedings. While the Biden administration largely reversed the policies of the previous administration in several areas, it also inherited important aspects of Trump's foreign and security policies.

One of them was the policy of withdrawal from Afghanistan, in which "Biden was working from a script inherited from the administration of Donald Trump" (Richard Haass, president of the Council on Foreign Relations).[1] President Trump had made public his intention to pull out of Afghanistan in the election campaign, but he heeded the advice of Secretary of Defense James Mattis and other officers. In a speech on August 21, 2017, seven months after taking office, he stated that "a hasty withdrawal would create a vacuum that terrorists...would instantly fill" and rejected a pullout strategy guided by "arbitrary timetables," citing the example of how pulling U.S. troops from Iraq in 2011 had allowed the Islamic State to grow more powerful there. In addition, he reportedly granted Secretary of Defense Mattis the authority to deploy additional troops.[2] Before long, however, Trump became frustrated with the situation in Afghanistan. By the summer of 2019, he had turned to the idea of withdrawing U.S. troops "as quickly as we can." The Trump administration began to negotiate with the Taliban without the participation of the Afghan government, while proceeding to reduce the number of U.S. troops stationed in Afghanistan. These negotiations resulted in the U.S.-Taliban Agreement for Bringing Peace to Afghanistan, or Doha Agreement, signed on February 29, 2020 between Zalmay Khalilzad, U.S. special representative for Afghanistan reconciliation, and Abdul Ghani

Baradar, head of the Taliban's political office in Qatar. In the agreement, the Taliban pledged to prevent terrorists, including al Qaeda, from using Afghan soil to attack the United States and its allies, to refuse cooperation with groups or individuals that threaten the security of the United States and its allies, and to prevent groups or individuals within Afghanistan from attacking the United States and its allies. In exchange, the United States pledged to fully remove all military forces of the United States, its allies, and Coalition partners, civilian personnel other than diplomats, and private security company personnel by May 1, 2021. The U.S. withdrawal was executed in line with the Doha Agreement, and on January 15, 2021, five days before the change of administration, acting Secretary of Defense Christopher Miller announced that the number of U.S. troops stationed in Afghanistan had been reduced to 2,500.

After taking office on January 20, the Biden administration, led by Jake Sullivan, assistant to the president for national security affairs, reportedly held 25 National Security Council (NSC) meetings over the two-plus month period from February through April, during which the Afghanistan strategy was intensively reviewed. Based on these meetings, President Biden announced in a speech at the White House on April 14 that the "final withdrawal" would begin on May 1, and that the redeployment of U.S., NATO allies, and partner troops from Afghanistan would be completed by September 11. Although the deadline for complete pullout was pushed back by a little more than four months, the Biden administration has nevertheless upheld the Trump administration's policy.

In an earlier intra-governmental review, Gen. Austin Miller, commander of the United States Forces-Afghanistan, had recommended that several thousand U.S. troops remain in the country. Likewise, Secretary of Defense Lloyd Austin presented two options: withdrawal according to the Doha Agreement, or continued presence in Afghanistan for an indefinite period. He asserted that the latter option, continuing to station U.S. troops in Afghanistan, would enable the United States to provide Ashraf Ghani's administration with vital intelligence to govern the country and would allow the United States to gain "situational awareness" on the ground. In response, President Biden made it clear that maintaining the

Secretary of Defense Lloyd Austin (left) and JCS chairman, Gen. Mark Milley (center) greet Gen. Austin Miller, commander of the United States Forces-Afghanistan (right), at Joint Base Andrews, as he returns to the United States on July 14, 2021 (DOD photo by Navy Petty Officer 1st Class Carlos M. Vazquez II)

current regime was not the objective of the military operation, stating in a meeting at the White House, "If the mission is to preserve the Ghani government, I would not send my own son."[3]

From the start, President Biden recognized that the military operation in Afghanistan, which was initiated to prevent the recurrence of terrorist attacks against the United States, had become unclear in its objectives. It had expanded to include efforts to rebuild the nation of Afghanistan, and he believed that the time had come for the operation to return to its original objectives.[4] Biden expressed this sentiment in a speech on April 14, when he said that as a result of the U.S. forces' continued presence in Afghanistan after the killing of Osama bin Laden, the mastermind of the terror attacks on the United States, "our reasons for remaining in Afghanistan are becoming increasingly unclear." In contrast to the insistence of the Department of Defense (DOD) on a limited, but continued presence in the area, Biden believed that "a troop presence became a magnet for more troops," and that the situation could spiral out of hand if the Taliban—which had refrained from attacking U.S. troops in accordance with the Doha Agreement—resumed attacks once it learned that the U.S. forces were there to stay. Thus, maintaining a continued presence would ultimately require the deployment of additional forces.[5]

President Biden's understanding draws from his experience as vice president in the Barack Obama administration, where he participated in the White House reviews of the Afghanistan-Pakistan strategy in the spring of 2009 and the

Afghanistan surge in the summer and fall of the same year. In one notable instance, Biden visited Pakistan and Afghanistan in January 2009, just before he took office as vice president.[6] There, during talks and dinner with President Hamid Karzai, he reportedly came to the conclusion that the Afghan government did not have the willpower to resolve its country's governance problems, including its corruption and internal divisions, nor a sense of commitment in the fight against the Taliban, and that there was no hope of turning the situation around in Afghanistan.[7] On this point, former President Barack Obama noted in his memoir that Biden's January 2009 visit to Afghanistan "convinced him [Biden] that we needed to rethink our entire approach to Afghanistan."[8]

Once the review of the Afghanistan surge had begun, Gen. Stanley McChrystal, commander of the International Security Assistance Force stationed in Afghanistan, called for an additional 40,000 U.S. troops to be sent to Afghanistan to conduct a "comprehensive counterinsurgency (COIN) campaign." This request was supported by David Petraeus, commander of the U.S. Central Command, and Mike Mullen, chairman of the Joint Chiefs of Staff (JCS). According to former President Barack Obama, Vice President Biden "viewed McChrystal's proposal as just the latest attempt by an unrestrained military to drag the country deeper into a futile, wildly expensive nation-building exercise, when we could and should be narrowly focused on counterterrorism (CT) efforts against al-Qaeda."[9]

Former President Trump held similar views to President Biden regarding the continued presence of U.S. troops in Afghanistan. According to John Bolton, Trump's national security advisor, Trump "opposed a continuing US presence in Afghanistan" and "was frustrated with what he called 'his' generals," namely, Secretary of Defense Mattis and others who repeatedly urged him to keep the troops in Afghanistan.[10] In addition, during an interview with Bob Woodward at the *Washington Post*, he expressed strong dissatisfaction with "four generals" (Secretary of Defense Mattis, White House Chief of Staff John Kelly, JCS Chairman Joseph Dunford, and National Security Adviser H.R. McMaster), saying that if he followed their advice, "does this mean we're going to be there [in

A member of the U.S. Air Force 23rd Security Forces Squadron plays ball with Afghan children evacuated from Afghanistan to Ramstein Air Base, Germany, as part of Operation Allies Refuge (August 31, 2021, Ramstein Air Base, Germany)

Afghanistan] for the next 100 years?"[11] In this light, it seems rather natural that former President Trump would respond the way he did to Biden's April 14 decision. In a statement on April 18, Trump criticized Biden's extension of the withdrawal deadline, but called the 19-year-long campaign in Afghanistan "enough, in fact, far too much and way too long" and described the decision to pull out from Afghanistan "a wonderful and positive thing to do." In doing so, he made it clear that he disagreed with many Republican officials.

Another topic of debate was whether the United States should limit its presence in Afghanistan to counterterrorism missions. Regarding this, in an article he contributed to the March/April 2020 issue of *Foreign Affairs*, President Biden, then one of the Democratic presidential candidates, called for an end to military operations in Afghanistan, reiterating that the United States should bring home the majority of its troops from the wars in Afghanistan and the Middle East and "narrowly define" its mission as defeating al Qaeda and the Islamic State. Even if the U.S. military were to limit its role to counterterrorism missions, the fact would remain that Afghanistan's share of the war on terror was declining relative to other countries. In his April 14 speech, President Biden noted that "over the past 20 years [after the September 11 attacks], the threat has become more dispersed, metastasizing around the globe: al-Shabaab in Somalia; al Qaeda in the Arabian Peninsula; al-Nusra in Syria; ISIS attempting to create a caliphate in Syria and Iraq and establishing affiliates in multiple countries in Africa and Asia." In such a situation, "keeping thousands of troops grounded and concentrated in just one country at a cost of billions each year makes little sense."

The same view had already been expressed in President Obama's "Drone Speech" at the U.S. National Defense University on May 23, 2013. In this speech, President Obama, referring to the outbreak of al Qaeda affiliates, pointed out that "from Yemen to Iraq, from Somalia to North Africa, the threat today is more diffuse." He then revealed that he had signed the Presidential Policy Guidance (PPG), a framework for reviewing direct actions taken unmanned aerial vehicles (UAVs) and by Special Forces in areas other than Afghanistan, Iraq, Syria, and parts of Libya, which are designated "areas of active hostilities."[12]

Efforts to scale back and reorganize combat missions have also been taking place with regard to Iraq. On July 26, 2021, President Biden announced an agreement with the Iraqi government to end the U.S. combat mission in Iraq by the end of 2021, based on negotiations in the U.S.-Iraq Strategic Dialogue that began on June 11, 2020, under the Trump administration. In Iraq, as in Afghanistan, the Biden administration completed the work begun under the Trump administration.

Behind President Biden's decision to take over President Trump's policy of complete withdrawal from Afghanistan and make it a reality was the foregone conclusion that the Afghan government, which the United States had propped up for many years, would at some point reach the brink of collapse. It was a choice that he dared to make, being fully aware of possible criticism he would take and in defiance of the recommendations of the DOD and senior military leadership. In the aforementioned contribution to *Foreign Affairs*, President Biden wrote, "staying entrenched in unwinnable conflicts drains our capacity to lead on other issues that require our attention, and it prevents us from rebuilding the other instruments of American power." In light of this, the withdrawal from Afghanistan can be interpreted instead as a decision to allocate more resources to more critical issues, such as strategic competition with China. In his April 14 speech, President Biden stated that he was the fourth president to preside over the war in Afghanistan, and that "I will not pass this responsibility on to a fifth." Such a statement should be seen as a demonstration of Biden's strong political will to follow through with this decision.

(2) "Strategic Competition" with China

Matt Pottinger, who oversaw the Trump administration's Asia policy, first as NSC senior director for Asia, and then as deputy national security advisor, said the Biden administration "has largely maintained its predecessor's policy" toward China, a point made clear early in the administration.[13] The Interim National Security Strategic Guidance (INSSG) released by the White House on March 3, 2021, states that the "distribution of power across the world is changing," creating "new threats" such as China, Russia, North Korea, Iran, and terrorism and violent extremism. Among them, China is positioned as "the only competitor potentially capable of combining its economic, diplomatic, military, and technological power to mount a sustained challenge to a stable and open international system" (emphasis added).

This remarkable continuity in perception on China can be attributed to a shared recognition across party lines that the United States can no longer expect deeper engagement with China to encourage its transformation. This expectation had formed the basis of China policies of the successive U.S. administrations since Richard Nixon. In the March/April 2018 issue of *Foreign Affairs*, Kurt Campbell, currently the NSC coordinator for Indo-Pacific affairs in the Biden administration, and Ely Ratner, who serves as the assistant secretary of defense for Indo-Pacific security affairs, mentioned that since Nixon, the United States has "put too much faith in its power to shape China's trajectory," and that despite trade with China and the country's integration into the international economy, "China has instead pursued its own course, belying a range of American expectations." The same perception was shared by the Trump administration's Secretary of State Mike Pompeo, who said that since Richard Nixon's presidency, the United States presumed it to be "so inevitable" that as China became more prosperous, it would open up, and that the freer it became, the less of a threat it would present to the international community—but "that age of inevitability is over" (July 23, 2020 speech at the Richard Nixon Presidential Library and Museum). In the

September/October 2019 issue of *Foreign Affairs*, Campbell and Sullivan, who would serve as President Biden's national security advisor, observed that both Republican and Democratic foreign policy officials "have mostly, and rightly, discarded some of the more optimistic assumptions that underpinned the four-decade-long strategy of diplomatic and economic engagement with China."

Continuing in the line of the Trump administration, the Biden administration has positioned relations with China as "strategic competition." However, it does not consider strategic competition to consist solely of adversarial elements, and has made its position clear, saying in the INSSG: "strategic competition does not, and should not, preclude working with China when it is in our national interest to do so." Likewise, during his "A Foreign Policy for the American People" speech at the State Department on March 3, 2021, the same day the INSSG was released, Secretary of State Antony Blinken explained that the relationship with China has "competitive," "collaborative," and "adversarial" aspects. These three aspects of the relationship with China make it a "complicated one" (Secretary of State Blinken, MSNBC interview, February 1, 2021), but the key to meeting these challenges, he says, is for the United States to demonstrate its leadership through diplomacy and in its engagement with international organizations.

In fact, on February 4, shortly after taking office, President Biden declared in his State Department address on U.S. foreign policy, "America is back," followed by, "Diplomacy is back at the center of our foreign policy." These remarks expressed his desire to strengthen U.S. leadership in addressing a variety of challenges. The same message was demonstrated symbolically when President Biden signed two documents on January 20, his first day in office: one retracting the Trump administration's decision to withdraw the United States from the World Health Organization (WHO), and the other bringing the United States back into the Paris Agreement (the United States formally rejoined on February 19). As stated by Secretary of State Blinken in his March 3 speech, in terms of engagement in diplomacy and international organizations, "where we have pulled back, China has filled in." One can note that underlying all of this was the country's strategic competition with China for international leadership.

Regarding the Biden administration's relations with China, concrete examples of continuity with the previous administration can be seen in several areas. The Trump administration, in its final days, prohibited U.S. persons from the transaction and possession of publicly traded securities of any company identified as a Communist Chinese Military Company (CCMC), including their derivatives (Executive Order 13959 (November 12, 2020), Executive Order 13974 (January 13, 2021)). A total of 44 companies were designated as CCMCs under the Trump administration. In contrast, with Executive Order 14032 of June 3, 2021, President Biden reorganized President Trump's regulations and expanded the ban on trading and holding publicly traded securities and their derivatives to include "Chinese Military-Industrial Complex Companies" (CMIC), which also cover "the surveillance technology sector," citing their "use of Chinese surveillance technology to facilitate repression or serious human rights abuse." As of the end of 2021, 68 Chinese companies have been designated as CMICs, more than under the Trump administration. These include SenseTime Group Limited, which was identified as a CMIC on December 10, 2021, International Human Rights Day, for providing China with systems that made use of facial recognition technology to monitor ethnic minorities in the Xinjiang Uyghur Autonomous Region.

As exemplified by the expansion of the ban on trading and holding publicly traded securities and their derivatives to encompass CMICs, including those in the "surveillance sector," the Biden administration, following the steps taken by the Trump administration, has increased sanctions on China in connection with the human rights situation in the Xinjiang Uyghur Autonomous Region. During the Trump administration, the Treasury Department designated senior Communist Party and public security officials for the first time in July 2020, freezing their assets in the United States pursuant to the Global Magnitsky Human Rights Accountability Act. Following this, under the Biden administration, two more individuals were added to the Global Magnitsky sanctions program on March 22, 2021, and again on December 10, 2021. On December 23, President Biden also signed into law the Uyghur Forced Labor Prevention Act, which prohibited the import of "goods made with forced labor in the Xinjiang Uyghur

Autonomous Region."

As for Taiwan, the Biden administration has been making moves to strengthen relations with Taiwan while maintaining its existing policy positions. On March 25, 2021, the American Institute in Taiwan signed a memorandum of understanding to establish a Coast Guard Working Group with the Taipei Economic and Cultural Representative Office in the United States. Following this, on April 9, the State Department issued the Guidelines on Relations with Taiwan. Intended to serve as a guide for U.S. government officials in interactions with "Taiwan counterparts," it positions Taiwan as "a vibrant democracy and an important security and economic partner that is also a force for good in the international community" and "liberalize[s] guidance on contacts with Taiwan." The guidelines were drafted in accordance with the Taiwan Assurance Act of 2020, enacted on December 27, 2020, which directed the State Department to review the department's current guidance that governs relations with Taiwan with "the intent to deepen and expand United States-Taiwan relations." In a press statement dated May 7, 2021, Secretary of State Blinken also stated that "Taiwan is a reliable partner, a vibrant democracy, and a force for good in the world," and insisted that Taiwan be invited to the World Health Assembly, the highest decision-making body of the World Health Organization (WHO).

In addition, on June 16, 2020, nearing the end of the Trump administration, the official Facebook account of the U.S. Army 1st Special Forces Group (Airborne) posted a promotional video showing a training exercise in which U.S. operators carried wounded soldiers into a UH-60 helicopter with what appeared to be the "Blue Sky with a White Sun" and the Chinese characters "Lujun [Army]" on it. The media responded to the post, saying it showed that the United States had sent special operations forces to Taiwan and was training with the Taiwanese military. In November of the same year, it was reported that marines from the Marine Special Operations Command had been sent to Taiwan and that they were training the Taiwan Marine Corps. In response, a U.S. DOD spokesman commented to *Stars and Stripes* that such reports were "inaccurate." Then, on October 7, 2021, well into the ninth month with President Biden in office, the

Wall Street Journal offered some perspective on the continued provision of training by U.S. special-operations forces for the Taiwan military even after the change of administration, reporting that "about two dozen members of U.S. special-operations and support troops are conducting training for small units of Taiwan's ground forces" and that "the American forces have been operating in Taiwan for at least a year."[14]

The Biden administration is aware that it must also properly manage strategic competition with China to prevent the situation from escalating in an undesired manner. One example of this was President Biden's appeal to President Xi Jinping at the U.S.-China summit held online on November 15, 2021, when he noted the need for "common-sense guardrails" to ensure that competition does not veer into conflict and to keep lines of communication open. In that regard, there has been a growing sense in China that the United States has been in decline ever since the 2008 financial crisis. Events such as the COVID-19 pandemic in 2020 and the January 6 attack on the U.S. Capitol Building have only increased the momentum behind such arguments.[15] How the United States works on these perceptions in China through its words and actions will also be critical in managing the competition.[16]

(3) Rallying Allies and Partners in the Indo-Pacific

According to the INSSG, in order to advance strategic competition with China, the United States must confront China from "a position of confidence and strength." To this end, the United States must "rally our allies and partners to join us, pooling our negotiating leverage and showing our collective power and resolve." Such efforts to strengthen ties with allies and partners began soon after the Biden administration took office. On March 12, 2021, the Japan-Australia-India-U.S. Leaders' Video Conference was held, where participants pledged to "commit to promoting a free, open rules-based order, rooted in international law" and respond to "challenges to the rules-based maritime order in the East and South China Seas." At the subsequent Japan-U.S. Security Consultative Committee meeting on March 16 and the Japan-U.S. summit on April 16, participants expressed concern about "Chinese activities that are inconsistent with the international rules-based order" and opposed China's unlawful maritime claims and activities in the South China Sea and "any unilateral attempts to change the status quo." They also expressed "serious concerns" about the human rights situation in Hong Kong and the Xinjiang Uyghur Autonomous Region and emphasized "the importance of peace and stability across the Taiwan Strait."

The United States is also seeking cooperation with European allies on Indo-Pacific issues. One such effort was President Biden's June 2021 trip to Europe, which he described as "America rallying the world's democracies."[17] At the G7 summit held in Cornwall, the United Kingdom, from June 11 to 13, and at the U.S.-EU summit held in Brussels on June 15, leaders called on China "to respect human rights and fundamental freedoms, especially in relation to Xinjiang and those rights, freedoms and high degree of autonomy for Hong Kong," and underscored "the importance of peace and stability across the Taiwan Strait," stating that they "remain seriously concerned about the situation in the East and South China Seas." Then, at the North Atlantic Treaty Organization (NATO) summit held in Brussels on June 14, NATO allies stated that "China's stated ambitions and assertive behavior present systemic challenges to the rules-based international order and to areas relevant to Alliance security." In addition, in 2021, the United States symbolically demonstrated its cooperation with European countries on Indo-Pacific security issues through joint training exercises with ships sent by these countries to the Indo-Pacific (see Section 2 (1)).

One of the most notable examples of U.S. cooperation with concerned nations on Indo-Pacific security was the creation of the Australia-United Kingdom-United States trilateral security partnership (AUKUS), which President Biden jointly announced with Australian Prime Minister Scott Morrison and UK Prime Minister Boris Johnson at the White House on September 15, 2021. According to the joint statement released that day, AUKUS is an "an enhanced trilateral security partnership" whose purpose is "to deepen diplomatic, security, and defense cooperation in the Indo-Pacific region." Furthermore, it described trilateral cooperation on the acquisition of conventionally armed, nuclear-powered submarines for the Royal Australian Navy as "the first initiative under AUKUS." Prime Minister Morrison revealed that Australia intends to build nuclear submarines in Adelaide, Australia, in close cooperation with the United Kingdom and the United States, which have experience in operating nuclear submarines. The three countries would hold talks over the next 18 months to determine "an optimal pathway" to develop a nuclear submarine capability for the Royal Australian Navy.

It is worth noting that Australia plans to build eight nuclear submarines at the Osborne Naval Shipyard in Adelaide through the 2040s, according to the Australian Department of Defence. On November 22, in Canberra, the governments of the three countries signed the Agreement for the Exchange of Naval Nuclear Propulsion Information concerning the provision, management, and protection of information on naval nuclear propulsion, including the nuclear reactors needed to build nuclear submarines. In a media statement explaining the purpose of creating AUKUS, released on September 16 (Australian time; the day that AUKUS' creation was announced), Prime Minister Morrison, Defence Minister Peter Dutton, and Foreign Affairs Minister Marise Payne stated that with the decision to cooperate with the United States and the United Kingdom in building nuclear submarines, Australia would be discontinuing development of the *Attack*-class conventionally powered submarines, which it had been carrying out jointly with the French defense company Naval Group in order to replace its six existing *Collins*-class conventional submarines.

On October 30, 2021, Vice Admiral Jonathan Mead, chief of the Nuclear Powered Submarine Taskforce, Australian Department of Defence, explained in comments posted on the Department's website that the decision to introduce nuclear submarines was due to "a rapid deterioration of the strategic environment of the Indo-Pacific region" as well as the fact that "military modernization is occurring at an unprecedented rate. Capabilities are rapidly advancing, and their reach is expanding. As a result, our technological edge is narrowing." According to Vice Admiral Mead, to deal to this situation, the Australian government will "allow us to hold potential adversaries at risk from a greater distance and influence their calculus of the costs involved in threatening Australia's interests" as well as "develop a more capable military force" that includes nuclear submarines.

Vice Admiral Mead did not specify which country he was referring to when he spoke of "military modernization" occurring at an "unprecedented rate." However, the introduction of nuclear submarines to Australia by AUKUS is generally perceived to be with China in mind, as pointed out by Michael Gilday, chief of naval operations, who stated in a September 23, 2021 webinar that AUKUS is a "brilliant stroke with respect to our posture in the Pacific, particularly vis-à-vis China."

Furthermore, AUKUS is expected to increase the interoperability of the militaries of the United States, United Kingdom, and Australia. In a speech at the United States Institute of Peace on November 19, 2021, Kurt Campbell, coordinator for Indo-Pacific affairs, said that AUKUS would lead to further integration among the militaries of the three countries, especially their naval forces through the exchange of personnel. Campbell believes that integration will progress to a point where there is "almost a melding" of their forces.

While trilateral cooperation on nuclear submarines through AUKUS has attracted the most external interest, cooperation in AUKUS is not limited to nuclear submarines alone. The September 15 joint statement listed the following areas of cooperation through AUKUS: 1) promote deeper information and technology sharing, 2) foster deeper integration of security and defense-related science, technology, industrial bases, and supply chains, and 3) deepen cooperation on a range of security and defense capabilities.

Specifically, it mentions Australia's acquisition of long-range strike capabilities. A September 16 media statement by Prime Minister Morrison and other ministers revealed that "Australia will rapidly acquire long-range strike capabilities" through AUKUS, including Tomahawk Cruise Missiles, Joint Air-to-Surface Standoff Missiles (Extended Range) (JASSM-ER), Long-Range Anti-Ship Missiles (Extended Range) (LRASM), and precision strike guided missiles with a range of over 400 kilometers for its land forces, and that it will cooperate with the United States to develop hypersonic missiles for its air capabilities.

Furthermore, in the 2020 Defence Strategic Update (released in July 2020), Australia's Department of Defence identified sovereign manufacturing capabilities for advanced guided weapons among objectives it was pursuing in addition to the acquisition of long-range strike capabilities. This challenge was addressed in a joint statement released after the Australia-U.S. Ministerial Consultations (AUSMIN) held at the U.S. State Department on September 16, the day after the creation of AUKUS was announced. It revealed that discussions were held on Australia's sovereign manufacturing capabilities for guided weapons, and that the two countries had agreed to work together on it in the future. The statement also incorporated cooperation between the U.S. and Australian defense departments on research, development, testing, and evaluation, and mentioned that the two countries had signed a Statement of Intent on Strategic Capabilities Cooperation and Implementation in order to expand joint development efforts on "advanced defense capabilities." Similarly, during the joint press conference after the AUSMIN, Secretary of State Blinken stated that through AUKUS, the United States and Australia would promote cooperation in cyber, AI, quantum technologies, and additional undersea capabilities.

U.S. Secretary of Defense Austin (back right) welcomes Australian Defence Minister Dutton (back left) to the U.S. DOD on September 15, 2021, ahead of the Australia-United States Ministerial Consultations (AUSMIN) the following day (DOD photo by Jim Garamone)

Obviously, AUKUS also carries foreign policy objectives. One is to strengthen ties with the United Kingdom. This was evident when President Biden announced the creation of AUKUS side-by-side with the United Kingdom and Australian prime ministers, saying that AUKUS "reflects a broader trend of key European countries playing an extremely important role in the Indo-Pacific." Seeking a global role post-Brexit, the United Kingdom, in its *Global Britain in a Competitive Age* report published in March 2021, set out a new "Indo-Pacific tilt" and its intention to strengthen cooperation with Indo-Pacific countries through "persistent engagement by our armed forces and our wider security capacity-building." AUKUS incorporates both of these developments in the United Kingdom.

Australia, on the other hand, has been subject to China's "economic coercion"—its ability to "leverage its economic influence to impose cost and alter the behavior of targeted actors, as well as discourage others from pursuing similar actions" (U.S. DOD, *Military and Security Developments Involving the People's Republic of China 2021* report). In particular, in April 2020, when Prime Minister Morrison pointed out the need for an investigation to determine the origin of COVID-19, China launched what has been described as "an economywide assault" on Australia, imposing significantly stricter tariffs, import restrictions, and other measures.[18] Regarding this, Campbell, coordinator for Indo-Pacific affairs, in an interview with the *Sydney Morning Herald* on March 16, 2021, stated that the United States put China on notice that the United States would not improve bilateral relations as long as China continues to engage in economic coercion with Australia, and that President Biden himself conveyed the same message to Prime Minister Morrison at the Japan-Australia-India-U.S. Leaders' Video Conference on March 12. Furthermore, after mentioning China's "economic coercion" targeting Australia at the post-AUSMIN joint press conference, Secretary of State Blinken stated that "the United States will not leave Australia alone on the field—or better yet, on the 'pitch.'" In doing so, he emphasized that AUKUS was formed with the notion of supporting Australia, which had become a target of Chinese economic coercion. His statement likely reflects the recognition that the future of the United States' international leadership depends on the support it provides to allies in the face of economic coercion by China.[19]

2. U.S. Military Forces in the Indo-Pacific

(1) Deployments in the Western Pacific

In 2020, the United States cancelled, postponed, or scaled back various military exercises in response to the spread of COVID-19. Among these, in March 2020, aircraft carrier USS *Theodore Roosevelt* suspended its Western Pacific deployment due to a COVID-19 outbreak on board. In contrast, 2021 saw rapid vaccination progress and an easing in infections, which made it possible to hold various large-scale exercises involving allied forces and actively deploy ships in the Western Pacific. These included training and test and evaluation thought to simulate high-end warfighting with China and Russia.

Exercise Northern Edge 2021 (NE 21) took place in Alaska from May 3 to 14. NE 21 was a Pacific Air Forces-led exercise sponsored by the U.S. Indo-Pacific Command (INDOPACOM) for the purpose of "high-end, realistic war fighter training." In addition to the U.S. Air Force, NE 21 brought together participants from the U.S. military services of the Army, Navy, and Marine Corps. On May 11, as part of "Large Force Employment training," the High Mobility Artillery Rocket System (HIMARS) battery, which was deployed by transport aircraft, conducted fire training from an airfield secured by airborne brigade. Exercise Lightning Edge was conducted from May 10 to 14 in conjunction with NE 21. During Exercise Lighting Edge, the 25th Infantry Division based in Hawaii remotely connected to the Multi-Domain Task Force (MDTF) (see (2) on MDTF) at Joint Base Lewis-McChord in Washington state through the all domain operations center (ADOC) in order to enable a common operating picture (COP), which was then used to take action against simulated targets on the island of Oahu. In the March 2021 chief of staff of the Army (CSA) paper, *Army Multi-Domain Transformation*, ADOC was described as a MDTF "command node," currently under construction, that "will enable 24/7 oversight of adversary contact in all domains." Its capabilities were verified at Exercise Lighting Edge.

Also participating in NE 21 were the carrier strike group (CSG) led by USS

Theodore Roosevelt and the amphibious ready group (ARG) led by USS *Makin Island*. These groups participated in the training exercise to prepare for the possibility of naval operations becoming possible in the Arctic Region due to global warming. The U.S. Navy has explained that participation in NE 21 by the CSG and ARG reflects the policy set out in *A Blue Arctic* (January 2021), the strategic blueprint released by the Department of the Navy on January 5, 2021, which states that the Department will "build more capable naval forces for the Arctic Region."

As "one of only a handful of exercises that combine GPC [great power competition]-level threat complexities with the joint interoperability necessary to realistically inform our test data," NE 21 also provided an opportunity for operational testing of equipment designed for high-end warfighting. One such test was the performance evaluation of the Eagle Passive Active Warning Survivability System (EPAWSS), which was developed to be equipped on F-15 fighter aircraft. EPAWSS is a state-of-the-art electronic warfare and protection system that collects and processes electromagnetic energy to create a comprehensive, 360-degree picture of threats in the battle space so that countermeasures can be taken quickly. The test was conducted by F-15EX and F-15E aircraft that had actually been equipped with EPAWSS. Incidentally, the Air Force announced earlier on December 31, 2020, that it had placed an order with Boeing for low-rate initial production of EPAWSS.

Also conducted at NE 21 was an experiment to verify the kill chain— the sequence from target detection to engagement— for the Air-Launched Rapid

An F-35B with the Marine Fighter Attack Squadron 211 deployed aboard the U.K. aircraft carrier HMS *Queen Elizabeth* operating in the South China Sea on October 6, 2021 (Photo by 1st Lt. Zachary Bodner, 3rd Marine Aircraft Wing)

Response Weapon (ARRW), a hypersonic glide weapon under development by the Air Force. For this experiment, a B-52 received target data from sensors via the All-Domain Operations Capability experiment (ADOC-E), more than 1,000 nautical miles (1,852 km) away. The bomber then took a simulated shot of the target from 600 nautical miles away using an ARRW.

Following NE 21, the U.S. Indo-Pacific Command hosted the Large Scale Global Exercise 2021 (LSGE 21) from August 2 to 27, taking place "across the Indo-Pacific region with our global partners." LSGE 21, which emphasized cooperation with "global partners," saw participation not only by regional allies such as Australia and Japan, but also the United Kingdom, which deployed the U.K. Carrier Strike Group (CSG-21), led by HMS *Queen Elizabeth*, to the Indo-Pacific. Specifically, beginning on August 20, bilateral training was conducted in the Philippine Sea by CSG-21 and an expeditionary strike group (ESG) led by USS *America*. During this training, HMS *Queen Elizabeth* carried the Royal Air Force 617 Squadron and U.S. Marine Fighter Attack Squadron 211, both of which are equipped with F-35Bs. Together with the F-35Bs of the Marine Fighter Attack Squadron 121 aboard USS *America*, they exhibited "dual-carrier—and triple-F-35 squadron—capability." On August 13 and 14, the *America* ESG and CSG-21 conducted fire support coordination training on Farallon de Medinilla, an uninhabited island in the Mariana Islands. Upon the request from joint terminal air controllers (JTAC) with the 31st Marine Expeditionary Unit, F-35Bs provided ground support and a Dutch frigate, HNLMS *Evertsen*, which was a part of CSG-21, provided naval gunfire. Furthermore, "multinational advanced aviation operations" by the *America* ESG and CSG-21 carrier-based aircraft were conducted on August 20, followed by "continuous flight operations for 48 hours" from August 22 to 24. On August 24, the U.S. Air Force's KC-135 aerial refueling aircraft and F-15C fighters from the Kadena Air Base, as well as ships and aircraft of Japan's Self-Defense Forces, including the destroyer JS *Ise*, conducted training with the *America* ESG and CSG-21. On August 26, the *Carl Vinson* CSG, which had departed San Diego on August 2, and CSG-21 launched their respective carrier-based aircraft, including F-35Cs and F-35Bs, for bilateral flight training in the Philippine Sea.

Originally scheduled for summer 2020, Large Scale Exercise 2020 (LSE 2020) was postponed due to COVID-19. Renamed Large Scale Exercise 2021 (LSE 2021), it was instead conducted from August 3 to 16, 2021, within the framework of LSGE 21. LSE 2021 was conducted by the U.S. Navy and Marine Corps in order to assess and test modern warfare concepts. With the participation of five naval fleets, five carrier strike groups (CSGs), and four amphibious ready groups (ARGs) in the Pacific, Atlantic, and Mediterranean oceans, it "showcased the ability of our fleets to synchronize and integrate across the globe" (Vice Admiral Steve Koehler, commander of the 3rd U.S. Fleet) on a scale unprecedented in recent years. The exercise was also unique in that it was conducted as a live, virtual and constructive (LVC) exercise: some ships conducted live maneuvers, others participated in the exercise remotely away from them while moored, and computer-generated ships and units were also part of the exercise.

Meanwhile, the 3rd Fleet (San Diego, California) and 2nd Fleet (Norfolk, Virginia), both of which participated in LSE 2021, moved their respective headquarters to Joint Base Pearl-Harbor-Hickam in Hawaii and a base near Norfolk for the duration of the exercise, where they oversaw operations from expeditionary maritime operations centers set up in large tents. These efforts to have personnel "practice in war-like conditions," and to take "Marines and sailors out of garrison mode and immers[e] [them] into a wartime scenario," suggests that LSE 2021 was designed for a great power conflict, in which fixed U.S. military command and control facilities could be easily targeted.

On August 15, during LSE 2021, the 1st Battalion, 12th Marine Regiment, which is planned to be reorganized into a Marine Littoral Regiment (MLR), maneuvered the Navy Marine Expeditionary Ship Interdiction System (NMESIS) to the Barking Sands Missile Range on the Hawaiian island of Kauai using air-cushioned landing craft (LCAC) and MV-22B aircraft. There, it fired Naval Strike Missiles (NSM) and struck a target ship at sea. Although the Marine Corps has used HIMARS in past exercises premised on maritime theater, such exercises were either aimed at rapid deployment of HIMARS by transport aircraft or LCAC, or involved the firing of land-attack rockets or training projectiles without anti-ship strike capabilities. The fact that live-fire training was conducted at LSE 2021 using NSM anti-ship missiles, which actually flew for 100 nautical miles and struck a target ship, indicates that the Marine Corps is making steady progress toward acquiring anti-ship strike capabilities (see (2) for further details on MLR, NMESIS, and NSM).

The U.S. Navy describes LSE 2021 as the largest exercise conducted since the Cold War. Rather than its scale, however, the main point of LSE 2021 was how it integrated operations "across the globe" in the Pacific, Atlantic, and Mediterranean. The exercise is understood to have been conducted in order to ensure that the United States is capable of responding to a two-front war in the Pacific and in Europe, such as in the hypothetical event of an armed conflict with China that triggers Russia to take up arms.[20]

Addressing complex situations that occur across multiple regions and combatant commands was one of the themes of a series of hearings on DOD reform held by the Senate Armed Services Committee from October to December 2015. These hearings resulted in the Fiscal Year 2017 National Defense Authorization Act (enacted December 23, 2016), which added providing advice on "global military integration" and preparing plans for allocation and transfer of forces among combatant commands to the JCS Chairman's role.[21] The enactment of this law prompted the Joint Staff to work on the issue of globally integrated operations (GIO). In an April 2018 contribution to the *Joint Force Quarterly*, then-JCS Chairman Dunford stated that while "most crises could be contained to one region" in the past, "this assumption no longer holds true."[22] Likewise, when Lieutenant General Dan O'Donohue, director of J7 (Joint Force Development), Joint Staff, spoke at a conference at the U.S. National Defense University on October 31, 2018, he explained the need for GIOs, citing concerns that "our threats act with the global unity of effort." Both of these instances touched upon the possibility of coordination between China and Russia during a crisis.[23] As for GIOs, globally integrated exercises (GIE) involving multiple combatant commands have been conducted since October 2017, and globally integrated wargames (GIWG) that take emerging technologies into account have been conducted since 2019. LSE 2021 is positioned as one of the GIEs.[24]

While LSGE 21, which encompasses LSE 2021, was not included in the FY2021 budget request, it was included in the FY2022 budget request and will be held annually through FY2026. LSGE 21 was hosted by the U.S. Indo-Pacific Command and focused geographically on the Western Pacific. For FY2022 and beyond, however, there are plans to expand the exercise so that it "will link multiple CCMDs [combatant commands] with allies and partners in order to exercise warfighting plans on a global scale" (emphasis added). Like GIEs, it seems set to become an exercise emphasizing "global integration" of the U.S. forces in "dispersed geographical areas."

In 2021, U.S. naval ships were also actively deployed in the South China Sea (see Table 7.1). In February, dual carrier operations were conducted in the South China Sea by two CSGs: the *Nimitz* CSG, which was returning from deployment in the Middle East and waters off Somalia, and the *Theodore Roosevelt* CSG, which departed San Diego in December 2020. In April, dual operations were conducted by the *Theodore Roosevelt* CSG and the *Makin Island* ESG, with F-35Bs onboard. Solo carrier operations were also conducted by the *Carl Vinson*, *Ronald Reagan*, and *Theodore Roosevelt* CSGs. Then, in October, the *Carl Vinson* CSG conducted bilateral training in the South China Sea with JS *Kaga* of the Japan Maritime Self-Defense Force. Thus, even though the *Ronald Reagan* CSG was deployed to the Middle East from around late June through mid-September in order to support the withdrawal of U.S. forces from Afghanistan, one can say the United States continued to maintain an active presence in the South China Sea.

Table 7.1. Major U.S. naval activities in the South China Sea during 2021

Duration	Participating units [1]	Activities in the South China Sea [1]
Jan. 23–25	TRCSG	After leaving San Diego Dec. 23, 2020, TRCSG entered the South China Sea, Jan. 23, 2021 for "routine operations." Conducted flight operations in the South China Sea.
Feb. 5– around 18	NIMCSG, TRCSG	After completing deployment to Middle East, Indian Ocean, off the Somali coast (July 24, 2020–Jan. 29, 2021), NIMCSG transited the Malacca Strait and entered the South China Sea, Feb. 4. President Biden called NIMCSG operating in the South China Sea, and talked with its commander and some of the crew members, Feb. 8. Around Feb. 9, TRCSG joined NIMCSG in the South China Sea, where they conducted dual CSG operations. Feb. 10, NIMCSG moved to the Philippine Sea. TRCSG continued flight operations in the South China Sea toward Feb. 17 and moved to the Pacific Ocean.
Apr. 4–12	TRCSG, MKIARG	Apr. 4, TRCSG entered the South China Sea. TRCSG conducted a bilateral exercise with the Royal Malaysian Air Force, Apr. 6 and 7. After deployment to Middle East and off Somali coast (Dec. 21, 2020–Mar. 31, 2021), MKIARG entered the South China Sea, Apr. 8. On the same day, F-35Bs deployed onboard USS *Makin Island*, conducted joint training with F-15SGs and F-16Ds from the Republic of Singapore Air Force. Apr. 9, TRCSG and MKIARG joined forces in the South China Sea to conduct "expeditionary strike force operations." TRCSG and MKIARG, thereafter conducted training in the South China Sea, moved to the Pacific Ocean, and returned to San Diego toward the end of May.
June 14–18	RRNCSG	After departing Yokosuka May 19, RRNCSG conducted bilateral training with Japan Maritime Self-Defense Force JS *Ise* in the Philippine Sea, and entered the South China Sea, June 14. June 17, RRNCSG conducted integrated bilateral training with Republic of Singapore Navy frigate and corvette. After transiting the Malacca Strait, June 18, RRNCSG conducted joint maritime training with the Indian Navy in the Indian Ocean and deployed to Middle East in support of U.S. withdrawal from Afghanistan (June 25–Sept. 17).
Around July 6– around 10	USS *Tulsa* (LCS), USS *Kidd* (DDG)	USS *Tulsa* and USS *Kidd* formed a SAG, while underway in the South China Sea July 9, and practiced surface warfare, mine countermeasure, and anti-submarine warfare.
Early Aug.– Late Aug	USS *Tulsa*	Aug. 4, USS *Tulsa* conducted replenishment-at-sea from underway replenishment oiler USNS *Tippecanoe* in the South China Sea. It participated in SEACAT exercise, conducted Aug. 10–20. Aug. 23, Vice President Harris visited USS *Tulsa* during its port call at Changi Naval Base. USS *Tulsa* continued to operate in the South China Sea toward Aug. 30.
Sep. 5–14	VINCSG	After a port call at Yokosuka (Aug. 28–31), VINCSG deployed to the South China Sea, Sep. 5, as "part of the U.S. Navy's routine presence in the Indo-Pacific." Sep. 7, USS *Tulsa*, which returned to the South China Sea after receiving supplies in Okinawa, joined VINCSG. It marked the first time an LCS operated as part of a CSG. VINCSG continued to operate in the South China Sea until Sep. 14, and moved to the Philippine Sea.

Sep. 24–26	RRNCSG	Sep. 24, on the return trip from the Middle East, RRNCSG entered the South China Sea, where it conducted flight operations, maritime strike exercises, anti-submarine operations, and coordinated tactical training. After conducting operations until Sep. 26, RRNCSG move to the Philippine Sea.
Oct.– Nov. 23	USS *Milius* (DDG)	Oct. 19–23, USS *Milius* conducted bilateral training with JS *Akizuki* in the South China Sea. Oct. 30, USS *Milius* joined VINCSG, JS *Kaga*, and JS *Murasame* in the South China Sea (see box below). Nov. 14–17, USS *Milius* conducted bilateral training with JS *Kaga* and JS *Murasame* in the South China Sea. Nov. 20, USS *Milius* conducted small boat operations with USS *Chafee* and transited the Taiwan Strait, Nov. 23.
Oct. 24 –Nov. 6	VINCSG	Oct. 24, VINCSG entered the South China Sea, after participating in Japan-U.S.-Australia-UK Maritime Partnership Exercise in the Bay of Bengal. Oct. 25–27, VINCSG conducted flight operations. Oct. 30, USS *Carl Vinson*, USS *Shiloh*, USS *Lake Champlain*, and USS *Milius* navigated in the South China Sea with JS *Kaga* and JS *Murasame*. Nov. 2–3, USS *Milius* operated in the Sulu Sea and returned to the South China Sea, Nov. 4. USS *Milius* continued operations in the South China Sea until Nov. 6, and moved to the Philippine Sea, Nov. 7, arriving in Guam, Nov. 11.
Late Oct.– Nov. 17	USS *Jackson* (LCS)	Oct. 28, USS *Jackson* formed a SAG with JS *Yudachi*, and trained in the South China Sea. USS *Jackson* continued operations in the South China Sea until Nov. 17, and moved to the Philippine Sea, Nov. 18.
Nov.– Dec.	USS *Chafee* (DDG)	USS *Chafee* conducted underway replenishment (Nov. 9, 17, 23, 30, and Dec. 6), flight operations (Nov. 16), antiterrorism force protection drill (Nov. 27 and Dec. 1) in the South China Sea.

Sources: Compiled by the author based on U.S. Navy releases, Fleet Tracker (https://news.usni.org/category/fleet-tracker)

Note: For freedom of navigation operations and Taiwan Strait transits, see Table 7.2.

Note 1: ARG (amphibious ready group), CG (guided-missile cruiser), CSG (carrier strike group), DDG (guided-missile destroyer), ESG (expeditionary strike group), LCS (littoral combat ship), MKIARG (Makin Island ARG), NIMCSG (Nimitz CSG), RRNCSG (Ronald Reagan CSG), SAG (surface action group), TRCSG (Theodore Roosevelt CSG).

In the Philippine Sea and the Bay of Bengal, located east and west of the South China Sea, there was an increased level of naval activities by the United States, allies, and partners, including those within the framework of LSGE 21. On October 3, the *Ronald Reagan* CSG and *Carl Vinson* CSG engaged in "multiple carrier strike group operations" in the Philippine Sea with JS *Ise* of the Japan Maritime Self-Defense Force and CSG-21. In addition, from November 21 to 30, the *Carl Vinson* CSG conducted multinational exercises in the Philippine Sea with Japanese, Australian, Canadian, and German ships, according to the U.S. Navy. The CSG also participated in Phase II of Exercise MALABAR 2021 that took place in the Bay of Bengal from October 11 to 14, during which it conducted training with ships and aircraft of the Indian Navy, JS *Kaga* and JS *Murasame* of the Japan Maritime Self-Defense Force, and a frigate of the Royal Australian Navy. Having completed the Phase II exercise, the naval forces from Australia, Japan and the United States, also joined by CSG-21, conducted the Maritime Partnership Exercise 2021 in the Bay of Bengal from October 15 to 18.

In addition, the U.S. Navy continued to conduct Freedom of Navigation operations (FONOP) in the South China Sea and transits through the Taiwan Strait, just as they did during the Trump administration (see Table 7.2). According to the U.S. Navy, FONOPs in the South China Sea were conducted five times, and transits through the Taiwan Strait were conducted 11 times in 2021 (all under the Biden administration). That the U.S. Navy itself has begun to publicize these specific individual operations is an indication of its willingness to demonstrate its commitment to maintaining stability in the region.

Table 7.2. Taiwan Strait transits and freedom of navigation operations (FONOPs) in the South China Sea conducted by U.S. Navy ships during 2021

Date[1],[2]	Participating units[3]	Activities
Feb. 4 (Taiwan-1), 5 (FONOP-1)	USS *John S. McCain*	Feb. 4, USS *John S. McCain* transited the Taiwan Strait, Feb. 5, conducted FONOP in the vicinity of the Paracel Islands, Feb. 5. It joined NIMCSG and TRCSG, which were conducting dual CSG operation in the South China Sea. USS *John S. McCain* moved to the Philippine Sea, Feb. 10.
Feb. 17 (FONOP-2)	USS *Russell*	Around Feb. 9, USS *Russell* entered the South China Sea, as part of TRCSG, which then conducted dual CSG operations with NIMCSG. Feb. 17, USS *Russell* conducted FONOP in the vicinity of the Spratly Islands.
Feb. 24 (Taiwan-2)	USS *Curtis Wilbur*	Feb. 24, USS *Curtis Wilbur* transited the Taiwan Strait.
Mar. 10 (Taiwan-3)	USS *John Finn*	Mar. 9–10, USS *John Finn* proceeded from the Pacific Ocean to the East China Sea. Mar. 10, USS *John Finn* transited the Taiwan Strait, and Mar. 11 12, moved from the South China Sea to the Pacific Ocean.

Apr. 7 (Taiwan-4)	USS *John S. McCain*	Apr. 7, USS *John S. McCain* transited the Taiwan Strait and proceeded to the South China Sea.
May 18 (Taiwan-5), 20 (FONOP-3), June 22 (Taiwan-6)	USS *Curtis Wilbur*	May 18, USS *Curtis Wilbur* transited the Taiwan Strait, and May 20, conducted FONOP in the vicinity of the Paracel Islands. It continued operations in the South China Sea including underway replenishment (May 23 and June 6), and bilateral operations with Royal Australian Navy frigate HMAS *Ballarat* (June 6–11). June 22, USS *Curtis Wilbur* transited the Taiwan Strait, and moved to the Philippine Sea to conduct underway replenishment, June 23. Back in the South China Sea, it operated with ocean surveillance ship USNS *Victorious*, June 24.
July 12 (FONOP-4), 28 (Taiwan-7)	USS *Benfold*	USS *Benfold* entered the South China Sea after conducting bilateral training with Republic of Singapore Navy in the Philippine Sea until July 7. July 12, it conducted FONOP in the vicinity of the Paracel Islands and navigated in the South China Sea with USS *Kidd*. Afterwards, it conducted "routine operations" in the South China Sea including underway replenishment on July 26, transited the Taiwan Strait, July 28, and operated in the East China Sea, July 29.
Aug. 27 (Taiwan-8)	USS *Kidd*	Aug. 27, USS *Kidd* transited the Taiwan Strait with U.S. Coast Guard National Security Cutter USCGC *Munro*.
Sep. 8 (FONOP-5)	USS *Benfold*	USS *Benfold* operated in the South China Sea, Sep. 2, and conducted FONOP in the Spratly Islands (within 12 nautical miles of the Mischief Reef), Sep. 8.
Sep. 17 (Taiwan-9)	USS *Barry*	After operating in the Philippine Sea, USS *Barry* transited the Taiwan Strait, Sep. 17 and moved to the East China Sea.
Oct. 14–15 (Taiwan-10)	USS *Dewey*	USS *Dewey* transited the Taiwan Strait with Royal Canadian Navy HMCS *Winnipeg*.
Nov. 23 (Taiwan-11)	USS *Milius*	After operating in the South China Sea (see Table 7.1), USS *Milius* transited the Taiwan Strait and moved to the East China Sea.

Sources: Compiled by the author based on U.S. Navy releases.
Note: NIMCSG (Nimitz Carrier Strike Group), TRCSG (Theodore Roosevelt Carrier Strike Group).
Note 1: Dates are all those indicated in the sources.
Note 2: "Taiwan" in parentheses indicate Taiwan Strait transits, while "FONOP" indicates freedom of navigation operations. Numerals after "Taiwan" or "FONOP" indicate cumulative numbers of cases of Taiwan Strait transits or FONOPs conducted including the particular case in question.
Note 3: Participating U.S. units shown in this table are all *Arleigh Burke*-class guided-missile destroyer.

(2) The Pacific Deterrence Initiative (PDI) and the Force Posture in the Indo-Pacific

The National Defense Strategy (NDS) released by Secretary of Defense Mattis in January 2018, positioned the "long-term, strategic competition" with China and Russia as "the principal priorities" for the DOD given "the magnitude of the threats they pose to U.S. security." Mark Esper, succeeding Mattis, reinforced this position when he stated in his speech on August 26, 2020, that "focus[ing] the Department on China" was one of the "ten targeted goals" of the NDS. Under the Biden administration, Secretary of Defense Austin has also expressed his intention to prioritize the response to the China threat. In the advance policy questions statement he submitted for his confirmation hearing before the Senate Armed Services Committee on January 19, 2021, he praised the 2018 NDS for "correctly [identifying] strategic competitions with China and with Russia as the primary challenges animating the global security environment" before stating that he believes "China is the top priority."

Thus, from the Trump administration to the Biden administration, the DOD's policy has consistently been prioritizing the response to the China threat. The problem, however, is in its implementation, a concern that has been raised from the beginning: while "the NDS generally reflects the right priorities and objectives, it is not supported by adequate investments" (2018 NDS Commission report).[25] Regarding implementation of the NDS, Senators Jim Inhofe and Jack Reed, ranking member and chairman of the Senate Armed Services, said that "the progress to date has been insufficient to achieve the 'urgent change at significant scale' that is required," and added that "America's ability" to "maintain a credible balance of military power" is "at risk" in Asia.[26]

These concerns are what led Congress to create a provision on the Pacific Deterrence Initiative (PDI) in section 1251 of the FY2021 National Defense Authorization Act, enacted January 1, 2021. Intended to enhance the United States deterrence and defense posture in the Indo-Pacific region, assure allies and partners, and increase capability and readiness in the Indo-Pacific region, the PDI is to be established by the secretary of defense and will carry out prioritized activities to improve the design and posture of the Joint Force (meaning U.S. forces) in the Indo-Pacific region in the five categories shown in Table 7.3.

Furthermore, section 1251 directs that the secretary, in consultation with the commander of the U.S. Indo-Pacific Command, shall compile a report on the PDI that includes a description of its activities and estimated expenses for the fiscal year in which the budget request is made and the plan for not fewer than the four following fiscal years; a summary of progress made towards the purposes of the PDI; a summary of the activity, resource, capability, infrastructure, and logistics requirements necessary to reduce risk to the joint force's ability; as well as a detailed timeline. This report is to be submitted to the congressional defense committees by February 15, 2021, and every year thereafter. Section 1251 also stipulates that when the DOD submits its annual budget request to Congress, it shall pick up budget items that fit the purpose of the PDI and organize them by the above five categories.

The PDI is not the first time Congress has asked the DOD to provide information on military investments in the Indo-Pacific. Prior to the 2021 National Defense Authorization Act, section 1253 of the FY2020 National Defense Authorization Act, enacted in December 2019, required that not later than March 15, 2020, the commander of the U.S. Indo-Pacific Command submit to the congressional defense committees a report containing the independent assessment with respect to the activities and resources required, for FY2022 through 2026, to achieve the implementation of the NDS with respect to the Indo-Pacific region, the maintenance or restoration of the comparative military advantage of the United States with respect to China, and the reduction of risk of executing contingency plans of the DOD. In response, Admiral Philip Davidson, INDOPACOM commander, submitted the report *Regaining the Advantage* (thereafter, Section 1253 Assessment) to Congress on April 1, 2020. His report requested $1.6 billion for FY2021 and $18.4 billion for FY2022-26 in the five categories of Joint Force lethality; force design and posture; strengthening allies and partners; exercises, experimentation, and innovation; and logistics and security enablers.

The PDI does not, in and of itself, mean an increase in budget. Its purpose is to tag items that are included in the service/agency budget requests and are deemed consistent with the purposes of the PDI and arrange them according to the purposes of the PDI. This was expected to facilitate transparency of the extent to which the department as a whole plans to invest in the Indo-Pacific. This is also what the December 3, 2020 Conference Committee report for the FY2021 National Defense Authorization Act refers to when it explains the significance of the PDI: "the availability of budgetary data organized according to regional missions and the priorities of the combatant commands is critical for the ability of the Department and the Congress to assess the implementation of the National Defense Strategy."[27] This approach to making the budget "visible" by having each branch and agency's budget requests—which are not originally itemized by region—reorganized by a specific region and presented to Congress, has also been used in the European Deterrence Initiative (EDI), for which budget requests have been made from the DOD's budget for FY2016 onward. The PDI follows the example set by the EDI.

In the FY2022 budget request, which the DOD submitted to Congress at the end of May 2021 in response to the FY2021 National Defense Authorization Act, PDI-related expenditures were summarized as separate budget justification material, and approximately $5.08 billion was allocated for these expenditures.[28] As indicated by the key items in the PDI established by the Act, the PDI's emphasis is on clarifying where and how U.S. military forces will be deployed and how they will be maintained logistically. This is consistent with the policy of transitioning from "large, centralized, unhardened infrastructure" to "smaller, dispersed, resilient, adaptive basing" set forth by the 2018 NDS. Regarding the force posture in the Indo-Pacific, the April 2020 Section 1253 Assessment called for distributed forward-deployed forces that "balances lethality and survivability," and a force posture and joint force laydown "properly positioned to defend in depth," claiming that "forward-based air and naval forces need the ability to disperse to expeditionary airfields and ports." The assessment further estimated that over the six-year period from FY2021 through 2026, a total of approximately $5.86 billion, divided between U.S. territories, Oceania, Pacific island countries, and Southeast Asia, would be required to transform the U.S. force posture.

Table 7.3. Areas of prioritized activities within the Pacific

Pacific Deterrence Initiative (PDI)	▶ Modernizing and strengthening the U.S. military presence
	▶ Improving logistics and maintenance capabilities and the pre-positioning of equipment, munitions, fuel, and materiel
	▶ Carrying out a program of exercises, training, experimentation, and innovation for the joint force
	▶ Improving infrastructure to enhance the responsiveness and resiliency
	▶ Building the defense and security capabilities, capacity, and cooperation of allies and partners

Source: William M. (Mac) Thornberry National Defense Authorization Act for Fiscal Year 2021, Public Law 116-283, 116th Cong., 2nd sess. (January 1, 2021), § 1251 (b).

The issue of force posture, however, was virtually absent in the FY2022 PDI budget justification material submitted to Congress by the DOD at the end of May 2021. Instead, 96 percent of the approximately $5.08 billion in PDI-related expenses was allocated to "Joint Force Lethality," an item that refers to weapon modernization, including $1.02 billion to upgrade F-35B/C fighter aircraft and $2.02 billion to upgrade *Arleigh Burke*-class destroyers. A Senate staffer criticized the FY2022 PDI budget request, which is heavy in weapons, but light in force posture, saying that even if it is "an important platform," it would be "ultimately useless without the theater posture and logistics in place to support it."[29] In the first place, the DOD has also acknowledged that the aforementioned PDI budget request document does not provide a complete picture of the allocation of resources to the Indo-Pacific. In this regard, the PDI has been insufficient in "enhanc[ing] budgetary transparency and oversight" (Senate Armed Services Committee) in the manner hoped for by Congress. The criticism that "Congress should rewrite the Pentagon's Pacific deterrence budget request" also touches on this point.

Even though the PDI budget request document did not meet Congress's expectations, there are some areas in the FY2022 budget request where an enhanced military posture in the Indo-Pacific is evident. One of these is the strengthening of Guam's defenses.

At the Senate Armed Services Committee hearing on March 9, 2021, Admiral Davidson, commander of the U.S. Indo-Pacific Command, stated that Guam is a U.S. territory with 170,000 U.S. citizens, a "deep-water strategic port, major fuel stores, munitions stores, command and control," as well as a "major power projection airfield," and that this "Guam is a target today." Calling for enhanced defense of Guam, he proposed building up the Guam Defense System (GDS) as a "360-degree, persistent, air and missile defense capability on Guam." According to Davidson, the GDS will defend against ballistic missiles, cruise missiles, and even hypersonic weapons, and is envisioned as providing full 360-degree defense against threats posed by Chinese surface task groups and submarines that "make circumnavigations of Guam and the Commonwealth of the Northern Marianas." Following this, in the FY2022 DOD budget request submitted to Congress at the end of May 2021, $118.3 million in GDS-related expenses were appropriated for the Missile Defense Agency (MDA) for the first time (see Table 7.4).[30]

Strengthening the defense of Guam had also been proposed as the Homeland Defense System-Guam (HDS-G) a year earlier in the Section 1253 Assessment submitted to Congress by Admiral Davidson in April 2020. This assessment estimated that $77 million was needed for FY2021, and $1.59 billion for FY2022 to FY2026. Although it was not included in the FY2021 DOD budget request submitted to Congress at the same time, it was included in the unfunded priority list (UPL) (items that each service, combatant command, National Guard Bureau, and MDA are required to report to Armed Services and Appropriations Committees of both houses, as those deemed necessary but not included in the budget request due to budgetary limitations) submitted to Congress by the commander of the U.S. Indo-Pacific Command together with the FY2021 request.[31] On the other hand, $76.8 million was included in the Senate bill under the FY2021 Defense Authorization Act at the request of the U.S. Indo-Pacific Command, but this request was shelved after negotiations in the Conference Committee. Thus, the strengthening of Guam's defenses finally got underway with the inclusion of GDS expenses in the FY2022 budget, albeit for MDA.

However, since the GDS is expected to be able to provide 360-degree defense against threats from cruise, ballistic, and hypersonic missiles, the components that should comprise the system are still under consideration. Through Section 1650 of the National Defense Authorization Act for Fiscal Year 2021, Congress required the secretary of defense to conduct a comparative assessment of existing deployed interceptor systems and those under development that could be used to defeat ballistic, hypersonic, and cruise missile threats to Guam, and report to Congress within 120 days after enactment of the Act.

Admiral Davidson proposed a system based on the Aegis Ashore as a "mature" and operationally proven system, but it is believed that the Aegis Ashore alone would not meet GDS requirements for countering a wide range of threats. On June 22, 2021, in a speech at the Center for Strategic and International Studies (CSIS), Vice Admiral Jon Hill, MDA director, stated that "a lot of folks just think Aegis Ashore right away. But that may not be sufficient for what we need" for GDS, and that given the breadth of the threat, it "automatically drives you to the multi-mission systems." MDA Director Jon Hill also mentioned the possibility of integrating the Army's Lower Tier Air and Missile Defense Sensor (LTAMDS), which is said to be capable of defeating hypersonic weapons; the Navy's SPY-6 radar, which is capable of defeating both cruise and ballistic missiles; and the Army's THAAD, into the GDS. The MDA's FY2022 budget request includes the development of a Joint Track Management Capabilities (JTMC) Bridge between the IAMD Battle Command System (IBCS), which links the Army's various sensors and shooters; the Navy's Aegis Weapon System (AWS); and the Command and Control, Battle Management, and Communications (C2BMC) system. It is listed as a research, development, test, and evaluation (RDT&E) cost "to promote greater integration between Army and Navy assets."[32] A JTMC Bridge is necessary because each U.S.-developed system for missile defense has been developed separately with its own unique command and control architecture. Harry Harris, former U.S. ambassador to South Korea and Davidson's predecessor as commander of the U.S. Indo-Pacific Command, warned that a stovepiped system would "promise mission failure at first contact with an enemy fielding advanced 21st Century missiles." He noted that "enormous sensor-to-weapon integration across multiple domains, including cyber and space" is needed to defeat hypersonic, cruise, and ballistic missile threats.[33]

New developments in strengthening the military posture in the Indo-Pacific were also seen in the Marine Corps and the Army. The Marine Corps, under General David Berger, who became commandant of the U.S. Marine Corps in July 2019, is advancing measures to realize the Expeditionary Advanced Base Operations (EABO) concept. The EABO concept seeks to sustain operations inside anti-access/area denial (A2/AD) zones with the chief aim of countering "the predominantly maritime threat posed by China" (General Berger). It calls for divesting some infantry battalions, medium tiltrotor squadrons and light attack squadrons supporting these infantry battalions, and howitzer batteries, abolishing entire fleets of tank companies, and substantially adding rocket batteries that would contribute to Marine Corps' long-range strike capability. In February 2021, a *Tentative Manual for Expeditionary Advanced Base Operations* was published that provided an outline of EABO operations and the organization of the units involved.[34]

In particular, the "main focus-of-effort" for the Marine Corps' reorganization efforts is the III Marine Expeditionary Force (III MEF), which is in charge of the

Table 7.4. DOD budget requests for Guam Defense System

FY2021 DOD Budget Request (Feb. 2020)	Section 1253 Assessment (Apr. 2020)	FY2021 National Defense Authorization Act (Jan. 1, 2021)	FY2022 DOD Budget Request (May 2021)
—	$77 million for FY 2021, and $1,594 million for FY2022–26.	— (Senate bill included $76.8 million for GDS, which was later dropped in conference negotiation)	$118.3 million (Includes $40 million in procurement account for purchasing items that will be commonly used for any of the proposed IAMD architectures, and $78.3 million in research, development, test and evaluation account for developing IAMD system on Guam against air-breathing, ballistic, and hypersonic missile threats)

Sources: Compiled by the author based on Missile Defense Agency budget justification materials, FY2021 National Defense Authorization Act, and others.

Indo-Pacific region.[35] During FY2022, the Marine Corps plans to reorganize the 3rd Marine Regiment (Kaneohe Bay, Hawaii) of the 3rd Marine Division into a Marine Littoral Regiment (MLR), optimized for operation in the littorals. The 4th Marine Regiment (Camp Schwab, Okinawa) and the 12th Marine Regiment (Camp Hansen, Okinawa) are slated to follow and begin MLR reorganization once the 3rd Marine Regiment has completed MLR reorganization, the unit design has been tested in experimentation, and the necessary adjustments have been made.[36] The MLR is "the base unit for our future force" according to General Burger, and MLR reorganization may extend beyond the III MEF.

The MLR is designed to persistently operate across the competition continuum, from competition below armed conflict to armed conflict, inside the adversary's A2/AD zone, while evading detection and attacks. The Littoral Combat Team (LCT), which is the core of MLR, is formed around an infantry battalion and an anti-ship missile battery. LCT will conduct long-range anti-ship strikes and establish and maintain multiple expeditionary advance bases (EABs) in support of forward arming and refueling point (FARP) and intelligence, surveillance, reconnaissance (ISR) operations.[37] The heart of the anti-ship missile battery within MLR will be NMESIS, which combines unmanned and remotely piloted Joint Light Tactical Vehicle (JLTV) and two Kongsberg's NSMs with a range of over 100 nautical miles, or 185.2 kilometers.[38]

Since NMESIS brings together existing subsystems with proven track records, such as JLTV and NSM, it has been swiftly implemented in the field since the development began in 2019. The Marine Corps' FY2022 budget request included $47.89 million to procure 29 NSMs for eight NMESIS units to be deployed to the 3rd Marine Regiment, the first regiment to be converted to an MLR. However, since these are scheduled for phased delivery after December 2023, according to the request document, the MLR will not actually acquire anti-ship strike capability until after that.[39]

The MLR will launch these NSMs from the islands, but because their range is limited to over 100 nautical miles (185.2 km), General Berger made public a plan to introduce longer-range Tomahawk Land Attack Munitions (TLAM), Maritime

Strike Tomahawks (MST), and SM-6 containerized anti-ship missiles, which would give the Marine Corps "the ability to influence the vast maritime area." In fact, the UPL that the Marine Corps submitted to Congress as part of its FY2022 budget request included 48 Tactical Tomahawks ($96 million), along with 35 additional NSMs ($57.8 million).

Anti-ship strike capability is not the only thing expected of the MLR. In an article contributed to the May/June 2021 issue of *Military Review*, a journal published by the U.S. Army Command and General Staff College, General Berger noted that while the Force Design program pursued by the Marine Corps to date has focused exclusively on its anti-ship strike capability, what is "becoming clearer" is that the role required of the Marine Corps as a stand-in force is rather "*reconnaissance and counterreconnaissance* applied in all domains and across the competition continuum." According to Berger, the MLR will play an important role in reconnaissance and counterreconnaissance. Its ISR capability will provide "deterrence by detection" by placing an adversary under persistent surveillance, discouraging coercive behavior even in competition below armed conflict. Furthermore, should the competition escalate to armed conflict, the MLR will be able to "identify and track" targets such as "key reconnaissance platforms, scouting units, and other elements of the adversary's command, control, communications, computers, cyber, intelligence, surveillance, reconnaissance, and targeting (C5ISR-T) complex" and provide targeting data to guide the long-range strike capabilities of the Joint Force.

Berger points out that the MLR's utility as an ISR force linking to the entire U.S. military is more important than having attack capabilities in its own right. While the *Tentative Manual for Expeditionary Advanced Base Operations* published in February 2021 reflects this point, it is also being tested in actual exercises.[40] During Exercise Noble Jaguar conducted around Japan from September 27 to 30, 2021, the participating 3rd Battalion, 12th Marine Regiment, shared targeting data from its multipurpose radar with the aircraft carrier USS *Carl Vinson* and destroyer USS *Howard*, which were sailing in the Philippine Sea, and F/A-18s with Marine Aircraft Group 12 operating in the surrounding airspace, enabling "joint strikes against maritime and land-based targets."

The Army, on the other hand, has organized an MDTF around the 17th Field Artillery Brigade (Joint Base Lewis-McChord, Washington) and an intelligence, information, cyber electronic warfare and space (I2CEWS) unit as an ongoing pilot program in 2017, and has conducted

A crewmember of a UH-1Y with the Marine Light Attack Helicopter Squadron 267 deploys a sonobuoy during Exercise Summer Fury 21 (July 20, 2021, near San Clemente Island, California) (U.S. Marine Corps video by Cpl. Levi Voss)

various exercises and test and evaluation. In September 2021, based on the lessons learned from this experience, it formed a second MDTF around the 41st Field Artillery Brigade (Grafenwoehr, Germany) and an I2CEWS unit. *Army Multi-Domain Transformation*, released in March 2021 by Gen. James McConville, chief of staff of the Army, revealed that the Army plans to build a total of five MDTFs: one positioned in the Arctic and one aligned for global response, in addition to the two aligned to the Indo-Pacific and one aligned to Europe, whose formation and deployment plans had been disclosed previously. Positioned as "theater-level maneuver elements," each MDTF is assigned to support a specific combatant command and is organized, trained, and operated according to the requirements of that combatant command. Since the first MDTF was formed around a HIMARS brigade, it was well known that the MDTF will include HIMARS and the Precision Strike Missile (PrSM) (with a range of 60 to 499 km) that can be launched from HIMARS. However, the *Army Multi-Domain Transformation* made it clear that the MDTF formation will also include a Strategic Fires Battalion with the Long-Range Hypersonic Weapon (LRHW), which is said to have a range of over 2,775 kilometers, and a Mid-Range

Table 7.5. Long-range strike capabilities planned to be deployed
with Multi-Domain Task Forces

Category	Purpose/range	Remark
Long-Range Hypersonic Weapon (LRHW)	Surface-to-surface, 2775 km and above	Developed based on Common Hypersonic Glide Body (C-HGB). Mar. 2021, the U.S. Army began delivering training canisters to the LRHW prototype battery. Two flight tests are planned for FY2022, one for FY2023. In FY2023, LRHW missiles will be fielded.
Mid-Range Capability (MRC)	Anti-ship and surface-to-surface, 500–1500 km or approx. 1800 km	In FY2023, MRC prototype, consisting of missiles, launchers, and battery operations center, will be fielded to an operational battery. Nov. 2020, contract was awarded to Lockheed Martin to build MRC prototype based on SM-6 and Tomahawk missiles.
Precision Strike Missile (PrSM)	Surface-to-surface (anti-ship strike capability to be retrofitted), 60–499 km	Initial 30 PrSM missiles ordered in FY2021 are planned to be delivered Feb.–Nov. 2023. Fielding will begin in FY2023. Anti-ship strike capability will be added through "Spiral One" upgrade by 2025. Deployed on HIMARS.

Sources: Compiled by the author based on Department of the Army budget justification materials and news reports.

Capability (MRC) in addition to HIMARS/PrSM (see Table 7.5).

The Marine Corps' MLR, as its designation suggests, is expected to operate in "littorals" (which in U.S. military terminology includes both the "seaward" area from the open ocean to the shore, and the "landward" area <u>inland</u> from the shore that can be supported and defended directly from the sea) as a "naval force" with anti-ship, ASW, and ISR capabilities ("naval" in this context connotes close integration between the Navy and Marine Corps).[41] In contrast, the MDTF places greater emphasis on its ground attack capability rather than its anti-ship strike capability, as well as on having the means of striking with greater range, as suggested by the name Strategic Fires Battalion. In particular, the LRHW, whose warhead uses the Common Hypersonic Glide Body (C-HGB), which has been jointly developed by the Army, Navy, Air Force, and MDA, is said to have a range of over 2,775 kilometers. It is positioned as "a prototype strategic strike weapon system" to "defeat Anti-Access/Area Denial (A2/AD) capabilities, suppress adversary Long Range Fires, and engage other high payoff/time critical targets."[42] The current Army Operating Concept, *The U.S. Army in Multi-Domain Operations in 2028*, released in November 2018, stated that the ability to first "penetrate" A2/AD systems by neutralizing and destroying the enemy's long-range systems to ensure freedom of maneuver was necessary for subsequent operations. Likewise, the *Army Futures Command Concept for Maneuver in Multi-Domain Operations 2028*, released in July 2020, revealed that the LRHW will be used to strike enemy long-range fires systems.[43] In the 2019 Army Modernization Strategy, the Army had positioned long-range precision fires that "penetrate and neutralize enemy A2/AD capabilities" as its top modernization priority.

In addition, the MRC is expected to have a strike range of 500 to 1,500 kilometers, or even up to 1,800 kilometers, bridging the gap in range between the PrSM and LRHW. In November 2020, the SM-6 and Tomahawk missiles were selected as the initial MRC prototypes. It should be noted that the LRHW, MRC, and PrSM are all expected to be deployed to the forces by the end of FY2023.

The introduction of LRHW into the Army's inventory will mark the first time the service has operated a long-range strike capability since it withdrew medium-range ballistic missile Pershing-II from service in West Germany in late 1980s. The Army's plan to deploy LRHW drew criticism from the inside and outside the military. In an online interview on March 31, 2021, General Timothy Ray, commander of the Air Force Global Strike Command, brought further attention to the issue when he criticized the Army's plan to newly acquire a long-range strike

A LRHW training canister being delivered to the 17th Field Artillery Brigade (Joint Base Lewis McChord, Washington) on September 15, 2021

capability in the Pacific, calling it "stupid" when equipping Air Force bombers with hypersonic weapons is a more effective long-range strike option, and especially because the Air Force already has years of experience in operating missile-equipped bombers.[44]

Some have pointed out that there is interservice rivalry in the development of hypersonic weapons.[45] At an online lecture hosted by the CSIS on February 23, 2021, General John Hyten, vice chairman of the JCS, responded to such criticism as raised by General Ray of the Army's hypersonic weapons program with the understanding that each service, not just the Army, is expanding the domain in which it operates with good reason. At the same time, he maintained that "the problem is making sure that everybody can operate together, can maneuver effectively in all domains seamlessly." However, the duplication of efforts itself is undeniable, and is reportedly under analysis at the Office of Cost Assessment and Program Evaluation (CAPE) at the Office of the Secretary of Defense.[46]

As discussed in this chapter, the Biden administration is taking steps to better engage in the strategic competition with China while inheriting policies advanced under the prior administration. However, even though the Biden administration's highest priority challenge is China, the United States has security interests in various parts of the world, where it is committed to maintaining stability. This leaves the United States unable to devote time and energy solely on any single challenge. Rather, it has to strike a balance among competing priorities by appropriately allocating resources—including diplomatic, military, economic, time-based, or political capital and other intangible resources. From this perspective, the United States will also need to allocate appropriate resources to Europe, to deal with another great power, Russia. Also important is how it will balance the need to respond to urgent crises with longer-term strategic competition with China. Within past Democratic administrations, calls for a more robust, proactive U.S. response, including the use of military force, have tended to be more vocal when humanitarian crises occurred abroad. Furthermore, the administration will need to strike a balance between domestic agendas and foreign policy objectives. While U.S. domestic agendas are often perceived as being at odds with pursuing leadership abroad, calls by President Biden and his team since the election campaign for "a foreign policy for the middle class" or "A Foreign Policy for the American People" can be viewed as an attempt to bridge that gap between international and domestic issues. These are the perspectives from which it will be necessary to closely monitor how the Biden administration promotes its domestic and international agenda in 2022.

NOTES

1) Richard Haas, "Op-Ed: The Modest U.S. Presence on Afghanistan Was Working," *Los Angeles Times*, August 16, 2021.

2) Bob Woodward, *Fear: Trump in the White House* (New York: Simon & Schuster, 2018), 229.

3) Bob Woodward and Robert Costa, *Peril* (New York: Simon & Schuster, 2021), 339.

4) Ibid., 337.

5) Special Inspector General for Afghanistan Reconstruction, *Quarterly Report to the United States Congress* (Washington, DC, July 2021), 51; Woodward and Costa, *Peril*, 339.

6) Michael Hirsh, "From Moral Responsibility to Magical Thinking: How Biden Changed His Mind on Afghanistan," *Foreign Policy* (online), April 16, 2021.

7) Bob Woodward, *Obama's War* (New York: Simon & Schuster, 2010), 67-69.

8) Barack Obama, *A Promised Land* (New York: Crown, 2020), 318.

9) Commander, *NATO International Security Assistance Force, Afghanistan, Commander's Initial Assessment* (Kabul, 2009), 1-1; Ibid., 432, 433; Kikuchi Shigeo, "'Gunjiteki opushon' wo meguru seigun kankei—gunjiryoku koshi ni kakaru ishikettei ni okeru beikoku no bunmin shidosha to gunjin" [Political-military relations regarding the 'military option': U.S. civilian leaders and military personnel in decision-making regarding the use of military force], *Boei Kenkyujo Kiyo* [NIDS Journal of Defense and Security] 16, no. 2 (February 2014): 19-30.

10) John Bolton, *The Room Where It Happened: A White House Memoir* (New York: Simon & Schuster, 2020), 215.

11) Bob Woodward, *Rage* (New York: Simon & Schuster, 2020), 194.

12) The White House, "Remarks at National Defense University," May 23, 2013, DCPD201300361, Govinfo; Kikuchi Shigeo, "Gunji sakusen wo meguru Howaito Hausu=Kokubosho kankei—Obama seiken oyobi Toranpu seiken no hikaku wo chushin ni—" [White House-Department of Defense relations on military operations:

A comparison of the Obama and Trump administrations], *Boei Kenkyujo Kiyo* [NIDS Journal of Defense and Security] 21, no. 2 (March 2019): 39-41.

13) Matt Pottinger, "Beijing's American Hustle: How Chinese Grand Strategy Exploits U.S. Power," *Foreign Affairs* 100, no. 5 (September/October 2021): 110.

14) Gordon Lubold, "U.S. Troops Have Been Deployed in Taiwan for at Least a Year," *Wall Street Journal*, October 7, 2021.

15) Jude Blanchette, "Beijing's Visions of American Decline," *Politico*, March 11, 2021.

16) Michèle A. Flournoy, "How to Prevent a War in Asia: The Erosion of American Deterrence Raises the Risk of Chinese Miscalculation," *Foreign Affairs* (online), June 18, 2020; Gerald F. Seib, "Biden's China Challenge: Counter Its Perception of American Decline," *Wall Street Journal*, March 29, 2021.

17) Joe Biden, "Opinion: Joe Biden: My Trip to Europe Is about America Rallying the World's Democracies," *Washington Post*, June 5, 2021.

18) Jeffrey Wilson, "Australia Shows the World What Decoupling from China Looks Like," *Foreign Policy* (online), November 9, 2021.

19) Michael Schuman, "China Discovers the Limits of Its Power," *Atlantic* (online), July 28, 2021.

20) Steven Stashwick, "US Navy, Marines Conclude Giant Two-Ocean Exercise," *Diplomat*, August 27, 2021.

21) Stephen M. Gallotta, James A. Covington, and Timothy B. Lynch, "Globally Integrated Exercises: Optimizing Joint Force C2 Structure," *Joint Force Quarterly*, no. 89 (2nd quarter 2018): 20.

22) Joseph Dunford, "The Character of War and Strategic Landscape Have Changed," *Joint Force Quarterly*, no. 89 (2nd quarter 2018): 2.

23) Dan O'Donohue, "Globally Integrated Operations," briefing slides presented to the Military Education Coordination Council, October 31, 2018.

24) Ibid., 20; Francis J.H. Park, "Deconflicting Exercises and Experimentation under Global Integration," *Joint Force Quarterly*, no. 102 (3rd quarter 2021): 55, 56.

25) Kikuchi Shigeo, "Bei kokubo keikaku ni okeru 'Pacing Threat' toshite no Chugoku" [China as a 'Pacing Threat' in U.S. defense planning], *NIDS Commentary* (September 1, 2021): 3-5.

26) Jim Inhofe and Jack Reed, "The Pacific Deterrence Initiative: Peace through Strength in the Indo-Pacific," *War on the Rocks*, May 28, 2021.

27) House of Representatives, *William M. (Mac) Thornberry National Defense Authorization Act for Fiscal Year 2021 Conference Report to Accompany H.R. 6395*, 116th Cong., 2nd sess., H. Rep 116-617, 1790.

28) Office of the Under Secretary of Defense (Comptroller), *Pacific Deterrence Initiative Department of Defense Budget Fiscal Year (FY) 2022* (Washington, DC, 2021), 13.

29) Dustin Walker, "Congress Should Rewrite the Pentagon's Pacific Deterrence Budget Request," *Defense News*, June 2, 2021.

30) Department of Defense (DOD), *FY 2022 Missile Defense Agency Defense-Wide Justification Book Procurement, Defense-Wide (Includes O&M and MILCON)*, vol. 2b (Washington, DC, 2021), 105; DOD, *FY 2022 Missile Defense Agency Defense-Wide Justification Book Research, Development, Test & Evaluation, Defense-Wide*, vol. 2 (Washington, DC, 2021), 527, 529.

31) Senate Armed Services Committee, *National Defense Authorization Act for Fiscal Year 2021 Report [To Accompany S. 4049] on To Authorize Appropriations for Fiscal Year 2021 for Military Activities of the Department of Defense, for Military Construction, and for Defense Activities of the Department of Energy, to Prescribe Military Personnel Strengths for Such Fiscal Year, and for Other Purposes*, S. Rep. 116-236, 116th Cong., 2nd sess., June 24, 2020, 119.

32) DOD, *FY 2022 MDA RDT&E*, 529.

33) Harry Harris, "Aegis Ashore Too Limited for Guam: Former INDO-PACOM Head," *Breaking Defense*, July 9, 2021.

34) David H. Berger, "The Case for Change: Meeting the Principal Challenges Facing the Corps," *Marine Corps Gazette* 104, no. 6 (June 2020): 10.

35) David H. Berger, *Commandant's Planning Guidance: 38th Commandant of the Marine Corps* (Washington, DC, 2019), 3.

36) *USNI News*, June 4, 2020; United States Marine Corps, *Force Design 2030 Annual Update* (Washington, DC, 2021), 10.

37) Headquarters, Marine Corps, "Marine Littoral Regiment (MLR)," updated August 2, 2021; Senate Armed Services Committee, *Statement of General David H. Berger Commandant of the Marine Corps as Delivered to the Senate Armed Services Committee on the Posture of the United States Marine Corps*, 117th Cong., 1st sess., June 22, 2021, 13; Headquarters, Marine Corps, *Tentative Manual for Expeditionary Advanced Base Operations* (Washington, DC, 2021), A-1.

38) Department of the Navy, *Department of Defense Fiscal Year (FY) 2022 Budget Estimates Navy Justification Book Procurement, Marine Corps*, vol. 1 (Washington, DC, 2021), 34.

39) Ibid., 31, 32, 34, 39, 40.

40) Headquarters, Marine Corps, *Tentative Manual*, 1-4, 3-20.

41) Joint Chiefs of Staff, *Department of Defense Dictionary of Military and Associated Terms* (Washington, DC, 2021), s.v. "littoral."

42) Department of the Army, *Department of Defense Fiscal Year (FY) 2022 Budget Estimates Justification Book Research, Development, Test & Evaluation, Army RDT&E – Budget Activity 4* (Washington, DC, 2021), 639.

43) Army Futures Command, *Army Futures Command Concept for Maneuver in Multi-Domain Operations 2028* (Fort Eustis, VA, 2020), v, figure 1.

44) "Questions and Answers: Bombs Away," *Air Force Magazine* 104, no. 5 (May 2021): 11.

45) Government Accountability Office, *Hypersonic Weapons: DOD Should Clarify Roles and Responsibilities to Ensure Coordination across Development Efforts, GAO-21-378* (Washington, DC, 2021), 33-34.

46) *Breaking Defense*, April 8, 2021.

Chapter 8

Japan

Facing the Political Choices in an Era of Great Power
Competition

TAKAHASHI Sugio

Japan Maritime
Self-Defense Force's
JS *Ise*, USS *Carl
Vinson*, USS *Ronald
Reagan*, and HMS
Queen Elizabeth
conducting a
multilateral exercise
in the Western
Pacific (©Mc2
Jason Tarleton/U.S.
Navy/Planet Pix via
ZUMA Press Wire/
Kyodo News Images)

Summary

An era of "great power competition" has returned with the escalation of U.S.-China and U.S.-Russia rivalries. This great power competition has two aspects. One is competition for comprehensive national strength centered on science and technology; the other is competition for geo-strategic balance of power. Japan, which adopts the same strategic position as the United States, is a party to both of the great power competitions.

A key element in the latter competition is the extent to which Japan allocates resources to defense. Japan's defense spending has long remained unchanged at roughly 1% of GDP, or about 5 trillion yen in real terms. Even so, Japan's defense expenditure accounted for 38% of East Asia's total in 2000, although it is now down to 17%. The ratio of defense spending of Japan to China, the largest spender on defense in East Asia, was nearly 1:1 in 2000. By 2020, it had widened to 1:4.1.

In military strategy, the so-called 3:1 rule postulates that the attacker needs three times the force as the defender. In Japan's periphery, including the Senkaku Islands, China has continued and intensified its unilateral attempts to change the status quo, along with expanding and stepping up military activities. If the rule were simply applied to Japan and China, Japan's defense spending would be at least one-third the level of China's. Considering the current Japan-to-China ratio and the growth of China's defense expenditure in the future, Japan's defense spending could be on a scale of 10 trillion yen to maintain the one-third level. Such defense spending level must take into consideration the balance between the risk of fiscal insolvency and the risk of deterrence failure.

In the United States, the Joseph Biden administration took office, while in Japan, the Kishida Fumio administration succeeded the Suga Yoshihide administration. The Biden administration held a Japan-U.S. Security Consultative Committee (2+2) meeting in March 2021 and a Japan-U.S. summit meeting in April, laying a clear path for strengthening the Japan-U.S. Alliance. It is expected that progress in the roles, missions, and capabilities consultations will enhance tangible defense cooperation.

Keywords

great power competition   defense spending   Japan-U.S. Alliance

Taiwan Strait   roles, missions, and capabilities

1. Great Power Competition and Japan

(1) Great Power "Competition" and "Cooperation"

There are two main schools of thought in international relations, realism and liberalism. Realism holds that interstate relations are based on conflict between states, while liberalism describes a cooperation-based paradigm. The former tries to understand the reality of endless wars and conflicts "as it is" and emphasizes the balance of power among states mainly in terms of military and economic power. Liberalism, in contrast, emphasizes international law and institutions that support international cooperation and encapsulates a broad discourse on the world "as it should be."

The two schools offer not so much theoretical frameworks as viewpoints that are unique to international relations. Some events in history are easier to understand from a realist perspective; other events are easier to understand from a liberal perspective. A strict realist view focusing on interstate conflict may overlook opportunities for cooperation, even when there is momentum for international collaboration. Conversely, a strict liberal view emphasizing international cooperation may fail to stop an aggression, even when order is being challenged.

The period between World War II and the Cold War was an era characterized by confrontation across the globe. The ensuing Cold War period saw a bitter contest between the United States and the Soviet Union, raising fears of human extinction from all-out nuclear war. During this period, a realist worldview assumed a prominent place, and security studies evolved especially around deterrence theory.

But after the Cold War ended due to the collapse of the Soviet Union, the liberal worldview gained influence, and scholars began to assert the need for a post-Cold War security policy that focuses on international cooperation.[1] Specifically, the security policy discourse grounded in "cooperative security" was extensively debated.[2] A paper that attracted particular attention at the time was Michael Mandelbaum's "Is Major War Obsolete?"[3] He contended that great powers will no longer fight wars over the international order and that a major change in strategic thinking was thus needed.

Two decades later, however, the international landscape underwent a renewed transformation. The United States, which for a time enjoyed prosperity as the "sole superpower" partly because of the September 11 terrorist attacks in 2001, saw its state power wither. In addition, Russia's annexation of Crimea in 2014 caused a sharp deterioration in U.S.-Russia relations. And, above all, China's rapid economic growth and modernization of its military capabilities made "great power competition," especially U.S.-China strategic competition, a key strategic issue. In his paper, Mandelbaum himself self-criticizes his failure to predict China's activities in particular.[4] Such escalation of U.S.-China and U.S.-Russia confrontations has brought back an era of "great power competition." Fears have surfaced that a large-scale war could occur between the United States and China over the Taiwan Strait, or between the United States and Russia over the Baltic states, ushering in the return of realism as the dominant world paradigm.

(2) The Return of Great Power Competition

The international landscape was relatively stable for some time after the Cold War. Following Iraq's invasion of Kuwait in 1990, the United Nations' collective security mechanism functioned—the coalition forces led by the United States defeated Iraqi forces and liberated Kuwait. In the wake of the September 11 terrorist attacks in 2001, Russia cooperated indirectly with the U.S. military operation in Afghanistan by allowing U.S. aircraft to transit Russian airspace. China, too, cooperated with the United States by sharing information on Islamic extremist movements in the Xinjiang Uyghur Autonomous Region. On the issue of North Korea's nuclear development, stakeholders including the United States, China, and Russia cooperated within the framework of the Six-Party Talks, and a denuclearization agreement was reached in September 2005 under China's chairmanship.

Yet U.S. tensions with China and Russia continued to simmer during this period, including U.S.-Russia confrontation over the expansion of the North Atlantic Treaty Organization (NATO), differences in U.S. and Chinese positions on the Taiwan issue, and confrontations between the United States and China/Russia over the development and deployment of ballistic missile defense systems. These tensions took a distinctly confrontational turn in the 2010s. China's coercive and unilateral actions, such as rapid construction of artificial islands in the South China Sea and pressure on Japan over the Senkaku Islands in the East China Sea, brought a further backlash from regional countries and heightened U.S. wariness toward China. Furthermore, Russia's annexation of Crimea in 2014 and subsequent pressure on Ukraine triggered a decisive deterioration in U.S.-Russia relations.

In light of this deteriorating international security environment, the Donald Trump administration of the United States formulated the National Security Strategy (NSS) in December 2017, the year the administration took office. The NSS presented a worldview referred to as the "return of great power competition," labelling China and Russia as "revisionist powers."[5] During the Trump administration, China continued to take unilateral actions in the East and South China Seas and intensified diplomatic and military pressure on Taiwan under the administration of Tsai Ing-wen of the Democratic Progressive Party. In Europe, Eastern European countries were feeling increasingly threatened by Russia's re-expansion, while concerns over human rights issues and the security of 5G mobile networks heightened wariness toward China. The United States, in particular, was concerned about the loss of U.S. dominance, fueled by tensions in international relations, coupled with a shifting balance of power due to the rise of China. These concerns were manifested concretely in the 2018 report of the National Defense Strategy Commission, an expert panel that Congress established to review the Trump administration's National Defense Strategy following its release in January 2018. The report candidly notes that the United States could suffer a "decisive military defeat" against China or Russia.[6]

Against this backdrop, the Joseph Biden administration took office in 2021. In March of its inaugural year, the administration released the Interim National

Security Strategic Guidance. It mentions the escalation of confrontations with states, such as China and Russia, and upholds the Trump administration's worldview of the United States being in strategic competition with China and other countries.[7]

There are seemingly two aspects to the great power competition that is currently unfolding in this manner. First concerns comprehensive national strength centered around science and technology. An example is the 5G mobile network. Chinese companies outpace Western companies in the market, and the technological superiority of Japan, the United States, and other Western countries is no longer regarded as a given. Furthermore, China is leading moves toward "digital authoritarianism," an authoritarian digital revolution that gives top priority to public security, and to this end, strives to control personal information, and in some cases, restrict human rights. But such a social system conflicts with democratic values, such as privacy and basic human rights. For this reason, it is considered critical to rebuild Western technological superiority, including emerging technologies, in order to promote a digital revolution that underscores democratic values. In this context, importance is attached to economic security.

The other is competition over the geo-strategic balance of power. In the Indo-Pacific region—more specifically, in Taiwan, the East China Sea, and the South China Sea—regional countries that seek to maintain the status quo are engaged in a conflict with China that seeks to alter it. Military balance plays a key factor in this aspect.

(3) Japan and "Great Power Competition"

In Japan, there are debates over the country becoming entangled in the ongoing great power competition and its repercussions on the country's position. Japan, however, is not a neutral third party in the U.S.-China competition.

As mentioned above, the present great power competition has two aspects. One is competition over the post-digital revolution social system. The other is balance of power in China's periphery areas, including the Western Pacific, or put more bluntly, a power game of establishing a "sphere of influence." Regarding the former, there is no doubt that Japan should aim for digital revolution that emphasizes democratic values. Regarding the latter, it is in Japan's national interest to maintain the status quo, especially in the East China Sea. In this sense, Japan's position is the same as the United States' from the start, and it is not fitting for Japan to view the U.S.-China competition from a third-party perspective.

In the first place, the Japan-China confrontation played a significant part in increasing the competitive nature of U.S.-China relations since the Barack Obama administration. In 2010, when tensions erupted after Japan seized a Chinese fishing boat, which rammed Japan Coast Guard patrol vessels near the Senkaku Islands, some in the United States worried about becoming embroiled in a Japan-China confrontation over the Senkaku Islands. This was largely because Washington at the time adopted a "shaping and hedging" policy toward China, i.e., inducing China to become a responsible great power through economic engagement, while simultaneously developing military deterrence and preparing to counter conflict should the outcome be different.[8] Nevertheless, as noted above, due to the key factors of the Japan-China confrontation in the East China Sea and China's unilateral actions, the United States viewed the current international order as a "return of great power competition," and perceived that averting China's status quo-breaking actions was an important strategic objective. Thus, so long as Japan-China relations are partly responsible for shaping the U.S.-China competitive relationship, Japan can by no means take a bystander's position in the great power competition.

At the same time, however, Japan needs to note that the U.S.-China confrontation in the great power competition is unfolding over the abstract concept of "hegemony." So long as it is abstract, an equilibrium point might exist somewhere. Beijing proposed, for example, to reach an equilibrium in the form of U.S. recognition of China's sphere of influence. This was the so-called "new model of major country relations." Although this was not accepted by Washington, some in the United States for a time advocated forming a Group of Two (G2) with China. It should be kept in mind that it is thus logically possible for the United States and China to set an equilibrium point. If the status quo could be maintained only for Taiwan's status, the United States could theoretically choose to concentrate its defense east of Guam, while de facto accepting China's dominance west of the first island chain that includes the South China Sea.

Senkaku Islands, Okinawa Prefecture (Kyodo)

Meanwhile, there are specific issues between Japan and China, such as the Senkaku Islands and the East China Sea gas fields. In this light, it is clear that Japan is positioned as a party to the great power competition more than the United States, in that Japan seeks to maintain the status quo in the geo-strategic competition while finding itself in direct confrontation with China.

2. Relative Decline and Challenges of Japan's Defense Spending

(1) Current Situation of Japan's Defense Spending

The extent to which Japan can allocate resources to national defense comprises a key element of great power competition, especially the power politics dimension where military balance is of great significance. As is well known, Japan's defense spending is roughly 1% of GDP, or approximately 5 trillion yen in real terms. The so-called "1% ceiling" originated in a 1976 cabinet decision of the Miki Takeo administration that stipulated the "1% GNP defense spending cap," but it is not defined as an official rule today since it was abolished by the Nakasone Yasuhiro administration's cabinet decision in 1986.

On the flip side, defense spending has rarely exceeded 1% of GDP. The reason is not so much an institutional cap as budget ceilings which were imposed in a severe fiscal environment, curbing increases in spending. The security environment, too, was stable for some time after the Cold War ended in the late 1980s. Therefore, significant increases in defense spending were not needed in the first place.

In order to accelerate defense power reinforcement and significantly enhance defense capabilities from FY2021, the FY2022 defense budget will implement projects to be included in the FY2022 initial budget ahead of schedule on an unprecedented scale. The FY2021 supplementary budget and the FY2022 initial budget were integrated into the "defense power reinforcement and acceleration package." The total amount budgeted for the "defense power reinforcement and acceleration package" is 5,866.1 billion yen. This represents an increase by 6.5% or 355.9 billion yen from the amount of the FY2021 supplementary budget and the FY2022 initial budget combined (excluding U.S. forces realignment-related expenses). In addition, new deferred burden increased by 2.0% or 49.3 billion yen to 2,458.3 billion yen, which is much higher than previous growth rates. Both increases are the largest on record. Deferred burden applies to multiyear contracts of no more than five years in principle. They are entered into for many defense capability enhancements because they require several years to complete, including procurement of major equipment, such as vessels and aircraft, and construction of hangars and barracks.

Among these priorities, particularly in strengthening the capabilities for cross-domain operations, are the acquisition and enhancement of capabilities in the space, cyber, and electromagnetic domains as well as the enhancement of capabilities, sustainability, and resilience in the conventional domains. Priorities in strengthening the core components of defense capabilities include enhancing the human resources, strengthening the defense technological and industrial base, and enhancing intelligence capabilities.

(2) Decline in Japan's Defense Spending Relative to East Asia's Total
Figure 1 compares the 2020 and 2000 defense expenditures of Japan, China, the Republic of Korea (ROK), and Taiwan as a percentage of East Asia's total. The data are taken from the *Military Balance*, published annually by the British

think tank the International Institute for Strategic Studies (IISS). In 2000, as the chart illustrates, Japan's defense expenditure accounted for 38% of defense expenditures in East Asia, slightly more than China's 36%. The ratio of Japanese to Chinese defense spending was roughly 1:1. Two decades later, however, Japan's share decreased to 17%. Meanwhile, China's share reached 65% boosted by continued large-scale military buildup, widening the ratio to 1:4.1.

That is to say, Japan's defense spending as a share of East Asia's total fell by half, dropping from nearly equivalent to China's share to less than a quarter of it. This stems from the fact that Japan's defense spending remained at around the 5 trillion yen level for the past 20 years, whereas China continued to increase its spending at a high growth rate. Note that Taiwan's share declined from 15% to 5%, while like China, the ROK increased its share, up from 11% to 13%. The ROK has consistently increased its defense spending, and if this trend continues, is expected to surpass Japan in a few years.

As the buildup of defense and military capabilities takes some time, it is not

Figure 8.1. Defense expenditure as % of East Asia's total

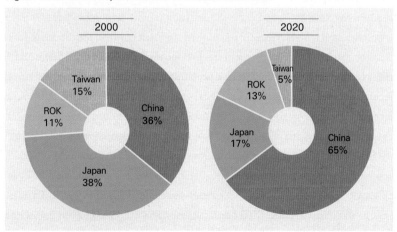

Sources: Compiled by the author based on IISS, *Military Balance 2001/2002*; IISS, *Military Balance 2021*.

Chapter 8

Japan

hugely meaningful to compare single-year differences alone. However, the fact that significant disparities have emerged over the past two decades has critical implications for the military balance in the region. They affect not only Japan but even the United States, which has serious concerns about facing a "decisive military defeat" in a war with China, as stated in the aforementioned National Defense Strategy Commission report.

That said, Japan, too, has increased its defense spending. Japan's defense spending contracted under the austerity measures of the Koizumi Junichiro administration and subsequent administrations, which were aimed at balancing the primary balance. In FY2008, defense spending fell to about 4.7 trillion yen in nominal terms. But since then, the amount has increased to 5,123.5 billion yen in the FY2021 budget and to 5,178.8 billion yen in the FY2022 initial budget. In other words, in a little over a decade, defense spending grew by more than about 17%. It is a fact that efforts have been made, considering Japan's difficult fiscal situation. This is evident by comparing defense to other budgeted items.

Figure 2 shows Japan's budgeted expenditures in FY2019 on a settlement basis. The data is based on settlement information reported to the Diet. Rather than budgeted expenditures, actual expenditure figures are used to examine the overall cash flow. Budgeted expenditure is the sum of the initial budget and the supplementary budget. Actual expenditure represents the budgeted expenditure, plus the amount carried over from the previous fiscal year, reserve funds used, and changes such as transfers and appropriations. As of writing, the most recent settlement information available is that for FY2020. The FY2020 trend, however, diverges significantly from that of earlier years due to the introduction of a large supplementary budget for responding to the novel coronavirus disease (COVID-19). Total expenditure (actual) amounted to 182 trillion yen in FY2020, compared to 109 trillion yen in FY2019.[9] Notably, social security expenditure was about 49 trillion yen in FY2020, compared to about 34 trillion yen in FY2019. Due to these discrepancies, this analysis uses FY2019 figures from before the COVID-19 pandemic.

In an ordinary context, defense spending refers to defense expenditure in the

Figure 8.2. FY2019 Japan's budget expenditures (settlement basis)

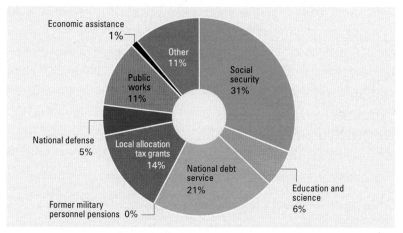

Source: Compiled by the author based on Ministry of Finance's settlement information.

main budget. It is expressed on a contract basis and often includes expenditures on equipment and other items under deferred payment contracts. The reason is that contract basis is more useful for knowing the total expenses per project. This method, however, does not include any supplementary budget that was spent after the approval of the main budget. Settlement, on the contrary, presents the amount of expenditures made during the fiscal year in question and includes the supplementary budget. It does not, however, include expenditures borne in the future through deferred payment contracts. In this sense, it should be noted that the items included in the settlement and the main budget are different. In order to examine the supplementary budget and other cash flows for the relevant fiscal year, the actual expenditure as shown in the settlement is used as a guide here.

Since a meaningful analysis cannot be conducted looking only at a single fiscal year, comparisons with other expenditure items are made based on past data. Figure 3 compares FY2019 data from before the COVID-19 pandemic and FY2000 data from 20 years ago (in real terms with price adjustments). As the figure shows, defense spending increased by 123.9% in real terms from FY2000 to FY2019. Over the last 20 years, only social security spending (195.0%) grew at a higher pace than defense spending among the major budgeted items.

That said, defense spending and public works spending decreased in the meantime due to fiscal austerity policies implemented since the Koizumi administration through the global financial crisis. If the comparison timeframe is narrowed from a 20-year period to a 10-year period from FY2010 to FY2019, the growth rate of defense spending becomes 128.9%. Compared to other budgeted items, only public works spending (157.6%) grew at a higher rate than defense spending during this 10-year period. Over the decade from FY2010 to FY2019, social security spending increased by 125.8%, slightly less than defense spending

Figure 8.3. Comparison of FY2000 and FY2019 expenditures

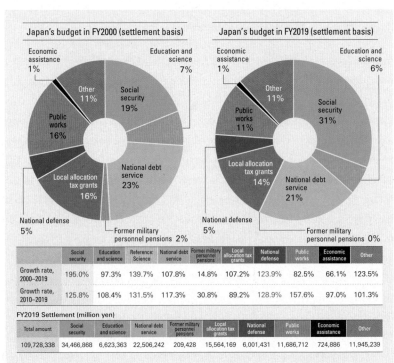

	Social security	Education and science	Reference: Science	National debt service	Former military personnel pensions	Local allocation tax grants	National defense	Public works	Economic assistance	Other
Growth rate, 2000–2019	195.0%	97.3%	139.7%	107.8%	14.8%	107.2%	123.9%	82.5%	66.1%	123.5%
Growth rate, 2010–2019	125.8%	108.4%	131.5%	117.3%	30.8%	89.2%	128.9%	157.6%	97.0%	101.3%

FY2019 Settlement (million yen)

Total amount	Social security	Education and science	National debt service	Former military personnel pensions	Local allocation tax grants	National defense	Public works	Economic assistance	Other
109,728,338	34,466,868	6,623,363	22,506,242	209,428	15,564,169	6,001,431	11,686,712	724,886	11,945,239

Source: Compiled by the author based on Ministry of Finance's settlement information.

growth (however, if FY2010 and FY2020 are compared, defense spending growth becomes 127.4% and social security spending growth 177.4% due to a surge in social security spending in FY2020).

The significant growth in social security spending was inevitable in an aging Japanese society. The increase in public works spending was also unsurprising, especially considering that large cuts were made during the Koizumi administration and public works spending was necessary for reconstruction following the Great East Japan Earthquake.

Conversely, budgeted items that grew slower than defense spending from FY2000 to FY2019 were principally government national debt service (107.8%) and local allocation tax grants (107.2%). This shows defense spending has been given relative importance within the overall budget, even if it accounts for only 5% of the total national budget. The growth rate suggests that, albeit the difficult fiscal situation, Japan has made a degree of efforts to address the current security environment. In terms of absolute cash flow expenditures in FY2019, defense spending represents only about one-sixth of social security spending, less than one-third of government national debt service expenditure, about two-fifths of local allocation tax grants, and about one-half of public works spending.

(3) The Necessity of Political Choice

China has increased its defense spending at a pace far exceeding Japan's, and the gap is only widening. In 2019, U.S. Secretary of Defense Mark Esper of the Trump administration said allies, including Japan, should ideally spend 2% of GDP on defense.[10] This was not without reason, looking at the share of defense expenditures in East Asia shown above. Twenty years ago, Japan's defense spending, even at less than 1% of GDP, accounted for 38% of East Asia's total defense spending. Now it has dropped to less than half to 17%. The ratio of Japan to China, the largest spender on defense in East Asia, has widened from nearly 1:1 in 2000 to 1:4.1 in 2020. If Japan's defense spending were 2% of GDP, or double the current level, the ratio would be 1:1.95 in 2020, which is still disproportionate compared to the 2000 level but would significantly close the gap.

In military strategy, the so-called 3:1 rule postulates that the attacker needs three times the force as the defender. Additionally, Japan's security objective is to maintain the status quo. In other words, this objective can be achieved if the status quo can be maintained through defensive operations, not occupying some land through offensive foreign operations.

Of course, Japan has an alliance with the United States and can expect U.S. forces in Japan as well as U.S. reinforcements. Nevertheless, Japan has primary responsibility for defending its own territory as stated in the Guidelines for Japan-U.S. Defense Cooperation: "Japan will maintain primary responsibility for defending the citizens and territory of Japan and will take actions immediately to repel an armed attack against Japan as expeditiously as possible." In this light, one way to think of it would be to raise Japan's defense spending level to at least one-third but slightly less than one-half of China's defense spending, with the aim of securing stable deterrence for countering China's unilateral attempts to change the status quo near the Senkaku Islands.

If the rule were simply applied to Japan and China, and furthermore, if Japan's defense spending were 2% of GDP, or about 10 trillion yen, the Japan-to-China ratio would be 1:1.95. If Japan's defense spending were 7 trillion yen, the ratio would be 1:2.76, or about one-third. That said, China's defense spending has grown and is expected to continue to grow. From this perspective, it is not appropriate to use the FY2020 level as a given. Assuming that China's defense spending would continue to increase, Japan's defense spending set at one-third of that amount could reach the 10 trillion yen range.

Ten trillion yen corresponds to an expenditure level slightly less than public works spending (approximately 13 trillion yen) in FY2020 actual expenditures, which represent cash flow. In absolute terms, it is the fourth highest expenditure following social security, government national debt service, and local allocation tax grants. It is equal to about one-fifth of social security spending, about one-half of government national debt service, and about two-thirds of local allocation tax grants. Meanwhile, total expenditures in FY2020, expressed as actual expenditure, were approximately 182 trillion yen. Including the additional expenditure of 4 trillion yen that would be necessary if defense expenditure was 10 trillion yen, total expenditures would be approximately 186 trillion yen. While it is a well-known fact that Japan faces a difficult fiscal situation, an increase in spending from 182 trillion yen to 186 trillion yen would only translate into an increase of about 2.2% in overall expenditures. In FY2019, before the COVID-19 pandemic, total expenditure expressed as actual expenditure was 109 trillion yen. A 4 trillion yen increase in defense spending would represent about 3.5% of overall expenditures.

At the same time, if deterrence against China were to fail, the cost will likely not be contained at 4 trillion yen. Furthermore, it should be noted that if war were to occur in Japan, this fact would send shock waves to financial markets and could bring Japan closer to fiscal insolvency.

Japan cannot circumvent a debate over the following two options. One option is to increase defense spending to the same level as public works spending, or to about one-third the pre-pandemic social security spending, in order to fundamentally strengthen deterrence at the risk of increasing fiscal insolvency. The other option is to give emphasis to the fiscal insolvency risk and bear the risk of deterrence failure by accepting decisive inferiority in military balance. In examining this issue, consideration will need to be given to the extent to which priority will be given to defense over public works and other policy objectives.

Of course, Japan has entered into an alliance with the United States, meaning Tokyo does not have to fend for all its needs on its own. Yet the ongoing geo-strategic competition with China in East Asia is above all a Japanese problem rather than a U.S. problem, and Japan is a major party to the competition, especially in the East China Sea. The United States, too, has serious concerns regarding possible "decisive military defeat" in a contest with China. The extent of Japan's efforts in this regard will be a critical factor that shapes whether or not the future security environment will be favorable for Japan.

That said, defense spending cannot be increased haphazardly by setting some numerical target, nor is it even desirable to do so. Defense spending increases cannot improve Japan's security environment unless the specific force structure to be achieved and the strategic effects that they will deliver are clearly articulated. In particular, public understanding for defense spending increases cannot be attained without clarifying what specific capabilities will be used and in what form, and what the current shortfalls are.

Important in this context is "theory of victory," a concept which has recently gained currency among military experts. It describes how to fight a war to achieve its objectives should deterrence fail and war occur. In general, security strategies are considered to be hierarchically structured: grand strategy, followed by military strategy, followed by operational plan. "Theory of victory" lies between military strategy and operational plan.

Forming a "theory of victory" allows defense planners to know which capabilities are particularly essential. They can then clarify in what form those capabilities would be used and what the current shortfalls are, along with indicating more tangibly what strategic effects would result from increasing defense spending. In this sense, discussions are urgently needed for establishing a "theory of victory" through formulating Japan's new National Security Strategy and National Defense Program Guidelines.

3. The Strengthening of the Japan-U.S. Alliance Cooperation

(1) The Biden Administration and the Japan-U.S. Alliance

During the 2017 to 2021 Trump administration, the security environment in Japan's surrounding region continued to become more severe, as demonstrated by the North Korean missile crisis in 2017 as well as China's increased pressure on Taiwan and continued deployment of government vessels around the Senkaku Islands. Meanwhile, Japan-U.S. relations remained stable, due in part to the positive relationship enjoyed by Prime Minister Abe Shinzo and President Trump. The deterrence provided by the Japan-U.S. Alliance contributed significantly to regional stability. The Japanese prime minister has since been replaced by Prime Minister Suga Yoshihide and then by Prime Minister Kishida Fumio, while the

United States transitioned to the Biden administration. Despite some uncertainty about how the Japan-U.S. Alliance would fare on the heels of the favorable Abe-Trump relationship, the Biden administration dispelled such fears by putting forward a policy underscoring the alliance early in the presidency.

Prime Minister Suga and President Biden held their first in-person summit meeting on April 16, 2021. This was President Biden's first in-person meeting with a foreign leader amid the strict international travel restrictions caused by the pandemic. After the meeting, the two leaders released the joint statement, "U.S.-Japan Global Partnership for a New Era," as well as the annexed agreement documents, "U.S.-Japan Competitiveness and Resilience (CoRe) Partnership" and "Japan-U.S. Climate Partnership on Ambition, Decarbonization, and Clean Energy."

The first foreign leader to visit the White House during the Obama administration was also a Japanese prime minister, Prime Minister Aso Taro. While Prime Minister Abe met with President Trump after he was elected, he was the second leader after Prime Minister Theresa May of the United Kingdom to meet with President Trump after he was inaugurated. A joint statement was not released after the Aso-Obama meeting, while the joint statement of the first Abe-Trump meeting was no more than two pages long. In contrast, the three documents released after the Suga-Biden meeting in April were ten pages in total, with each document containing specific and substantive content one would be surprised to find only three months into the U.S. presidency. As this suggests, the Suga-Biden meeting was not a ceremonial first meeting but a meeting held to conduct substantive policy coordination.

Indeed, even before the Japan-U.S. summit meeting, the Biden administration immediately set out to conduct active diplomatic activities after assuming office, ahead of finalizing its China strategy. The Suga-Biden meeting in April was one tipping point in the administration's initial diplomatic campaign comprised of successive meetings: the Quad summit meeting held remotely on March 12, the Japan-U.S. Security Consultative Committee (2+2) meeting held in Tokyo on March 16, the U.S.-ROK 2+2 held in Seoul on March 18, and the U.S.-China

Foreign Ministers' meeting held in Alaska on March 18. As this reveals, Japan occupies a critical place in the Biden administration's Asia strategy. In holding the Japan-U.S. summit meeting at this timing, the Biden administration likely intended to align the basic stance with Japan to begin fully forming the China strategy.

In Japan, the prime minister changed, and the Kishida administration came to power in October. As early as on October 5, Prime Minister Kishida held a telephone talk with President Biden, during which the two leaders agreed to proceed along the same path as previously followed, including further strengthening the deterrence and response capabilities of the Japan-U.S. Alliance and President Biden's reiteration of the U.S. commitment to Japan's defense, such as application of Article V of the Japan-U.S. Security Treaty to the Senkaku Islands.

(2) Issues concerning the Taiwan Strait and the Strengthening of Deterrence

The joint statement released after the Suga-Biden meeting in April 2021 drew attention most of all to the reference to Taiwan, the first such reference in 52 years by a Japan-U.S. leaders' joint statement since the 1969 Joint Statement of Japanese Prime Minister Eisaku Sato and U.S. President Richard Nixon.

No simple comparison between the two is appropriate. Fifty-two years ago, both Japan and the United States did not have diplomatic relations with the People's Republic of China, and any references to the ROK and Taiwan concerned the Okinawa reversion negotiations. That said, the Suga-Biden joint statement has significant implication considering the 1996 Japan-U.S. Joint Declaration on Security (also called the "Hashimoto-Clinton Joint Declaration" because it was a declaration between Prime Minister Hashimoto Ryutaro and President Bill Clinton). This declaration, in which the leaders confirmed the importance of the Japan-U.S. Alliance in the Asia-Pacific region since the end of the Cold War, refers to "peaceful resolution of problems in this region" but does not mention Taiwan or the Taiwan Strait.

Meanwhile, on February 19, 2005, in the midst of the consultations on U.S. force realignment, the Japan-U.S. 2+2 defense and foreign ministerial consultations announced common strategic objectives that included "Encourage the peaceful resolution of issues concerning the Taiwan Strait through dialogue." For some time after that, Taiwan and the Taiwan Strait were not mentioned in any 2+2 document. Then, for the first time in a while, the joint document released after the 2+2 meeting on March 16, 2021, ahead of the Suga-Biden summit meeting, contained the wording, "[The Ministers] underscored the importance of peace and stability in the Taiwan Strait." While this 2+2 document states, "underscored the importance of peace and stability," the joint statement released after the April 16 summit meeting changed the wording to, "[We] underscore the importance of peace and stability across the Taiwan Strait and encourage the peaceful resolution of cross-Strait issues," adding "encourage the peaceful resolution" similar to the 2+2 document of 2005.

A sense of crisis over the rapidly deteriorating security environment surrounding the Taiwan Strait underlies why such references to Taiwan or the Taiwan Strait were made in Japan-U.S. official documents for the first time in a long time. China's unilateral and coercive behavior backed by its rapid economic growth and modernization of military capabilities was already heightening concern during the Obama administration, ushering in a shift in the United States' China strategy to "rebalance to the Asia-Pacific region." Around this time, however, the South China Sea was the main focus of China related concerns, and the issues surrounding the Taiwan Strait did not garner much attention except for from some experts. But with the advent of the Trump administration, a sense of crisis surged over the situation in the Taiwan Strait, stemming from the United States revising its strategy based on the perception that a "great power competition" is unfolding between the United States and China, China stepping up pressure on Taiwan including increased military activity around Taiwan, and rising concerns that China might be considering the option of using limited force.

In particular, there is a shared concern among experts recently that the balance of conventional forces in the Western Pacific may be tipping in China's favor, in part due to the dominance of short- and medium-range ballistic and cruise missiles that China has deployed in large numbers. Of course, U.S. military superiority will remain unchanged if resources are mobilized from all over the world. However, this will take at least six months to around a year. Without taking into account such global mobilization and assuming a short-term decisive battle scenario using only the assets currently deployed in the Western Pacific, China is considered to have an increasing chance of gaining the upper hand. Reflecting this situation, the aforementioned U.S. National Defense Strategy Commission report expressed concern that the United States could suffer a "decisive military defeat" in a contest with China or Russia.

In light of this reality, it is clear that deterrence must be fundamentally strengthened, and the Japan-U.S. Alliance has assumed an increasingly greater role in peace and stability in the Western Pacific region. A sense of imminent crisis based on this strategic reality lies behind the extremely rapid pace at which the Biden administration has conducted Asian diplomacy since its inauguration.

(3) The Challenges of Strengthening Japan-U.S. Alliance Deterrence

Strengthening deterrence in a severe security environment requires resource allocation. In this regard, progress has been scant for both Japan and the United States. As the previous section showed, Japan's defense spending in 2000 accounted for 38% of East Asia's total (Japan, ROK, China, and Taiwan). This percentage has halved in two decades and is now down to 17%. In Washington, the fiscal year 2022 budget request allotted $5 billion for the Pacific Deterrence Initiative. Yet a close look at the details reveals that the budget is limited to Marine Corps and other existing modernization programs, including the F-35 fighter or the Tomahawk cruise missile. Fundamentally, the U.S. allotment is not designed for building a new deterrence posture. Given the seriousness of the present circumstances, it is imperative for Japan and the United States to develop actual capabilities.

In this connection, of note is the following excerpts from the joint statement issued on the occasion of the 2+2 held on March 16, ahead of the Suga-

Biden meeting: "The Ministers acknowledged the importance of close coordination as the Department of Defense conducts its Global Posture Review"; "The Ministers recommitted to enhancing close coordination to align security policy, deepen defense cooperation across

Japan Air Self-Defense Force F-15s escorting U.S. bombers in a training exercise (ZUMA Press/Kyodo News Images)

all domains, and bolster extended deterrence by consulting on Alliance roles, missions, and capabilities."

The Global Posture Review (GPR) was conducted some 20 years ago, too, during the George W. Bush administration. At that time, the main objective was to adapt the global deployment posture of the U.S. forces to the post-Cold War strategic environment. The GPR's aim was to transform the U.S. forward-deployed presence into a "virtual presence." This shift envisioned force reductions in Europe, where many troops had been deployed during the Cold War, as well as contingency response through rapid deployment of forces from the U.S. mainland. The September 11 attacks in 2001, however, forced the United States to send large numbers of troops to Afghanistan and Iraq, and the United States could not realize the initial goal of concentrating its main forces on the U.S. mainland. Furthermore, Washington began to rethink its agenda of reducing permanent forward-deployed forces and responding to contingencies through rapid deployment. Reducing permanent presence would decrease the United States' contribution to the security of its allies in peacetime and could undermine allies' trust in the United States. Washington abandoned the virtual presence concept, stating in the 2010 Quadrennial Defense Review (QDR), "We cannot simply 'surge' trust and relationships [with allies] on demand."[11]

The GPR now underway was prompted by the withdrawal from Afghanistan and Iraq. In August 2021, the U.S. forces withdrew completely from Afghanistan and conducted a major drawdown of troops stationed in Iraq. The withdrawal does not simply mean reduced overseas involvement of the U.S. forces; the withdrawal is meant to lead toward the realignment of their deployment posture, with focus on strengthening the strategic deterrence posture against China. A premium will be put on countering China's rapid development of anti-access/area denial (A2/AD) capabilities.

The Bush administration's GPR announced 20 years ago emphasized "stand-off" systems against A2/AD threats, i.e., deploying assets to positions outside the adversary's strike range and counterattacking with precision strikes from remote locations. But with the enhancement of China's A2/AD capabilities, the notion has spread that assets cannot penetrate from outside the strike range. Therefore, the discourse has increasingly shifted to the "stand-in" concept of maintaining highly resilient bases within the A2/AD zone and deploying outside assets to the bases. Another idea that has been debated is the "Archipelagic Defense" concept of strengthening the Japan-U.S. Alliance's A2/AD capability with ground-based missile capabilities, mainly anti-ship and anti-aircraft missiles. In order to strengthen the deterrence posture against China, Washington must review and adapt the U.S. military presence to its geopolitical and strategic confrontations with China, taking into account the current trends in military technology.

As for the roles, missions, and capabilities (RMC) consultation, this was part of the U.S. military realignment discussions during the Bush administration's GPR. Notably, the joint document from the 2+2 in October 2005 lists 15 examples of cooperation, and RMC has continued to be discussed since then.

The Guidelines for Japan-U.S. Defense Cooperation are similar to RMC. The Guidelines identify situations that should be jointly addressed by the Japan Self-Defense Forces (JSDF) and U.S. forces and specify the JSDF and U.S. forces' roles for each situation in order to formulate joint operational plans. The Guidelines are agreed to at the 2+2, a consultative committee of Japanese and U.S. defense and foreign ministers. Hence, operational plans that are prepared based on the Guidelines are contingent upon political approval, and the Guidelines play a significant role in ensuring democratic control over defense policy. Conversely, RMC's key role lies not in operational planning but in redefining the basic direction of the Japan-U.S. defense strategy and repositioning individual issues within the overall defense strategy. For example, the areas of

U.S. PAC-3 and the Japan Ground Self-Defense Force's Type-03 medium-range surface-to-air missile deployed for a Japan-U.S. combined training exercise (Kyodo)

RMC cooperation agreed upon in the 2+2 document of 2005 transcended mere realignment of bases and redefined the direction of U.S. military realignment in the context of strengthening deterrence.

In light of the current security environment, the RMC consultation to be conducted based on the 2+2 Joint Statement of March 2021 may have the following prime objective: redefine the basic direction of the Japan-U.S. defense strategy and form a "theory of victory" for the Japan-U.S. Alliance, tailoring to the changing military balance due to North Korea's growing nuclear and missile threat and China's strengthening of military capabilities, including A2/AD capability.

I would like to highlight here three critical discussion items for the RMC consultation.

First is the question of how to develop a missile defense system against North Korea's nuclear weapons and missiles and China's precision-guided ballistic missiles, along with growing threats of hypersonic weapons and cruise missiles. Japan and the United States have engaged in ballistic missile defense (BMD) cooperation since the end of the 20th century. Japan has made steady progress in developing a system against ballistic missile strikes and has acquired some level of capability to defend itself against ballistic missiles. However, ballistic missiles are not the only threat. Hypersonic weapons and cruise missiles also pose increasing threats: hypersonic weapons have a higher likelihood of penetrating BMD by aerodynamically maneuvering in the atmosphere, while cruise missiles cannot be dealt with by BMD because they fly at low altitudes in the atmosphere. Japan has evolved the "comprehensive air and missile defense" concept to address these new missile threats and ballistic missiles in an integrated manner. Japan will very likely need to develop new hardware, especially against hypersonic weapons, as well as the concept. In addition, given the growing missile threat, Japan will need to conduct research and development of not only first-generation BMD, which focuses on kinetic energy interceptors, but also second-generation BMD, which focuses on directed energy weapons.

Secondly, with the expiration of the Intermediate-Range Nuclear Forces (INF) Treaty, the post-INF system needs to be discussed. The treaty prohibited 500-kilometer range U.S. and Russian ground-launched missiles, but those restrictions have lapsed with the termination of the treaty in 2019. Considering Japan's geographical conditions, surrounded by water, the consultation must examine what comparative advantages ground-based missiles have over sea-launched missiles and which missiles would bring high added value through deployment.

Third is what to infer from the changes in the nature of combat, especially air warfare, with the United States no longer having a monopoly over precision-guided weapons and with unmanned and stealth technologies under development and proliferation. The precision-guided ballistic missiles currently deployed by China can likely pinpoint and destroy aircraft on standby at airfields. Note that any aircraft, including fighters, are on the ground for most of the day. In this light, the very nature of air warfare could change significantly in the near future.

These three matters are issues of importance individually, and each has implications for the overall Japan-U.S. Alliance. Rather than examining each of the issues alone and individually, the two countries need to contextualize them into the "theory of victory" for the entire Japan-U.S. Alliance and clarify the strategic effects. To this end, the RMC consultations are expected to play an essential role.

NOTES

1) Kamo Takehiko, *Kokusai anzen hosho no koso* [The concept of international security] (Tokyo: Iwanami Shoten, 1990); G. John Ikenberry, *After Victory: Institutions, Strategic Restraint, and the Rebuilding of Order after Major Wars* (Princeton: Princeton University Press, 2001).

2) Janne Nolan, ed., *Global Engagement: Cooperation and Security in the 21st Century* (Washington, DC: Brookings Institution, 1994); Dora Alves, ed., *Cooperative Security in the Pacific Basin: The 1988 Pacific Symposium* (Washington, DC: National Defense University Press, 1990); Emanuel Adler and Michael Barnett, *Security Communities* (Cambridge: Cambridge University Press, 1998); Helga Haftendorn, Robert O. Keohane, and Celeste A. Wallander, eds., *Imperfect Unions: Security Institutions over Time and Space* (Oxford: Oxford University Press, 1999).

3) Michael Mandelbaum, "Is Major War Obsolete?," *Survival* 40, no. 4 (1998): 20-38.

4) Michael Mandelbaum, "Is Major War Still Obsolete?," *Survival* 61, no. 5 (2019): 65-71.

5) The White House, "National Security Strategy of the United States of America" (December 2017).

6) [U.S.] National Defense Strategy Commission, "Providing for the Common Defense: The Assessment and Recommendations of the National Defense Strategy Commission" (November, 2018), 14.

7) The White House, "Interim National Security Strategic Guidance" (March 2021).

8) Takahashi Sugio, "US Policy toward China," in *NIDS China Security Report 2018: The China-US Relationship at a Crossroads*, English edition (Tokyo: National Institute for Defense Studies, 2018), 24-27.

9) [Japan] Ministry of Finance, "Reiwa gannendo ippan kaikei sainyu saishutsu kessan (dai 203 kai kokkai teishutsu)" [FY2019 General account revenue and expenditure settlement (submitted to the 203rd Diet session)] (November 20, 2020); [Japan] Ministry of Finance, "Reiwa 2 nendo ippan kaikei sainyu saishutsu kessan (dai 207 kai kokkai teishutsu)" [FY2020 General account revenue and expenditure settlement (submitted to the 207th Diet session)] (December 6, 2021).

10) Mark T. Esper, "Secretary of Defense Engagement at RAND Corporation (Complete Transcript)" (September 16, 2020).

11) [U.S.] Department of Defense, "Quadrennial Defense Review Report" (February 2010), 63.

Editor

National Institute for Defense Studies

The National Institute for Defense Studies (NIDS) is a think tank of the Ministry of Defense. NIDS is Japan's only national institute for academic research and education of security issues. A team of approximately 90 researchers studies about security policy, international affairs, and military history. Designated as an official archive for historical documents under the Public Records and Archives Management Act, NIDS also manages and provides a large depository of historical documents concerning military history. In addition, NIDS runs education programs for senior officials and officers of the Ministry of Defense and Self-Defense Forces, as well as for other ministry and agency officials. NIDS actively participates in defense exchanges and security dialogues in both research and educational fields with foreign and regional research institutes of security and defense.

Contributors (Titles are as at the time of writing)

Kurita Masahiro	Senior Fellow, Asia & Africa Division, Regional Studies Department	Chapter 1
Nishino Masami	Senior Fellow, Asia & Africa Division, Regional Studies Department	Chapter 2
Iida Masafumi	Head, America, Europe & Russia Division, Regional Studies Department	Chapter 3
Iwamoto Hiroshi	Research Fellow, China Division, Regional Studies Department	Chapter 3
Akutsu Hiroyasu	Chief, Policy Simulation Division	Chapter 4
Murooka Tetsuo	Senior Fellow, Asia & Africa Division, Regional Studies Department	Chapter 4
Matsuura Yoshihide	Head, Government & Law Division, Security Studies Department	Chapter 5
Tomikawa Hideo	Senior Fellow, Security & Economy Division, Security Studies Department	Chapter 5
Hasegawa Takeyuki	Research Fellow, America, Europe & Russia Division, Regional Studies Department	Chapter 6
Sakaguchi Yoshiaki	Senior Fellow, America, Europe & Russia Division, Regional Studies Department	Chapter 6
Kikuchi Shigeo	Head, China Division, Regional Studies Department	Chapter 7
Takahashi Sugio	Head, Defense Policy Division, Policy Studies Department	Chapter 8